D0929894

WITHDRAWN

MENDELSSOHN
IN
PERFORMANCE

MENDELSSOHN
IN
PERFORMANCE

EDITED BY
Siegwart Reichwald

FOREWORD BY CHRISTOPHER HOGWOOD

INDIANA UNIVERSITY PRESS

Bloomington and Indianapolis

This book is a publication of

Indiana University Press
601 North Morton Street
Bloomington, IN 47404-3797 USA

http://iupress.indiana.edu

Telephone orders 800-842-6796
Fax orders 812-855-7931
Orders by e-mail iuporder@indiana.edu

The paper used in this publication meets the minimum requirements of American National Standard for Information Sciences—Permanence of Paper for Printed Library Materials, ANSI Z39.48-1984.

Manufactured in the United States of America

Library of Congress Cataloging-in-Publication Data

Mendelssohn in performance / edited by Siegwart Reichwald ; foreword by Christopher Hogwood.
    p. cm.
    Includes bibliographical references and index.
    ISBN 978-0-253-35199-9 (cloth : alk. paper) 1. Mendelssohn-Bartholdy, Felix, 1809–1847. 2. Performance practice (Music)—Germany—History—19th century. I. Reichwald, Siegwart, date
    ML410.M5M58 2008
    780.92—dc22
                                            2008013739

1 2 3 4 5 13 12 11 10 09 08

CONTENTS

FOREWORD

It is only recently that Mendelssohn has made the transition from being an "easy" composer to being a "composer with problems." In his lifetime he, like Mozart, outlived his reputation as a Wunderkind. However, whereas Mozart then proceeded to a career in which the public decided that his performing was a spectacle worth applauding, but his later compositions were simply too difficult, Mendelssohn (we were led to believe) inherited a lifestyle that was easy and untroubled, his upbringing elegant and catholic, his musical tours a fluent litany of *jeu perlé* performances, and his compositions effortless outpourings; even his watercolors were dismissed as evidence of "too much talent."

"Easy" composers don't rate a volume of studies, certainly not one of performance studies; but the last fifteen years have seen a sea-change in the understanding of Mendelssohn's achievements, prompted by greater availability of his correspondence (still an unfinished project), several splendid biographical studies, and the appearance of critically scrutinized editions of many major works. The activities of scholars have piqued the interest of the public and of the "historically informed" segment of the performing world, and the moment is now ripe for the question to be asked: "How was his music performed?"

Mendelssohn himself was an energetic performer in most categories. In 1827, for example, he took part in a strenuous concert conducted by Carl Loewe: to open the program his new overture to *A Midsummer Night's Dream* was played for the first time, followed by a second Mendelssohn premiere, the Concerto for Two Pianos in A-flat, with the composer and Loewe as soloists; then came Weber's F minor *Konzertstück* for piano and orchestra, played by Mendelssohn (from memory, to the surprise of the audience) and finally Beethoven's Ninth Symphony, for which the tireless composer joined the orchestral violins—by most accounts, a normal evening for our prodigy.

More than many composers of his generation, Mendelssohn had been taught (under Zelter) to appreciate the importance of performance studies.

Not only did he show unusual perspicuity in matters of older music—his much applauded (but rarely repeated) version of the *St. Matthew Passion* (1829), his historical concert-programming in Leipzig—but also as an editor he demonstrated an unconventional (for the period) belief in the sanctity of the composer's text. When asked to prepare a performance edition of *Israel in Egypt* for the Handel Society he told Moscheles that it was essential to preserve every aspect of Handel's score—including his tempi, dynamics, and figured bass; any changes or additions would need to be noted in the text.[1]

With each unveiling of a new volume of his correspondence, we become increasingly aware of his nagging self-doubts and constant agitation for things to be improved, plus an intolerance of "good enough" and of vested interests in music administration. As the complex source situation for almost all his major works is revealed by new editions, we can study and sympathize with (or deplore) his confessed *Revisionskrankheit*. Although it will be a long time before the general listening public are won over to his revised version of the *Italian Symphony* after so many years of enjoying the "imperfect" earlier version, there is already a strong appreciation that an interpretative style of honeyed sanctimoniousness does Mendelssohn no favors. A combination of the work of biographers and editors has led to a recategorization that reverses Weingartner's description of Mendelssohn as the "first of the moderns" and sees him more as the "last of the classics."

This reassessment means his music appears before the public in a different intellectual context—more searching programming, not infrequent use of period instruments, an interest in "earlier versions" and a realization that our assumptions of a Mendelssohnian ethos have been radically distorted. Hans von Bülow, who studied with Mendelssohn and attended his rehearsals in the Leipzig Gewandhaus in the 1840s, offers a firm corrective. He claimed—using Schiller's distinctions—that "Schumann is a sentimental poet, Mendelssohn a naïve one" and suggested that Mendelssohn's music stands apart from Schumann's or Chopin's "romanticizing" influence on the musical public. On the contrary, "the whole gamut of feelings that are generated and nourished by enthusiasm for the 'sentimental' artists . . . will, if transferred to the works of the 'naïve' ones, make them shallow, boring, sober, contentless—in short, insufferable. . . . One plays into Mendelssohn things that are completely foreign to him; and plays out the things that constitute his greatest virtue. If one wants to play Mendelssohn correctly, one should first play Mozart." In particular he counsels against a "passionately excited rubato" and asks for the strict observance of meter, with no *ritardani* added which were not marked, and even when marked, "restricted to their least possible extent."[2]

How different an approach is described here compared with the Mendelssohn we normally hear today. Outspoken as it is, this advice seems to have been blithely ignored for at least a century, largely through professional shortsightedness. Conservatoire training tends to produce performers with an all-purpose, one-size-fits-all philosophy who are as surprised to find Mendelssohn annoyed when his *agitato* was misinterpreted as a tempo change (Brahms was similarly upset) as they are reluctant to absorb the implications of Elgar's marking "cantabile e vibrato" in his Violin Concerto (another forgotten style requiring study).

The lack of a published version of the complete Mendelssohn family correspondence makes the concept of the present volume all the more pertinent. Since Mendelssohn was prudent with what he chose to make public, it is sometimes his more private views which help our need for (horrid word) "contextualization." On tempi, for example, we need to have available as much evidence as possible from all sources—metronome markings, timed lengths of performances, comments on the required effect. When even as close a friend as Moscheles could get the tempo of the *Melusine* overture wrong at the premiere, it is important that we should know the metronome mark the composer later suggested in a letter, even if his aversion to such props prevented him printing it in the score.[3]

In addition to being an introduction to the latest scholarship, these essays should also be an encouragement to enterprise, regardless of whether you regard Mendelssohn as a historical figure or not. Although it would be nice if the Mendelssohn-piano returned with as much prestige as the Mozart-piano currently enjoys, this is not exclusively a matter for period instruments; other types of curiosity and initiative would also be rewarding. The independent-minded violinist (with either ancient or modern equipment) who dared to program "solo" Bach with Mendelssohn's intriguing piano accompaniments would discover that it no longer spells professional death. Similarly, an orchestral conductor not only could adopt Mendelssohn's numbers and disposition of his instruments, he might also bring back the ophicleide or even the English bass-horn, and retire the disagreeable tuba. In his programs, moreover, he might note that part of the originality of Mendelssohn's concert overtures was the fact that he did not always design them to be placed at the beginning of concerts.

To deal successfully with a composer who was a genius by both nature and nurture requires all the assistance we can muster—and to this end a welcome array of stalwart scholars await your perusal in this volume.

Christopher Hogwood
Cambridge, June 2006

NOTES

1. Letter from 7 March 1845 to Ignaz Moscheles; *Letters of Felix Mendelssohn to Ignaz and Charlotte Moscheles,* trans. and ed. Felix Moscheles (London: Trübner, 1888), 251–52.

2. Hans von Bülow, *Ausgewählte Schriften* (Leipzig: Breitkopf & Härtel, 1896), 403–406; quoted in translation by Susan Gillespie in *Mendelssohn and His World,* ed. Larry Todd (Princeton, N.J.: Princeton University Press, 1991), 392–93.

3. Felix Mendelssohn, letter to Heinrich Conrad Schleinitz, 20 November 1835; Hellmut Meyer and Ernst Lagerkatalog 52, Nr. 441. See chapter 10 for details.

MENDELSSOHN
IN
PERFORMANCE

I

Mendelssohn's Audience

DOUGLASS SEATON

Reflecting on Mendelssohn shortly after the composer's death, Wilhelm Heinrich Riehl wrote,

> He was the first musician who actually made music for "fine society"—in the best sense of the term. He was . . . a versatile, cultivated, socially adroit, wealthy, exquisitely mannered man, personally known in almost the whole of Germany, in demand in all select circles. . . . Mendelssohn also wrote in the spirit of this cultivated society, which now spread itself evenly and by proxy into all classes. . . . It is the present North German delicacy and versatility of culture, with its smoothing out of all rough national characteristics, that found expression in Mendelssohn's music. . . . No other art can show a man who, in his artistic work, stood so much in the middle of the social life of our cultivated circles and who in addition was so comprehended and valued by them as Mendelssohn. . . . Mendelssohn's influence must forthwith become a universal one, for the "cultivated society" in which he worked and lived, in whose spirit he created, is the same throughout Germany.[1]

In approaching any music of the past, we should keep in mind the contexts of that music's historical performances. We commonly reconstitute music using period instruments, styles of ornamentation, choices of tempo. We take a less conscious attitude, however, toward reconstituting ourselves as period listeners. Not that we could ever succeed completely in such an undertaking, of course, but we should imagine music's intended listeners, at least to make ourselves conscious of the gap between them and us, for awareness of the differences between ourselves and others forms the necessary first step toward understanding both. Approaching the study of Mendelssohn in performance, it behooves us to reflect on the contexts in which his works were first heard and on the audiences for whom he intended them.

There are at least three ways to view Mendelssohn's audience. First, we can outline the demographics of the population generally, describing the audience in terms of economic situations, vocational and professional status, daily living conditions, education, and so on. Second, we can take snapshots of actual audiences, focusing on individual listeners who attended Mendelssohn's performances of his (and others') works. Third, we can consider the relationships of Mendelssohn's music to the audiences that it addressed. And we must observe the interplay among these perspectives.

When we describe the audience for Mendelssohn's performances in his lifetime, we easily make the generalized observation that his primary listeners were the German Bürger of the Vormärz or Biedermeier period. We would then extend our view to include the English middle class and, stretching further in time and place, peripheral publics in France, the United States, and other countries. Such observations become meaningful, however, only to the extent that we understand what these generalizations mean, for each of these populations encompasses a wide range of different people, and more narrowly defined audiences heard performances in different milieus. The present discussion concentrates on the primary audience of Mendelssohn's performances, the German Bürgertum of the 1820s–40s—as Riehl put it, "this cultivated society, which now spread itself evenly and by proxy into all classes."

For a start, we should take note of the sizes of the cities in which Mendelssohn was most importantly active. The urban population grew rapidly throughout Germany in the first half of the nineteenth century. In Berlin the population doubled from about 200,000 in 1815 to over 400,000 in 1850. During the same period Leipzig grew from 45,000 to 63,000. Among other cities at the end of this period the population of Cologne stood at 97,000; that of Frankfurt am Main at 65,000; and Düsseldorf's at 27,000.[2] These are, of course, small numbers by today's standards; thus the audiences for concert and operatic music were proportionately higher in the early nineteenth century than now.

The German word *Bürger* does not translate directly into the French *bourgeois*. It may be the equivalent of either *bourgeois,* literally a city dweller, or more restrictively a *citoyen,* one with the legal status of citizen.[3] Mendelssohn's audiences consisted of the educated urban society as a whole, but this comprised only about 5 percent of the German population. Nor did the Bürgertum form a homogeneous population. The Bürger were distinct from peasants and laborers, and less so from the aristocracy, but a general distinction also existed between the higher-status and the petty bourgeois.[4] Moreover, we may identify three subsidiary groups:

Besitzbürger, the ownership bourgeoisie, defined by wealth;
Bildungsbürger, the intellectual bourgeoisie, characterized by cultural sophistication;
Wirtschaftsbürger, the business bourgeoisie, comparatively late in developing, which strived through effort and education to achieve integration into the previous categories.[5]

For class mobility increased greatly in the 1800s. Prussian reforms opened all occupations to everyone, creating the opportunity for free social movement.[6] Capital also moved across status lines.[7] Tenants on large agricultural estates became members of the middle class, and previously unlanded urbanites could now buy land.[8] The most important source of upward mobility for the petty bourgeois came through education to civic administration and the professions, so that within a generation or two families could change their social status considerably. Moreover, one's position in the Bürgertum was importantly defined by individual achievement of cultivated character, Bildung. Thus, education and the arts helped to determine social class. This certainly included music, so that musical ability and support of musical activity functioned as an important social determinant.

The ideal of the Bürgertum gave the arts autonomy from the state and the aristocracy. The new social situation made culture a means toward personal satisfaction for the non-aristocratic individual, separate from the daily labor needed to sustain life. Karin Friedrich emphasizes that "in the Biedermeier period . . . literature and the arts left the ivory tower of its classic and Romantic predecessors by adopting a more popular tone, while libraries, museums, concert halls, opera houses and theatres opened their doors to a wider public."[9] This "embourgeoisement" of art culture certainly operated in two directions. On one hand there was the inculcation of artistic awareness and interest in the Bürger. On the other hand there came to be a clear split between high arts and light art.[10]

The nineteenth-century bourgeoisie created the nuclear family, separating work from the home. Formerly, the typical urban household served as both living and working place, perhaps with a workshop or retail shop in one part of a dwelling, where parents and children spent most of their time, all contributing to the family livelihood. The industrial revolution made the family a distinctly bourgeois institution, with separate roles for father as breadwinner and mother (who did not work, and delegated household chores to servants) as custodian of cultural values. Sons could attend school rather than work as apprentices in the family craft or trade. Daughters learned domestic arts as well as literature, painting, and music.

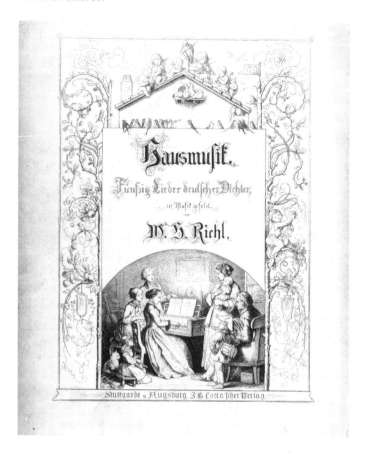

FIGURE 1.1. Ludwig Richter's title page design for Wilhelm Heinrich Riehl, *Hausmusik: Fünfzig Lieder deutscher Dichter* (Stuttgart and Augsburg, 1855).

Bourgeois family life included all sorts of new activities. In the drawing room there were conversation, including discussion of literature, culture, and public affairs; games, including board and card games; writing, including poetry; and painting. Out of doors families might take walks in local parkland or more extensive excursions in the countryside. Birthday celebrations and children's parties formed special occasions, and the family celebration of Christmas grew up. Whether at festive times or simply in general there could be music evenings at home or other types of domestic entertainments, including *tableaux vivants,* amateur plays, and readings. Such a drawing-room scene appears in the title illustration by Ludwig Richter for the 1855 collection *Hausmusik: Fünfzig Lieder deutscher Dichter* published by the same Wilhelm Heinrich Riehl quoted at the opening of this essay (figure 1.1).

Various bourgeois social activities took place outside the home. Men commonly gathered in coffee houses and pastry shops to converse and to read the latest news reports, including papers from other cities and countries. They also joined in outdoors activities in the *Herrengesellschaft*. Men and women together met at dinner parties, balls and dance parties, and "promenade concerts."[11]

Especially important was the rise of the social and functional association—*Gesellschaft* or *Verein*—such as museum associations, sports clubs (e.g., the *Schwimmverein*), and singing clubs (*Liedertafel*) or music societies (*Musikgesellschaft*). In fact, the Verein movement began in the 1820s with the founding of choral societies in numerous cities.

The Vereine provided an important sense of belonging in the context of the otherwise increasing individualization of the industrial society. One of the main characteristics of Vereine was that members were regarded as equals. Although these organizations were not democratic in the broad sense, because participation required wealth and leisure, they provided a leveling force for a certain part of the population, making no distinction between the Bürger and aristocratic participants.[12]

The financial demands of this bürgerlich life were considerable. In addition to the cost of one's home and maintaining the family and servants, one had to afford the coffee house bill; transportation for the family on excursions; the costs of giving dinner parties, if not lavish balls; fashionable clothes in which to attend social occasions; theater and concert subscriptions; and membership dues for the Vereine in which one participated.

Women held an important position in the Bürgertum. By creating the nuclear family, the nineteenth century developed the feminization of women. Although women could not rank as citizens, they were important participants and appreciators of art. Indeed, culture was increasingly turned over to women. The education of girls, whether in schools or at home, concentrated more than that of boys on music and culture. For the Bürger a piano-playing daughter became a symbol of cultural status; even the petty bourgeoisie aspired to the piano in the drawing room and the leisured daughter to play it. Women came to have new and important roles in society at large, through charitable work that could now be managed by a leisured and prosperous woman, as teachers, as admired and respectable professional artists (for example, Jenny Lind and Clara Schumann) or amateurs (Fanny Hensel), as writers, and as the hosts of salons.[13]

Education formed an important characteristic of Mendelssohn's bourgeois audience. Historian Thomas Nipperdey defines the Bürgertum as the class educated at the universities.[14] The Enlightenment and the early nineteenth century produced diverse viewpoints on education, which framed the bourgeois educational experience. Johann Heinrich Pestalozzi (1746–1827) based his influential educational theory on the principle that the purpose of education was to produce useful citizens, while Johann Gottlieb Fichte (1762–1814) and Friedrich Schleiermacher (1768–1824) valued the role of education in creating national cultural unity. The Prussian ministers Stein and Hardenberg regarded the purpose of the university as utilitarian preparation for civil service. Nipperdey points out that early nineteenth-century Prussian reform intended education to create a new elite based on meritocracy. Leadership in early nineteenth-century Germany thus came from a "small social class consisting of the educated, the civil servants and the liberal professions."[15] On the other hand, Wilhelm von Humboldt envisioned university education as humanist, aimed at philosophy and science, pursued through research and teaching, to uplift humanity both morally and materially. Humboldt conceived education not as preparation for a career but for its own sake and for intellectual emancipation. Thus the ideal of *Wissenschaft* stood in tension with functionalist conceptions of education aimed primarily at careers in civil service.[16]

Bourgeois education began in the home with preschool learning that included reading, already rooted in the literary canon; science play, collecting, and the use of mechanical toys; and songs. When children became old enough, they attended the Bürgerschule for elementary education, and, if the family's resources permitted, they would obtain private tutoring at home. In addition to practical subjects, children were educated to the collective *Lebenswelt* of the bourgeoisie. Cultural formation included reciting poetry, playing the piano, and writing. Although formal education tended to be oriented to boys, girls commonly attended their brothers' lessons, in addition to which they learned domestic crafts, leisure activities, and literature.[17]

For boys, education continued through the gymnasium and university. In addition to the value of education itself, the stages and activities associated with student life served as standard rites of passage for bourgeois men, part of the collective experience that bonded the Bürgertum.[18] Women did not matriculate at the universities, although they could attend certain public lectures by famous professors.

Germany consequently became a nation of readers. Pragmatic factors favored this: better education to literacy; expansion of publishing; the propagation of reading rooms and libraries, and of the culture of coffee houses, which supplied a wide range of journals; the enormous increase of writing; and the appearance of book peddlers, who helped to literatize even rural areas. In addition, gas lighting became increasingly available, first in Berlin in 1829, but by 1850 in over thirty-five German cities. Newspapers and other periodicals were vital to the development of the Bürgertum, as journalism and journal reading became guides to opinion.[19]

The exchange of ideas and growth of the intellect had notable forums outside schools and universities. Debate and discussion took place in the more formal environment of the academy, the casual atmosphere of the coffee house, and especially the sophisticated salon. The private salons replaced the courts as the upper bourgeois class's preferred milieu for intellectual exchange. The greatest of the literary salons were Berlin's counterparts to the Paris models, including those of Henriette Herz, Rahel Levin (later Varnhagen von Ense), and Fanny Arnstein. For music, the important salons were those of the Beers (Meyerbeer's family) and, of course, the Mendelssohns. In addition to their contribution to the flowering of ideas, the Berlin salons helped in the leveling of society, for they brought disparate groups together: Jewish and Christian, middle class and aristocracy, civilian and military.[20]

For the Bürgertum travel comprised a distinctive element of cultural identity. For young men, especially, travel formed a central part of their Bildung. In their travels they focused attention on nature—particularly the sublime mountainscapes of Switzerland; on art—visiting museums, churches, theaters, opera houses, universities, and archives; on the miracles of industry and technology—inspecting factories, bridges, ships, railroads, and mines; and on political sites—including government buildings and battlefields, including especially the battlefield memorial for the 1813 Battle of the Nations at Leipzig, the decisive defeat of Napoleon. The memoirs of publisher Otto Elben report the stages of his representative 1846 tour. It included theater and opera, the Lower Rhine Music Festival in Cologne (with Mendelssohn as conductor), and a song festival in Brussels, as well as societies, casinos, book clubs, museums, and the telegraph.[21] Mendelssohn and his father in England in the summer of 1833 visited the Royal Observatory in Greenwich and the naval dockyards at Portsmouth.[22]

Travel was not only an educational experience, but also a leisure activity for the Bürger. Families visited major events, such as the Lower Rhine Music Festivals that constituted such a significant part of Mendelssohn's activity, spas and resorts at the coast or in the mountains, and so on.

Facilitating travel were a number of recent improvements. Boat travel on the Rhine, Danube, Isar, Elbe, and Oder gave access to much of Germany. Steamboats plowed the Rhine from 1826 and the Danube from 1829. Otto Elben went to Cologne from Heilbronn by steamship on the Neckar and the Rhine along with some bourgeois choral groups.[23] From the time of Napoleon there were paved roads, which enabled faster and more reliable wheeled travel. The railway began to develop in 1835, with service between Leipzig and Dresden from 1837 to 1839 and between Berlin and nearby cities after 1840.[24]

The Bürgertum was integrated with the idea of the German nation. In the early nineteenth century patriotic resentment of Napoleon united a core population of bourgeois and aristocratic classes—mostly young men: civil servants and army officers; the educated elite; philosophers, journalists, and writers.[25] Nationalism became a driving force in social equalization,[26] and at the same time cultural activities reinforced nationalism. The "important appurtenances to the new state-bourgeois culture industry" included theaters, museums, and concert halls.[27] There was a conscious effort toward the establishment of the German *Kulturnation* with statues of national heroes. Ludwig I of Bavaria created the *Feldherrnhalle* to represent German military history (1841–44). Throughout Germany there were monuments to Martin Luther, who represented to the nationalists the rejection of Catholic hegemony.[28] Such hero-monuments also appeared in the field of music; they would certainly include Leipzig's monument to Bach, dedicated in 1843, to which Mendelssohn devoted considerable effort, and the Beethoven monument in Bonn, established in 1845. A nationalist thread ran through the repertoires and activities of music associations, singing academies, and public choir festivals.[29]

Religious identity characterized the Bürgertum in various ways. In Prussia theologians in the circle of Crown Prince Friedrich Wilhelm promoted the concept of the "Christian state." Friedrich Wilhelm IV, after 1840 the new King of Prussia, devoted some serious effort to creating new Protestant liturgy, and he recruited Mendelssohn to produce music for this purpose. The Enlightenment had established a rational Christian protestantism, based on interpreted revelation, intellectual truth, humane ethos, and the superiority of piety and morality over dogma. Romanticism craved a more emotional and spiritual faith experience, and some of the Romantic intellectual elite converted to Roman Catholicism. The German Bürger collectively would do no such thing, however. Those who sought a middle ground found their finest spokesman in Schleiermacher, who championed the application of reason in theology, historical contextualization of faith in the present, and interpretation as the role of the church.[30] To a large extent it was to this position that Mendelssohn's religious music spoke. Meanwhile, the nineteenth-century thirst for spiritual experience made culture and art the locus of spiritual fulfillment, producing a *Bildungsreligion* or *Kunstreligion*. The temples of culture and the rituals of art helped to satisfy the desire for subjective experience.[31]

Turning now to specific records of individual audience members who heard Mendelssohn's performances, one can produce extensive, if inevitably

Table 1.1. Some Members of Mendelssohn's Audiences at Weimar, 1821

Goethe and his family
  Johann Wolfgang von Goethe
  Ottilie, his daughter-in-law
  Ulrike von Pogwisch, her sister

Other notable women
  Adele Schopenhauer, writer of stories and poetry
  Johanna, her mother

Members of the nobility
  Grand Duke and Duchess
  Princess Luise
  Maria Pavlovna, tsar's sister

Scholars
  Friedrich Wilhelm Riemer, Greek scholar
  [for Mendelssohn's 1825 visit—Frédéric Jacques Soret, crystallographer and
    numismatist]

Musical figures who heard Mendelssohn's "test" performances included:
  Carl Eberwein, violinist and composer
  Ludwig Rellstab, music critic and poet
  Johann Christian Lobe, writer on music

partial, audience lists, including the nobility, other aristocrats, political figures, scholars and scientists, writers and artists, and other prominent members of society.[32] To list audience members from the lower social ranks presents more problems, but naturally many such did attend Mendelssohn's performances, whether at the concert halls in the major cities of his career, Berlin, Düsseldorf, Leipzig, and Frankfurt, at the Lower Rhine Music Festivals, or in smaller venues. It will be possible here only to mention a few representative, but contrasting, performances.

Let us begin with one of the first important audiences for Mendelssohn's performances, Goethe and his circle at Weimar, where Carl Friedrich Zelter, Mendelssohn's composition teacher, introduced his star pupil in 1821 (see table 1.1). In addition to Goethe himself, the audiences for Felix's various performances included Goethe's daughter-in-law Ottilie, who managed his household and had already heard Felix and Fanny at a dinner hosted by Zelter in Berlin in 1819,[33] and her sister, Ulrike von Pogwisch. The nobility were represented there by the grand duke and duchess and the Princess Luise, as well as the tsar's sister Maria Pavlovna. Philology was present in the person of Friedrich Wilhelm Riemer, Greek scholar, secretary to Goethe, and tutor to the poet's son August, who became the librarian of the Saxon grand ducal library.[34] There, too, were Arthur Schopenhauer's sister Adele, a writer of stories

Table 1.2. Some Audience Members at the Revival Performance of Bach's
St. Matthew Passion **in 1829 in Berlin**

Nobility and political and military leaders
    King Friedrich Wilhelm III and his retinue
    Joseph Maria von Radowitz, military general and important Bach collector

Scholars and writers
    Friedrich Daniel Ernst Schleiermacher, theologian
    Georg Wilhelm Friedrich Hegel, philosopher
    Johann Gustav Droysen, historian
    Heinrich Heine, writer and poet

Noteworthy women
    Rahel Varnhagen von Ense, salonnière
    Madame Liman
    Frau Radowitz (Marie Voss), wife of General Radowitz
    Frau von Cotta, wife of the Stuttgart publisher
    Doris Zelter, wife of Carl Friedrich Zelter
    Therese Devrient, wife of Eduard Devrient, who sang the role of Jesus

Musical figures
    Gasparo Spontini, royal Generalmusikdirektor
    Carl Friedrich Zelter, director of the Berlin Singakademie
    Georg Poelchau, important manuscript collector
    [probably Paganini, who was in Berlin at the time]

Reviewers
    Friedrich von Raumer, for the *Spenersche Zeitung*
    Ludwig Rellstab, for the *Vossische Zeitung*
    Friedrich Förster, historian and poet, and founder of the Berlin
        Wissenschaftlicher Kunstverein, for the *Berliner Conversationsblatt,* which he
        co-published
    Johann Philipp Samuel Schmidt, royal councilor for shipping, for the Leipzig
        Allgemeine musikalische Zeitung
    Adolf Bernhard Marx, for the *Berliner Allgemeine musikalische Zeitung*

[Possibly also at the first performance, though they may not have attended until the 22
March performance under Zelter, were historian Johann Wilhelm Loebell and Breslau
Singakademie director Theodor Mosewius.]

and poetry, and her mother Johanna.[35] To commemorate the occasion Adele demonstrated one of the charming practices of bürgerlich life, the artistic cutting of silhouettes from black paper, three of which appear in Felix's album. Goethe also contributed a poem.[36]

We also know some of the audience at Mendelssohn's revival performance of the St. Matthew Passion in 1829 (see table 1.2).[37] The attitude and behavior of the audience represents the extreme example of the idea of

Table 1.3. Some Audience Members at Fanny's Sonntagsmusik at
Leipzigerstrasse 3, 10 March 1844

Nobility
   Prince Antoni Henryk Radziwill, king's brother-in-law, governor of Poznań,
     amateur cellist and composer
   Count Westmoreland, English ambassador
   eight princesses

Scholars
   Friedrich von Raumer, history professor at the University of Berlin
   Johann Lukas Schönlein, physician to King Friedrich Wilhelm IV
   Henrik Steffens, Norwegian naturalist, philosopher, poet

Writer and artists
   Fanny Lewald, writer
   Karl Wilhelm Wach, painter
   Christian Friedrich Tieck, sculptor

Other notable figures
   two daughters of Bettina Brentano von Arnim
   Franz Liszt

Kunstreligion, perhaps exaggerated in this particular case but not entirely
out of keeping with the approach to high art more generally. Fanny
Mendelssohn wrote, "The room was crowded, and had all the air of a
church: the deepest quiet and most solemn devotion pervaded the whole,
only now and then involuntary utterances of intense emotion were heard."[38]
A sardonic view of the same observation emerges from the comments of
Rahel Varnhagen von Ense, who noted that Frau Radowitz and Frau von
Cotta "read the Bible passages as text, without being moved at all! No, they
studied it with phony expressions, as if it were difficult—something like
Kant's *Critique of Pure Reason*."[39]
    To get an idea of the audience at the Sonntagsmusiken at Leipziger-
strasse 3, we can turn to the record of Fanny's musical afternoon on 10
March 1844 (see table 1.3). Fanny wrote that "Liszt and eight princesses"
attended.[40] More specifically, the audience included University of Berlin
history professor Friedrich von Raumer; Johann Lukas Schönlein, physician to the king; the Norwegian naturalist, philosopher, and poet Henrik
Steffens, who was living in Berlin; the novelist Fanny Lewald; the painter
Karl Wilhelm Wach; and the sculptor Christian Friedrich Tieck; the king's
brother Prince Antoni Henryk Radziwill, governor of Poznań and an amateur cellist and composer, with his family; Count Westmoreland, the English
ambassador; two daughters of Bettina Brentano von Arnim; and others.
Lewald's autobiography identifies the audience members and reports how

impressed she was with Felix's performance, although Liszt's arrival seems to have made just as great an impression.[41]

Not all of Mendelssohn's audiences were as sophisticated as these lists represent, confirming Riehl's observation that bürgerlich culture spread itself into all classes. At the Lower Rhine Music Festivals entrance to rehearsals cost 10 groschen, well within the means of the Kleinbürger, and audiences ranged upward of one thousand at some performances. The operatic brouhaha in Düsseldorf in December 1833 was precipitated by a party opposed to increased ticket prices, "mostly beerhouse keepers and waiters," Mendelssohn wrote to Moscheles.[42] Chorley reports that attendance at the Gewandhaus concert of 30 October 1839 cost just 16 groschen.[43] At the Braunschweig Music Festival in September of 1839 Chorley observed

> [e]legantly dressed girls in the transparent and gay toilettes of an English ballroom . . . side by side with the gipsy-colored, hard-handed peasant women of the district, in their black caps gracefully displaying the head and picturesquely decorated with pendant streamers of ribbon. Here, again, was a comely youth, tight-laced in his neat uniform, and every hair of his moustache trimmed to an agony of perfection, squeezed up against a dirty, savage, half-naked student, with his long, wild hair half way down his back, and his velveteen coat, confined at the waist with one solitary button, letting it be clearly seen that neither waistcoat nor shirt was underneath.[44]

Some Mendelssohn performances served quite unusual audiences. At his uncle Nathan's foundry in Bad Reinerz he played a Mozart concerto to an audience of ironworkers. At Brandenburg in October 1828 he explained fugues to military officers and played music, including the Well-Tempered Clavier, on local church organs. At the Gutenberg festival in Leipzig in June 1840 Mendelssohn's Festgesang was performed in the town square while booksellers sold their wares.[45]

Given the breadth of his audiences, from the highest intellectual circles to the petty bourgeoisie and even peasants and laborers, Mendelssohn faced the task of composing for the public but never catering to popularity. He had a clear idea of his target audiences. And we can survey Mendelssohn's works and performances from this point of view, keeping in mind his bürgerlich listeners.

One must begin in Berlin, certainly a very musical city. Berlioz wrote in his Mémoires, "Music is in the air there. One breathes it; it permeates you. One finds it in the theater, in the church, in the concert hall, in the street, the public parks, everywhere. . . . Music in Berlin is respected by the rich and the poor, the clergy and the army, artists and amateurs; the common people and the King hold it in veneration."[46] The veneration with which Berliners approached music must have seemed characteristic, though, for he also emphasized that "in order to believe it, one must witness the attention, the respect, the reverence with which the German public listens to such a composition [as the *St. Matthew Passion*]. Each person follows the words in the libretto; not a movement in the auditorium, not a murmur of approval or of criticism; no applause. They are at a sermon, they hear the gospel sung, they listen in silence not to a concert but to the divine service."[47] When Rahel Varnhagen commented snidely that Frau Radowitz and Frau von Cotta listened to the Passion with their eyes glued to the gospel text, this apparently represented a general approach taken by many in the audience, and not necessarily only on that occasion. Ronald Taylor also observes that Berlin was unlike Vienna, in that the Berlin audience depended on critics to educate and guide musical taste.[48] This accounts for the importance of A. B. Marx's series of articles that prepared Berliners for the revival of the *St. Matthew Passion*. All of this helps explain something of the seriousness with which Mendelssohn took his performances' relationships to audiences.

Nor did Berlin have a monopoly on serious listeners. Seneca's saying "Res severa est verum gaudium" [True joy is a serious matter] stood as a motto over the orchestra in the Leipzig Gewandhaus. Chorley wrote that "A Leipsic audience seemed to me difficult, and perhaps over-exquisite, in its likings and dislikings, but not captious without the power of giving a reason."[49] Like Riehl, John Toews points out that Mendelssohn's " 'home' . . . extended far beyond the small-town world of the Leipzig Buergertum,"[50] just as it did beyond the cultured elite of the Prussian capital.

That there was a cultural mission to be fulfilled in Germany was a matter of philosophical principle for Fichte and Hegel, who espoused the idea that the destiny of the German nation included showing the future to the world.[51] We can interpret Mendelssohn's oeuvre in general as rooted in an artistic project for ethical and cultural education—that is, as *Bildungsmusik*. Toews relates this project to the ideas that Mendelssohn learned from Zelter and from his family and that he developed in discussions with the Prussian diplomat Baron von Bunsen, among others.[52]

In terms of the larger works in public forums—Toews focuses on the "Reformation" Symphony, *Paulus,* the *Lobgesang,* and *Elias* but also discusses, for example, *Antigone*—Mendelssohn understood music's mission to be the enlightenment of the audience. Like some of his Romantic contemporaries he had no patience with titillating the audience by empty virtuosity nor fascinating them with thrilling but morally empty opera plots. Specifically, as Toews puts it, he envisioned music as a means by which the listener would find "personal identity as an internalization of an essential humanity defined through its dependence on an absolute ground."[53] At the same time, this identity for Mendelssohn's German audience depended on connection with history, represented largely through the invocation of the

Table 1.4. Some Dedications of Published Collections of Vocal and Piano Songs

Songs
- op. 34 Julie Jeanrenaud
- op. 47 Frau Constanze Schleinitz
- op. 57 Livia Frege (German ed.); Charlote Dolby (English ed.)

Songs without words
- op. 30 Elise von Woringen
- op. 38 Rose von Woringen
- op. 53 Sophy Horsley
- op. 62 Clara Schumann
- op. 67 Sophie Rosen

chorale within great historical genres, the oratorio and symphony. In other words, despite Mendelssohn's personal repulsion at the rise of German chauvinism, the sense of nation permeated his concept of the relation of his music to its bürgerlich audience.

This meant that the appropriate audience response to such works was neither Romantic solipsism nor communal entertainment. Rather, the listener should experience in the music connections to the content of the great ideas of history, whether historical, biblical, or mythical, and experience the great forms, as represented by the chorale, fugue, and symphony. The music would thereby elevate the audience to consciousness of higher truth and power, the source of both personal and shared cultural identity.

The smaller, more intimate works had a different performance function. Rather than cultivate the listener's identity in relation to history and the ground of human nature, these works address the listener in a private and intimate manner. Most evidently bürgerlich are Mendelssohn's contributions to music for the family audience—the lieder, part songs, and songs without words. Although these occasionally appeared in performances in public concerts, in conception they addressed the household music maker, the young women with their pianos, playing and singing for their families in the evening, or family and friends singing *im Freien* on an excursion. Many of these pieces literally addressed particular individuals. Vocal and solo piano songs often had as direct audiences friends and social acquaintances to whom manuscripts were presented "zu freundlicher Erinnerung." The published songs and songs without words were characteristically dedicated to women whom Mendelssohn knew personally. Table 1.4 shows the dedications of some of the published collections; a list of autograph manuscripts given as album leaves and keepsakes would run to many dozens.

As travel formed such an important part of the formative activity of the bourgeois, Mendelssohn's music based on travel also played to the Bürgertum. We think of the *Hebrides* overture and the Scottish and Italian Symphonies as reflecting Mendelssohn's own travels. Equally, though, we should consider them as addressing a listenership that formed its own personality by travel—or at least idealized such cultivating travel and would gladly identify with travel as part of its culture, if not wealthy enough to undertake the full Grand Tour, then vicariously through reading travel books, through pictures of foreign scenes, or through music.

Then, too, much of Mendelssohn's music based on literature reflects the intention to appeal to a well-read audience and/or to encourage bourgeois literary culture. Again, we think of the *Midsummer Night's Dream* Overture as reflecting the high literary culture of young Felix and his family themselves, but it also addressed an ideal bourgeois audience or cultivated the audience through the appeal to literary sophistication. Among the works that belong to this repertoire would be obviously the incidental music for Shakespeare's play, for Sophocles's *Antigone* and *Oedipus in Colonus,* and for Racine's *Athalie,* components of the Prussian royal and administrative program for building a classic culture. The category should include the settings of Goethe's *Meeresstille und glückliche Fahrt* and *Die erste Walpurgisnacht.* Naturally, the songs belong here, as well.

The popularity and importance of the Verein obviously plays into the works for vocal ensembles, part songs, and other choral music. Mendelssohn dedicated the part songs "im Freien zu singen" op. 48 to two medical doctors and musical amateurs, Dr. Martin and Dr. Gustav Adolf Spiess of Frankfurt am Main, associated with the Cäcilienverein there.[54]

The ambition to build the German nation brought music that addressed historic occasions and the audiences at commemorative events. The 1828 Dürerfest cantata, the 1830 *Reformationsfest* Symphony, and the music for the Leipzig Gutenberg festival in 1840—both the *Lobgesang* and Gutenberg *Festgesang*—belong to this category.

The works in more traditional genres helped cultivate Bildung in the German bourgeois audience by adducing the nation's music-historical tradition. This certainly applies to the oratorios—not neglecting the *St. Matthew Passion,* but developing in Mendelssohn's own extension of the genre in *Paulus* and *Elias;* likewise, Mendelssohn's performance of Bach's organ works and his own preludes and fugues. The symphonies (taken as symphonies rather than as travel or literary works), chamber music, and sonatas would all come into play. This also relates to the "historical concerts" performances that Mendelssohn developed with the Gewandhaus Orchestra.

For reasons that are probably obvious but generally remain unconscious we habitually approach musical works from the point of view of what they tell us about the composer in the sense of self-expression. This is natural from the viewpoint of nineteenth-century Romanticism, where the subjective position underlay assumptions about how music acts. As this essay suggests, however, we should not become so preoccupied with the composer's voice that we neglect to consider the music also in relation to its audiences.

Here we have discussed audiences for Mendelssohn's performances and music from both historical and conceptual points of view. We have identified the general audience for which Mendelssohn's music was conceived, the German bourgeois of the third, fourth, and fifth decades of the nineteenth century, a listenership developing a sense of its national and cultural identity, of general education, art, and family life. We have observed some of the elite social and intellectual society for whom we have records of attendance at Mendelssohn's own performances, as well as his lower-class listeners. And we have considered the ways in which Mendelssohn's music responded to and contributed to the development of his audience, bringing into play both the way in which Mendelssohn's audience, or his vision of it, affected his music and musical activities and the manner in which his music participated in constructing the audience and its culture.

NOTES

1. Excerpted from Clive Brown, *A Portrait of Mendelssohn* (New Haven: Yale University Press, 2003), 465–67. Riehl (1823–97) pursued a varied literary career. Brown identifies the article as from either the Nassau or the Augsburg *Allgemeine Zeitung* between 1847 and 1850; it was republished in Riehl's *Musikalische Characterköpfe* in 1853.

2. Numbers taken from Ronald Taylor, *Berlin and Its Culture: A Historical Portrait* (New Haven: Yale University Press, 1997), 114; R. Larry Todd, *Mendelssohn: A Life in Music* (New York: Oxford University Press, 2003), 306; and David Blackbourn, *History of Germany 1780–1918: The Long Nineteenth Century* (Oxford: Blackwell, 2003), 152.

3. Jürgen Kocka, "The European Pattern and the German Case," in *Bourgeois Society in Nineteenth-Century Europe,* ed. Jürgen Kocka and Allan Mitchell (Oxford and Providence: Berg, 1993), 4. In early nineteenth-century Prussia citizen status had to be applied for and depended on period of residence, home ownership, or practice of a trade. Civil servants and those in "educated professions" were technically not citizens, nor were people without real estate, soldiers, or Jews. They could vote but not hold office. See Thomas Nipperdey, *Germany from Napoleon to Bismarck, 1800–1866,* trans. Daniel Nolan (Dublin: Gill and Macmillan, 1996), 27.

4. Kocka, 4–5. Also not to be overlooked, a "bourgeois-peasant" society existed in the countryside; Nipperdey, 25.

5. David Blackbourn, "The German Bourgeoisie: An Introduction," in *The German Bourgeoisie from the Late Eighteenth to the Early Twentieth Century,* ed. David Blackbourn and Richard J. Evans (London and New York: Routledge, 1991), 8; Kocka, 21.

6. Nipperdey, 31. In fact, restrictions applied in both directions, so the new situation not only permitted the lower classes to move upward but also would allow noblemen to practice a trade.

7. David Landes, "Industrialization and Economic Development in 19th-Century Germany," in *Readings in the History of Economic Growth,* ed. Malcolm E. Falkus (Nairobi: Oxford University Press, 1968), 155.

8. Nipperdey, 29.

9. Karin Friedrich, "Cultural and Intellectual Trends," in *Nineteenth-Century Germany: Politics, Culture and Society 1780–1918,* ed. John Breuilly (London: Arnold, 2001), 110.

10. Nipperdey, 472, 479.

11. Wolfgang Kaschuba, "Germany *Bürgerlichkeit* after 1800: Culture as Symbolic Practice," in *Bourgeois Society in Nineteenth-Century Europe,* ed. Jürgen Kocka and Allan Mitchell (Oxford and Providence: Berg, 1993), 400; Nipperdey, 119.

12. Christiane Eisenberg, "Working-Class and Middle-Class Associations: An Anglo-German Comparison, 1820–1870," in *Bourgeois Society in Nineteenth-Century Europe,* ed. Jürgen Kocka and Allan Mitchell (Oxford and Providence: Berg, 1993), 153–54.

13. Blackbourn, "Bourgeoisie," 11, 15; Nipperdey, 102, 105–106.

14. Nipperdey, 416.

15. Ibid., 46–47.

16. Friedrich, 98; Nipperdey, 44, 46, 419–20.

17. Kaschuba, 408.

18. Ibid., 408–10.

19. Nipperdey, 164, 520–26.

20. Ibid., 119, 222.

21. Kaschuba, 409, 417–20.

22. Todd, 282.

23. Kaschuba, 419.

24. Nipperdey, 164–66.

25. Ibid., 18–19.

26. Landes, 156.

27. Nipperdey, 116.

28. Friedrich, 113.

29. Ibid., 111.

30. Nipperdey, 374–79.

31. Ibid., 478.

32. The present essay does not list family members and mostly not professional musicians. The list of Mendelssohn relatives is long and includes a remarkable population—as Felix Gilbert titled his book about the family, *Bankiers, Künstler, und Gelehrte*—well representing the elite audience. Of course, the roster of musicians in Mendelssohn's audiences excludes hardly any significant musician of his time.

33. Todd, 47.

34. By the time of Mendelssohn's 1825 visit to Weimar, his performance there was heard by the Genevan natural scientist Frédéric Jacques Soret (1795–1865); Todd, 139 and 586n15. Soret was tutor to the Weimar Crown Prince Carl Alexander, a crystallographer, and an important collector and scholar of coins.

35. Todd, 86–87.

36. The silhouette of fairies riding a hobby horse that corresponds to Goethe's poem is reproduced in Felix Mendelssohn, *Letters,* ed. G. Selden-Goth (New York: Pantheon, 1945), 24, as is Goethe's poem. Mendelssohn's album is MS. M. Deneke Mendelssohn d. 8 in the Bodleian Library in Oxford.

37. See Martin Geck, *Die Wiederentdeckung der Matthäuspassion im 19. Jahrhundert: Die zeitgenössischen Dokumente und ihre ideengeschichtliche Deutung,* Studien zur Musikgeschichte des 19. Jahrhunderts 9 (Regensburg: Bosse, 1967).

38. Letter to Carl Klingemann, 22 March 1829; Sebastian Hensel, *The Mendelssohn Family (1729–1847) from Letters and Journals,* trans. Carl Klingemann, 2nd rev. ed. (New York: Harper, 1882; repr. New York: Haskell House, 1969), 1:172.

39. Quoted in Geck, 48, from Rahel's letter to her husband of 13 March 1829. Rahel and Heine both expressed themselves bored by much of the performance.

40. Letter to her sister Rebecka Dirichlet, 18 March 1844; Hensel, 2:260.

41. Fanny Lewald, *The Education of Fanny Lewald: An Autobiography,* trans. of *Meine Lebensgeschichte,* ed. Hanna Ballin Lewis (Albany: State University of New York Press, 1992), 253–54. It has not been possible to identify which of Bettina's daughters were present; the three were Maximiliane ("Maxe," 1818–94), Armgart ("Amra," 1821–80), and Gisela (1827–89).

42. Felix Mendelssohn Bartholdy, *Letters of Felix Mendelssohn to Ignaz and Charlotte Moscheles,* trans. and ed. Felix Moscheles (London: Trübner, 1888), 88.

43. Todd, 281; Henry F. Chorley, *Modern German Music* (London: Smith, Elder, 1854), 2:33. For comparison, advertisements in the *Neue Zeitschrift für Musik* in 1839 show that for 10 groschen one could purchase Sterndale Bennett's Allegro grazioso for Piano, op. 18; or Heinrich Panofka's Ballade for Violin and Piano, op. 20; or 3 songs for voice and piano by A. von Villers. For 16 groschen one could buy Sigismond Thalberg's Andante in D-flat, op. 32; or Six Etudes for Violin, op. 2, by the young violin virtuoso Charles Dancla; or A. B. Fürstenau's Reminiscences of *Les Huguenots* for Flute and Piano, op. 129; or a fine lithograph portrait of Robert Schumann.

44. Chorley, 1:20.

45. Todd, 122, 191, 396.

46. Berlioz, *Mémoires de Hector Berlioz: comprenant ses voyages en Italie, en Allemagne, en Russie et en Angleterre, 1803–1865* (Paris: Callman Lévy, 1896–97), 2:118.

47. Berlioz, 2:122.

48. Taylor, 151.

49. Chorley, 2:51.

50. John Edward Toews, *Becoming Historical: Cultural Reformation and Public Memory in Early Nineteenth-Century Berlin* (Cambridge: Cambridge University Press, 2004), 246.

51. Taylor, 92.

52. Toews, 207–15.

53. Ibid., 278.

54. I have not been able to find specific information on Dr. Martin. A brief note on Spiess (1802–75) appears in an online auction catalogue listing for Antiquariat Franz Siegle, http://www.antiquariat-siegle.de/kat42/351-400.htm (accessed 12 May 2005).

2

Mendelssohn and the Piano

KENNETH HAMILTON

IMAGES OF A STYLE

Even during Mendelssohn's lifetime, three distinct images of him as a pianist-composer had begun to develop that served to categorize his musical style for over a century after his death. The positive was based on direct knowledge of his own playing and performance-practice. It presented the picture of a serious, conscientious, and intensely musical performer, an opponent of affectation and sentimentality, who favored brisk tempi and strict adherence to the letter of the score. Two competing negative images, eventually to border on caricature, were also emerging. One was based on the growing popularity of Mendelssohn's Songs without Words among well brought-up young ladies. Through this he was considered to be—presumably by osmosis—an "effeminate" musician: one whose piano music was suited to be trotted out in the bourgeois parlor by affected amateurs of shaky technique and saccharine taste. The last image, rather different but almost equally harmful, was derived from the widening reputation of the Leipzig Conservatory, which Mendelssohn had helped to found and in which he had taught both piano and composition. This center of learning supposedly fostered—at least to those avant-garde artists disaffected with its aims—a dry, pedantic, and conservative performance style. Mendelssohn was by association a hopelessly old-fashioned composer who appealed merely to eager but uninspired "young philistines in the conservatories," as the waspish American critic Nathan Dole complained in 1891.[1] Although it was scarcely fair to judge Mendelssohn's musical aesthetic by the sins of his devotees, "by their fruits shall ye know them" remained a valid critical stance toward the hapless composer well into the twentieth century.

Exposure to numerous distorted and effete performances of Mendelssohn's music indeed led many to associate him with a lightweight performance style of amiable amateurish inadequacy, despite a doughty rear-guard action fought sporadically after his death by pianists as celebrated and influential as Liszt, Hans von Bülow, and (belatedly) Busoni. The testimony of the first two was especially important as they themselves had heard Mendelssohn play. Although Liszt's personal relations with the considerably more straitlaced Mendelssohn ranged from the over-effusively cordial to the extremely uneasy, he retained both a vast respect for him as a musician and keen memories of his performance style. Instructing his pupils in 1883 on the approach required for the principal Romantic piano composers, Liszt gave a summary that is even more useful today: "Schumann especially must be phrased well in details; and played very compact—rhythmically well articulated. With him ritenutos should be very great, as with Mendelssohn the accelerandos and animatos are great; Mendelssohn dashes out bright and quickly. Schumann has breadth, but Chopin has greater height."[2] Remembering Mendelssohn's reputation for swift performances, he added on a later occasion: "I am not in favour of extreme tempi, as often heard done by virtuosos of today. It is justifiable only in a few exceptions—perhaps with Mendelssohn."[3] Von Bülow had not only frequently heard Mendelssohn play, but even received a lesson from him. As he put it: "I had the honour of being Mendelssohn's pupil for exactly two hours,"[4] and his comments on what sometimes passed for Mendelssohn performance style were typically trenchant: "The ritardandos which are added to Mendelssohn have given him an undeserved reputation for lemonade-like sentimentality. It is, however, noble wine, not lemonade."[5] A Mendelssohn Song without Words was, according to von Bülow, "as Classical as a Goethe poem" and should be played as such.[6]

Unlike some, both Liszt and von Bülow were also able to distinguish between Mendelssohn's own performance aesthetic, which they respected, and the frigid style sometimes associated with his famous conservatory at Leipzig, which they roundly despised. Although Liszt enjoyed a well-deserved reputation for benevolence and graciousness, certainly in comparison with the acerbic von Bülow, the Leipzig Conservatory and occasionally the other conservatories at Frankfurt, Berlin, and Cologne were habitually referred to with humorous contempt and sarcasm during his masterclasses. A student playing Liszt's *Liebestraum* no. 1 in 1884 was instructed, "You must play that totally carried away as if you were not even seated at the piano, completely lost to the world, not 1, 2, 3, 4 as in the Leipzig Conservatory!"[7]

while a performer of the *Mephisto* Polka was told sarcastically: "This piece is composed especially for the Leipzig Conservatory. Play it only paying attention to yourself, and not at all brilliantly."[8] Liszt's most withering comments, however, were occasioned by inept attempts at performing Chopin's C-minor Nocturne op. 48 no.2, when his criticism extended far beyond the unfortunate performers to take in two celebrated pianists in Mendelssohn's former circle, including one of his teachers, Moscheles:

> The first lady played the theme at the beginning extremely sentimentally and fragmented, whereupon the master sat down and played the theme in an extremely broad and expansive manner. The young lady continually swayed along back and forth, to which Liszt said "Keep perfectly calm, child. This tottering is 'frankfurtisch,' just do not totter so." [Clara Schumann taught at the Hoch Conservatory in Frankfurt.] He sat down and said: "Even the wonderful [Clara] Schumann sways like that," and he humorously imitated it. Then he came to speak about the fashionable fragmenting of all themes and said. "Disgusting! I thank you, that is certainly the opposite of all good manners." . . . Then in an extremely droll manner he imitated Moscheles playing one of his etudes. . . . Then he said, "Yes, in Leipzig, or Frankfurt, or Cologne or Berlin at the 'great conservatories,' there you will make a success with that. One can say to you as to Ophelia: 'Get thee to a nunnery'—get thee to a conservatory."[9]

A picture of Mendelssohn as a favorite of Victoria and Albert (which indeed he was), as a conservative conservatory director, as a prim composer of music suitable only for the dusty syllabuses of these same ossified conservatories, and even as a man whose music and morals were hygienic enough for governesses in high-collared Victorian dresses, took a long time to die, if it ever quite has. It was substantially encouraged toward the end of the nineteenth century by such entertainingly insulting critics as George Bernard Shaw, whose notorious and oft-repeated excoriations of Mendelssohn's "monstrous platitudes," his "kid-glove gentility and conventional sentimentality," lingered long in the memory.[10] The necessarily restricted keyboard repertoire recorded in the early decades of the twentieth century did little to counter this view. Although most major pianists kept at least a handful of the longer, more "serious" Mendelssohn works in their active concert repertoire (for example Busoni the G-minor Concerto, Ignaz Friedman the *Variations Sérieuses,* Paderewski the Prelude and Fugue in E minor), and although the Liszt/Mendelssohn "Hochzeitsmarsch und Elfenreigen" maintained its crowd-pleasing place as an encore, the pieces actually put down on disk tended to be the more modest usual suspects, such as the Andante and Rondo Capriccioso, the Capriccio op. 16, no. 2, and the few Songs without Words with popular titles such as "Spinning Song," "Spring Song," or "Hunting Song."

The limitations of recording technology that made it prudent for Josef Hofmann to record an abridged version even of the hardly lengthy Rondo Capriccioso ensured that it was often both inconvenient and commercially unattractive to record a moderately long piece such as the *Variations Sérieuses* (a staple also of Paderewski's repertoire, and notably the first item on the program of his astoundingly successful 1922 "comeback" recital in the Carnegie Hall). This naturally encouraged the repetition of Mendelssohn's more approachable lyrical works, which could usually be fitted snugly on one side of a 78-rpm disk without brutal cuts or inappropriately hectic tempi. Some performers, such as Mark Hambourg, gradually began to baulk at insistent requests to record and rerecord what they considered to be hackneyed and tired short pieces, such as the elfin E-minor Capriccio (set down by several performers in addition to Hambourg, including Emil von Sauer and Moiseiwitsch). The frequent appearance on disk of Mendelssohn's miniatures had indeed compounded the taint of cliché already emanating from their popularity in the parlor. One can in fact still hear Hambourg's boredom with Mendelssohn in surviving disks, especially in his stiff and routine recording of the Mendelssohn/Liszt "On Wings of Song"—a case of an artist "telegraphing in his performance" if there ever was one. A more sympathetic pianist like Rachmaninoff, however, managed to set down a quite scintillating version (1928) even of the well-worn "Spinning Song." This, after what admittedly appears nowadays to be a rather eccentric pause on the anacrusis to the main theme, hurtles along with thrilling verve and accuracy. Rachmaninoff's recording of his own treacherous transcription of the Scherzo from the music to *A Midsummer Night's Dream* was no less dazzling, and hardly matched by the celebrated recording of the same piece by Moiseiwitsch made soon after. Despite the example of such magnificent playing, and indeed consistent descriptions of Mendelssohn's own brisk and vigorous playing from his contemporaries, his music remained for many decades more than usually at risk from a wayward performance-style that might be summarized as Paderewski-without-the-genius: copiously arpeggiated, willfully sentimental; in short, incompetence masquerading as rubato.

PIANOS AND TEACHERS

Even the earliest of early piano recordings were made on instruments substantially different from those known to Mendelssohn. On his death in 1847 the piano had not yet completed its evolution toward the steely Leviathan familiar by the end of the nineteenth century, and still dominant today. It was to be ten years before von Bülow would inaugurate an iron-framed

Bechstein in a recital in Berlin, and another decade before Steinways were to score an overwhelming success at the 1867 Paris International Exhibition with their iron-framed, over-strung concert grand that set the template for the modern instrument. The pianos available to Mendelssohn were all of a more modest size and volume.

Mendelssohn's occasional piano teacher, Marie Bigot, who taught the prodigy in Paris in 1816, perhaps prompted the early purchase of a Broadwood piano for the Mendelssohn family. Bigot had been admired as a player by Haydn and had enjoyed a close friendship with Beethoven in Vienna. She herself had initially owned an Erard but subsequently changed to a Broadwood. Mendelssohn's father purchased one of the latter pianos (which he later had taken to Germany), rather than the expected French instrument, during the family's Parisian stay. By the 1830s the Broadwood was still in the family home in Berlin, if supposedly somewhat the worse for wear. Nevertheless, according to Mendelssohn's mother (admittedly not an unbiased witness) he could still make it produce a "heavenly" tone.[11] A drawing by William Hensel from 1821shows Felix seated at the other piano in the Mendelssohn household, a more slender Austrian instrument dating from around 1810.[12]

Mendelssohn's principal piano teacher, Ludwig Berger—whose students included Mendelssohn's sister Fanny as well as Henselt and Döhler—had been influenced in his keyboard development mainly by Field, Clementi, and Cramer. The etudes of the two latter accordingly played a significant role in Mendelssohn's keyboard training, while the nocturnes of Field were not without influence on the later Songs without Words, as indeed were Berger's own characteristic piano compositions. Other occasional teachers were Hummel, widely considered to be the finest player and improviser in Europe in the 1820s, and Ignaz Moscheles, many years later to join his erstwhile pupil as a professor at the Leipzig Conservatory.

With the exception of the modest later incorporation of some "advanced" figurations derived from Thalberg, Mendelssohn's own piano writing rarely strayed beyond this solid technical foundation laid early in his life. However, partly owing to his traditional musical schooling by Carl Friedrich Zelter, he also developed fluency in a variety of older keyboard styles, and was well acquainted with a range of historical keyboard instruments. In the Berlin *Singakademie,* the rehearsals he attended were accompanied by a harpsichord, while at home he had access to a Silbermann clavichord, an instrument that he later kept in his study in his Leipzig apartment beside his grand piano. But although he was greatly feted as an organist, particularly in England, the majority of his time at the keyboard was certainly spent at the pianoforte, and both he and his sister Fanny were eager to try out the wide variety of instruments produced by renowned makers in England, France, Germany, and Austria. By the mid-1830s Mendelssohn had traveled widely enough to be familiar with examples of pianos from virtually every major European manufacturer. At Goethe's house in Weimar, for example, he performed frequently on the poet's Viennese grand piano by Nannette Streicher. This instrument, which still exists, had a span of five octaves and featured four pedals ("harp" and "bassoon" in addition to the now usual two). Few serious composers—and certainly not Mendelssohn—wrote explicit directions for the extra pedals, and many influential pedagogues such as Czerny regarded them with distaste. Nevertheless these, and some even more extravagant examples, could be found on pianos well into Mendelssohn's adulthood.

Soon after he had begun to establish a European reputation as a pianist, the first gifts appeared at his doorstep. The English branch of Erard presented him with one of their instruments on 22 June 1832. Moscheles had already given a concert in London on it before it was shipped to the continent, and Mendelssohn enthusiastically wrote to him in English, paraphrasing a Byron poem he would set to music the next year: "there be none of beauty's daughters with a magic like Erard."[13] Although Fanny Mendelssohn found at least one Erard piano she encountered a little too heavy, despite what she admitted was its magnificent tone, her brother seems to have been untroubled by this. Lest Fanny's opinion be regarded as merely a reflection of her own lack of physical strength, we should remember that by the 1840s even Liszt considered some Erards to have actions that were rather too heavy for comfort. There can indeed be a remarkable difference of action-weight in restored Erards from the same period and the same factory, although most are significantly lighter than modern pianos, and all have a noticeably shallower fall of key.

Although on many occasions Mendelssohn simply had to play on whatever piano was conveniently available, he seems to have considered only Broadwood instruments to be serious rivals to the Erards, even if the family's first Broadwood—according to his sister—had the fault that "one hears in playing something besides the note, which sounds very unpleasant."[14] We know of Mendelssohn performing without complaint on an Erard in London (from the local factory), on a Broadwood he happened to come across on a steamer anchored off Liverpool in 1826 (not much choice in that particular venue), and on a Parisian Erard in 1832, an occasion where his performance received especially warm praise from the critics.[15] When, however, he was explicitly given the choice between a Broadwood and an Erard for the Birmingham premiere of his D-minor Concerto in 1837, he decided in favor of the latter.[16] In fact, so thoroughly impressed was he by the instruments of this company that he had a new Erard grand delivered to his Leipzig home in 1839. A little while later he performed Beethoven's "Moonlight" sonata, an improvisation on the same composer's "Adelaide," and his own Rondo op. 29 at Gewandhaus concerts on this piano. Nevertheless, in a final twist that prevents an easy summary of the situation, the Broadwood Company sent a new piano to Leipzig for Mendelssohn shortly before his death in 1847, an instrument which he apparently greatly admired.

It would therefore be misleading to claim that Mendelssohn consistently favored the one make of piano (unlike Chopin with his Pleyel, or Alkan and the young Liszt with their Erards) for his own performances. He seems sensibly to have judged each instrument on its particular merits, and perhaps agreed with his sister that one could not expect perfection from any piano. Even in today's age of mass production and standardized design there can be big differences between individual instruments from the same company. In Mendelssohn's day, when virtually all components of a piano were made by hand and the specifications of the instrument itself were in constant development, the contrasts could be vast indeed.

Performing on Historical and Modern Instruments

I have played on at least one 1830s Broadwood piano used by Mendelssohn (now housed in the present Broadwood factory at Stowe in England) and on a range of other contemporary Broadwoods and Erards. As these are undoubtedly the generally appropriate historical instruments for Mendelssohn's music, his performance indications need to be evaluated in this context. The instruments do have certain broad advantages over the modern concert grand, in particular a mostly lighter touch and shallower fall of key—useful qualities when one wishes to play quickly and crisply; and certain notable disadvantages, including variable stability of tuning, inefficient bass damping, and an often weak high treble range. Vast differences in tone color among the bass, middle, and treble registers are also regularly to be found in early pianos. For some musicians this is a lovable and fascinating characteristic, for others a glaring inadequacy. Suffice it to say that there are times when this feature does seem to be an advantage (the gentle opening of the Andante and Rondo Capriccioso is automatically characterized by three different tone-colors) and occasions when one would very gladly do without it (the brilliant octaves at the end of the same piece lose too much in volume and bite as they climb toward the treble). Of course, all of Mendelssohn's instruments were of a more flimsy build than those of today, but this was hardly a problem given the deliberate restraint of his keyboard writing. No doubt he regarded Liszt's piano-smashing antics with horror.

Worthy of greatest attention on the early instruments is phrasing and the associated use of the sustaining pedal. The latter was for Mendelssohn still to some extent a special effect designed to change the tone-color and increase the volume of sound more than to guarantee a perfect legato. The composer's own piano-duet arrangement of the *Hebrides* Overture, for example, at times indicates lengthy pedalings, seemingly to create an appropriately stormy sonority, but at other points is remarkably free from any pedal markings at all. Although Mendelssohn's "Thalberg-style" writing, as found in the Prelude to the E-minor Fugue, obviously demands a copious application of the pedal, some pianists may be surprised at the reticence with which it was actually indicated in the original printings of most of his works, especially if they are accustomed to the numerous editions in which swathes of new pedaling are generously provided.

Much of the pedaling added by editors was of the syncopated variety, which later on in the century was regarded as indispensable for performing pieces such as the very first Song without Words, op. 19 no. 1. Indispensable it may indeed be for more modern pianos, with their impressively effective damping systems. For despite our present skepticism about "unauthorized" alterations to a composer's text, most interventionist editors were certainly not careless vandals, but often—like Theodor Kullak—fine pianists whose intentions were simply to fit the music, as they saw it, to the instruments of the day. Their instruments were not Mendelssohn's. The light dampers on earlier Erards and Broadwoods had often functioned inadequately in the bass range of the instrument, particularly during loud passages. Pedal therefore had to be used with much greater discretion than on a modern piano, for fear of yet further confusing the sound, a requirement reflected by Mendelssohn's careful and scanty original markings. Syncopated pedaling was rarely necessary on Mendelssohn's instruments—the lightness of the dampers frequently produced a slight overhang in the sound, whether one wanted it or not, particularly on Erards, where the dampers actually push fairly weakly onto the string from below. It is no accident that syncopation and generally more copious and complex pedaling only became fashionable with the increasing efficiency of damper action in the decades after Mendelssohn's death.

The famous "Spring Song" is an instructive example of Mendelssohn's adept approach to pedaling. In the original edition of this work, the main tune is performed with dabs of sustaining pedal only at the recapitulation for a subtle variation in the sonority. The first presentation of the celebrated melody is obviously intended to have a crisp unpedaled staccato accompaniment (indeed Mendelssohn's piquant staccato was especially remarked upon in his own performances), with the required melodic legato to be achieved by the fingers alone. This is certainly made easier if Mendelssohn's relatively short phrase-lengths are printed and observed. Several subsequent editors added copious pedal to the opening pages, and also lengthened the phrase markings, creating a late-Romantic broad legato and completely eliminating the contrasts of tone-color between pedaled and non-pedaled passages intended by the composer. This became for many years the "standard" interpretation of this piece, heard on early recordings and to some extent still with us today.

The present-day performer must therefore be aware of what Mendelssohn actually wrote in terms of phrase and pedal markings, but must also keep in mind that his instrument may react rather differently from any known by the composer. This could well necessitate sensitive adaptation to express the probable intention, if not the letter, of the score. If the "Spring Song" is played on a modern concert grand, it is often useful to very slightly extend, without pedal, the length of the bass octaves supporting the tune during its first presentation. In this way we can imitate the short overhang of bass sound produced by Mendelssohn's instruments, avoid an over-flippant staccato in the lower register, and yet still maintain a non-pedaled sonority. We can additionally gauge from this example the limitations of von Bülow's seemingly straightforward advice "in Mendelssohn you do not need to interpret, he wrote everything scrupulously and exactly as he wanted to have it."[17] This presupposes not only an accurate edition, but also (although von Bülow himself may have disputed this) a piano of Mendelssohn's own era. Some experience of playing Mendelssohn on a range of contemporary pianos is enormously informative for the interpreter, even if his or her public performances are always on a modern instrument.

MENDELSSOHN THE PIANIST

Despite his even greater luster as a composer and conductor, Mendelssohn was certainly one of the preeminent pianists of his era. Contemporary admirers—and they were legion—were anxious to hold his playing up as a particularly pure model to follow, and to contrast it with what they regarded as current threats to good taste—a decadent virtuoso approach associated with Liszt, and a sweetly vapid approach associated with well-brought-up young ladies. As a brief illustration we might turn to two articles by Henry Chorley that appeared on the front page of the Philadelphia *National Gazette* of 20 August 1841, closely related in topic, yet rather different in content:

"Liszt's Piano Forte Playing" and "Mendelssohn's Piano Forte Playing" (it must, admittedly, have been a quiet week for news). Both of these were excerpts from Chorley's first volume of *Music and Manners in France and Germany,* and they summarize cogently a commonly held view of the aesthetic differences between the two performers. Liszt made a tremendous impact, but went too far for the upright Englishman. He is chastised for lacking uniform richness and sweetness of tone—in search of effect he forgot the limits of his instrument. The actual variety of tone, however, was "remarkable, and, as far as I have gone, unexampled." Other admirable qualities included "rapidity and evenness of fingers," "the power of interweaving the richest and most fantastic accompaniments with a steadily moving yet expressive melody," and "velocity, fire, and poignancy, in flights of octaves and chromatic chords."[18] The description of Mendelssohn's performance style, which in *Music and Manners* is also directly compared to that of Chopin and Moscheles, has a very different, and more sober, tenor: "Solidity, in which the organ-touch is given to the piano without the organ ponderosity; spirit (witness his execution of the finale of the D minor Concerto) animating, but never intoxicating to the ear; expression, which making every tone sink deep, requiring not the garnishing of trills and appogiaturi, or the aid of changes of time, are among its outward and salient characteristics."[19]

Elsewhere, Chorley attempted to depict Mendelssohn's playing by telling us what it is not. Mendelssohn's performance

> has none of the exquisite *finesses* of Moscheles . . . none of the delicate and plaintive and spiritual seductions of Chopin, who sweeps the keys with so insinuating and gossamer a touch, that the crudest and most chromatic harmonies of his music float away under his hand, indistinct yet not unpleasing, like the wild and softened discords of the Aeolian harp;—none of the brilliant extravagancies of Liszt, by which he illuminates every composition he undertakes, with a living but lightening fire, and imparts to it a soul of passion, or a dazzling vivacity, the interpretation never contradicting the authors' intention, but more poignant, more intense, more glowing than ever the author dreamed of.[20]

Remarkably, Chorley was even at this stage, long before Mendelssohn's death, anxious to distance the composer from associations with his less-talented female admirers: "One more word, which is perhaps a half-definition; Mendelssohn's is eminently manly music."[21] "Eminently manly"—it would hardly have been necessary to say it about Liszt or Thalberg, and would hardly have been likely to be said about Chopin, whose introverted and poetic style was to some contemporaries redolent not just of effeminacy but of the sickbed. With Mendelssohn, however, one had to protest loudly against the abuses of his admirers.

So how, in detail, did this "eminently manly" pianist play, and expect his music to be played? In terms of broad questions of performance approach, we can rely on a number of fortunately mostly unanimous contemporary accounts. Despite his skill, Mendelssohn would have contemptuously, and perhaps somewhat primly, rejected the description "virtuoso pianist," owing to what he regarded as its connotations of superficiality. In 1837 he reacted indignantly to his sister's admiration of contemporary virtuoso playing, and while doing so conveniently summarized his own views in a letter to his mother:

> I was annoyed, however, to hear that Fanny says the new school of piano-playing has left her behind . . . but there is absolutely nothing to that. She really plays all the little fellows such as Döhler into the ground; they can manage a couple of variations and party tricks nicely, and then everything becomes terribly boring, and that never happens when Fanny plays the piano. Then there is something other than party-tricks. Thalberg and Henselt are a rather different matter, for they are supposed to be true virtuosi in the manner of Liszt (who outclasses them all); and yet it all amounts to nothing more than a Kalkbrenner in his heyday, and blows over during their lifetime if there is not some spirit and life in it, and something more than mere dexterity. . . . For my part I believe that Chopin is by far the most inspired of them all, although Liszt's fingers are yet more amazing and supple than his.[22]

However much the tone of the above comments was colored by family solidarity, they are of a piece with views that Mendelssohn expressed on other occasions. He later grew to admire Thalberg more and more for his "composure and restraint,"[23] while as far as the notably unrestrained Liszt was concerned, he wrote: "I have seen no musician whose musical sensitivity . . . so courses straight into his fingertips and then flows directly out from there. And with this immediacy and his enormous technique and skill, he would leave all others far behind him, if it were not that his own ideas always predominate in whatever he is playing, and at least up to now these seem to have been denied him by nature."[24] Liszt, for his part, thought that Mendelssohn's own playing had "more warmth than Thalberg's, but less technique."[25]

Sir George Grove, in his ground-breaking entry on Mendelssohn in the first edition of his dictionary, provided what is still one of the most fascinating—even if hagiographic—accounts of Mendelssohn's performance-style, culled from personal conversations with many witnesses, although he cautioned that: "In reading them it should be remembered that Mendelssohn was fond of speaking of himself as a player *en gros,* who did not claim (however great his right) to be a virtuoso, and that there are instances of his having refused to play to great virtuosi."[26]

Clara Schumann's recollections opened Grove's list. Fully aware that her remarks were for public consumption, she put on the greatest possible adulatory gloss:

> My recollections of Mendelssohn's playing are among the most delightful things in my artistic life. It was to me a shining ideal, full of genius and life, united with technical perfection. He would sometimes take the *tempi* very quick, but never to the prejudice of the music. It never occurred to me to compare him with virtuosi. Of mere effects of performance he knew nothing—he was always the great musician, and in hearing him one forgot the player, and only revelled in the full enjoyment of the music. He could carry one with him in the most incredible manner, and his playing was always stamped with beauty and nobility. In his early days he had acquired perfection of technique; but latterly, as he often told me, he hardly ever practised, and yet he surpassed every one. I have heard him in Bach, and Beethoven, and in his own compositions, and shall never forget the impression he made upon me.[27]

The phrase "but never to the prejudice of the music" sounds almost as if it had been added as an afterthought, and in fact entries in Clara Schumann's diaries show that her opinions on Mendelssohn's brisk tempi were not always so positive. After a performance of Beethoven's Kreutzer Sonata with Mendelssohn as the accompanist she wrote: "He played this like he plays everything—in a masterly manner, brilliantly, yet not, to my mind, grandly enough, on the whole too hurried."[28] Robert Schumann had reminisced after Mendelssohn's death that he always liked taking really fast tempi when playing duets with Clara, and especially when sight-reading, a fondness also marked in his conducting. Although in this regard—indeed in any— Wagner was hardly an unbiased witness, his comments on Mendelssohn's performances are consistent with this: "he personally informed me once or twice that a too slow tempo was the devil, and for choice he would rather things were taken too fast; a really good rendering was a rarity at any time; with a little care, however, one might gloss things over; and this could best be done by never dawdling, but covering the ground at a good stiff pace." The result, according to Wagner, was that with an orchestra rehearsed by Mendelssohn, "every allegro ended as an indisputable Presto."[29]

Ferdinand Hiller, a close friend and supporter, most vividly remembered the natural ease of Mendelssohn's keyboard performance, but tempered his glowing remarks with a thoughtful appraisal of his weaknesses:

> Mendelssohn's playing "was to him what flying is to a bird. No one wonders why a lark flies, it is inconceivable without that power. In the same way Mendelssohn played the piano because it was his nature. He possessed great skill, certainty, power, and rapidity of execution, a lovely full tone—all in fact that a virtuoso could desire, but these qualities were forgotten while he was playing, and one almost overlooked even those more spiritual gifts which we

call fire, invention, soul, apprehension, etc. When he sat down to the instrument music streamed from him with all the fullness of his inborn genius,—he was a centaur, and his horse was the piano. What he played, how he played it, and that he was the player—all were equally riveting, and it was impossible to separate the execution, the music, and the executant. This was absolutely the case in his improvisations, so poetical, artistic, and finished; and almost as much so in his execution of the music of Bach, Mozart, Beethoven, or himself. Into those three masters he had grown, and they had become his spiritual property. The music of other composers he knew, but could not produce it as he did theirs. I do not think, for instance, that his execution of Chopin was at all to be compared to his execution of the masters just mentioned; he did not care particularly for it, though when alone he played everything good with interest. In playing at sight his skill and rapidity of comprehension were astonishing, and that not with pianoforte music only, but with the most complicated compositions. He never practised, though he once told me that in his Leipzig time he had played a shake (I think with the 2nd and 3rd fingers) several minutes every day for some months, till he was perfect in it."[30]

As for technique, Mendelssohn evidently, and hardly unpredictably, eschewed the newer virtuoso developments of using arm and shoulder weight to increase power and volume of tone, an approach often heard today. According to Otto Goldschmidt,

His mechanism was extremely subtle, and developed with the lightest of wrists (never from the arm); he therefore never strained the instrument or hammer. His chord-playing was beautiful, and based on a special theory of his own. His use of the pedal was very sparing, clearly defined, and therefore effective; his phrasing beautifully clear. The performances in which I derived the most lasting impression from him were the 32 Variations [in C minor] and the last Sonata (op. 111) of Beethoven, in which latter the Variations of the final movement came out more clearly in their structure and beauty than I have ever heard before or since.[31]

Not all were impressed by Mendelssohn's op. 111, however. Franz Brendel, a fervent supporter of "the music of the future," found his touch in the first movement "too light and fleeting" to convey the "painful disunity" of the composition[32] and evidently would have preferred if the performer had strained the instrument a little more. What Mendelssohn's "special theory" of chord playing was exactly is nowhere recorded, but what it probably did not involve was indulgence in frequent unmarked arpeggiation, a common approach that, according to Bülow, Mendelssohn implacably opposed.

One notable feature of Mendelssohn's playing was his power of occasionally recalling an orchestral sound—a quality usually preeminently attributed to Liszt. This talent was already noticeable in the home performances of the young Mendelssohn at musical gatherings. Therese Devrient reported: "Felix presided confidently from the piano and amazed his listeners by playing with such skill that one could hear individual instruments of the orchestra."[33] Later sources confirm this impression. Among others, Macfarren commented that "[i]n playing at sight from a MS. score he characterised every incident by the peculiar tone by which he represented the instrument for which it was written."[34]

This variety of tone-color notwithstanding, Mendelssohn's fundamental approach to piano technique remained deliberately old-fashioned. His conservatism naturally also extended to keyboard figuration. He contemptuously dismissed Henselt's imaginatively if extravagantly written Concerto in F as "passagework with a tune over the top,"[35] and of the more up-to-date styles of piano writing, only Thalberg's "three-handed" technique was sometimes essayed, notably in the Finale to the Second Concerto, the Etude in B-flat minor, op. 104b no. 1, and the Prelude to the Fugue in E minor. Even in the last-named there is a certain feeling of reticence owing to the limited span of the figuration, which is mostly confined to broken chords in close position that seldom stretch more than an octave. Liszt, Chopin, or Thalberg would surely have ranged more widely than this. Hiller recalled his attempts to persuade the composer to modernize a little the passagework in the D-minor trio:

> Mendelssohn had just finished his great D-minor Trio, and played it to me. I was tremendously impressed by the fire and spirit, the flow, and in short the masterly character of the whole thing. But I had one small misgiving. Certain pianoforte passages in it, constructed on broken chords, seemed to me—to speak candidly—somewhat old-fashioned. I had lived many years in Paris, seeing Liszt frequently, and Chopin every day, so that I was thoroughly accustomed to the richness of passages which marked the new pianoforte school. I made some observations to Mendelssohn on this point, suggesting certain alterations, but at first he would not listen to me. "Do you think that would make the thing any better?" he said. "The piece would be the same, and so it may remain as it is." "But," I answered, "you have often told me, and proved to me by your actions, that the smallest touch of the brush, which might conduce to the perfection of the whole, must not be despised. An unusual form of arpeggio may not improve the harmony, but neither does it spoil it—and it becomes more interesting to the player." We discussed it and tried it on the piano over and over again, and I enjoyed the small triumph of at last getting Mendelssohn over to my view. With his usual conscientious earnestness when once he had made up his mind about a thing, he now undertook the lengthy, not to say wearisome, task of rewriting the whole pianoforte part. One day, when I found him working at it, he played me a bit which he had worked out *exactly* as I suggested to him on the piano, and called out to me, "That is to remain in remembrance of you." Afterward, when he had been playing it at a chamber concert with all his wonderful fire, and had carried away the whole public, he said, "I really enjoy that piece; it is honest music, after all, and the players will like it, because they can show off with it." And so it proved.[36]

Mendelssohn's almost monastic attitude to contemporary keyboard styles was a counterpart to his strictness in performing the music of the masters he most admired, and several accounts testify to his seeming zealotry in adherence to the letter of the score. What could count as zealotry in the nineteenth century, however, often falls far short of the even greater fanaticism of our Urtext-obsessed age, and one must take care to evaluate contemporary comments in context. For example, Mendelssohn's famous revival of Bach's *St. Matthew Passion* took—quite deliberately, and for quite understandable practical reasons—what would now be regarded as eyebrow-raising liberties with the score, including extensive cuts and radical re-orchestration. Mendelssohn was also perfectly happy to compose a piano accompaniment to Bach's Chaconne for (originally) unaccompanied violin. Yet, there can be little doubt that by the standards of his time Mendelssohn was an unusually faithful, even Puritanical, performer. A pupil adding simply an extra note to fill out a chord was apt to be met with the disapproving "Es steht nicht da!" while he preferred any tempo fluctuations within a piece to be restrained and unobtrusive, an attitude that, in conducting, contrasted strikingly with Wagner's ostentatiously flexible approach.

The metronome, however, he despised as unnecessary, telling Berlioz once: "It's an utterly useless invention. A musician who can't work out the correct tempo of a piece just by looking at it is a blockhead." (He later felt the full force of Berlioz's sarcasm when he asked for some idea of the correct tempo for the King Lear Overture.)[37] It might reasonably be argued that Mendelssohn's resistance to his pupils' unlicensed liberties and additions could well have stemmed as much from their ineptitude ("Quod licet Jovi non licet bovi") than from an outright opposition in principle, but this is to ignore what indubitably was a streak of fundamentalism in his nature. His pleasure in some of Liszt's concerts in Berlin in 1842 was marred by what he regarded as an inappropriately cavalier license in the music of the great Classical masters, in accordance with his almost fanatical comment to Joachim that it is "inartistic, nay barbaric, to alter anything they have ever written, even by a single note":[38]

> Even Liszt doesn't please me here half as much as he did elsewhere. He has forfeited a large degree of my respect for him through the ridiculous pranks he plays, not only on the public (that didn't do any damage) but rather on the music itself. He has played here works by Beethoven, Bach, Handel and Weber so wretchedly and unsatisfactorily, so impurely and so unknowledgeably, that I would have heard them played by mediocre performers with more pleasure: here six measures added in, there seven omitted; here he plays false harmonies, and then later these are cancelled out by others. Then he makes a horrible fortissimo out of the softest passages, and goodness knows what other kinds of dreadful mischief. That may be all well and good for the public at large, but not

for me, and that it was good enough for Liszt himself, that lowers my respect for him by a very great deal. At the same time my respect for him was so great, that there is still enough left.[39]

Not surprisingly, when a pupil arrived at Leipzig sporting long Lisztian locks, Mendelssohn's first instruction to him was "you must get your hair cut!"[40]

How do we reconcile Mendelssohn's absolute condemnation of Liszt's liberties with a willingness to indulge in freedoms of his own? The answer is, of course, that we cannot, if we are expecting the consistency one encounters in a computer rather than a human being. The most we can say with confidence is that in an era with considerably more relaxed attitudes to textual fidelity than those prevalent today, Mendelssohn was generally regarded as on one extreme and Liszt (or at least the young Liszt) on the other. Perhaps were we to hear them now, both would surprise us.

When performing his own music Mendelssohn reportedly not only adopted an especially straightforward style, but even played in a deliberately detached manner, as if trying to avoid anything approaching a flashy or affected execution. Friends attributed this to his essential modesty—he did not wish his composition to gain in effect from any unworthily superficial technical brilliance. This directness of approach went concomitantly with an abomination of anything bordering on sentimental playing. Hans von Bülow put it typically bluntly: "Whoever plays Schumann tolerably well will play Mendelssohn rather intolerably. . . . Schumann is a sentimental poet; Mendelssohn a naïve one." Warming to his theme, he went on in an authoritative manner that succinctly summarizes his view of the essence of Mendelssohn's performance style, and deserves extended quotation:

> If one wants to play Mendelssohn correctly, one should first play Mozart, for example. Above all, one should renounce all Empfindsamkeit of conception, despite the temptations that are provided by certain frequently recurring melismas peculiar to Mendelssohn. One should try, for example, to play passages of this apparent character simply and naturally in rhythm, with a beautiful and regular attack, and one will surely find that they sound, in this fashion, much nobler and more graceful than in a passionately excited rubato. The master was committed, above all, to the strict observance of meter. He categorically denied himself every ritardando that was not prescribed, and wanted to see the prescribed ritards restricted to their least possible extent. He despised, furthermore, all arbitrary arpeggiation (chords that could not be played without breaking them, a la Schumann, he did not write, or only when he wanted successive chords—see the introduction to op. 22). In op. 14 there is not a single arpeggio mark, despite the "brilliant" style. He permitted the use of the pedal only for certain tonal effects. What subtle caution was to be exercised in this matter can be gleaned from his specification of the appropriate symbols throughout. Finally, he also protested against that "thrilling" haste, against the

rushing and forcing of his pieces by players who believed that the best way they could meet the charge of "sentimental" interpretation was through this kind of speeded-up, summary behaviour. Here we must nonetheless observe very decisively that his most frequent comments while teaching were "lively, briskly, keep going . . ."[41]

While one should not infer from the above that the ideal Mendelssohn performance should resemble that of a pianola, von Bülow's general meaning could hardly be clearer—and is especially convincing coming from one of the chief proponents of "tempo rubato" interpretation in the late nineteenth century.

IMPROVISATION

Despite Mendelssohn's almost exaggeratedly modest demeanor at the keyboard, one thing that could not help but draw attention to itself was his prodigious musical memory. Although playing from memory was hardly the rule in his day, he was quite able to recall a large repertoire without the aid of the score, a talent for better or worse required of pianists now, but then frequently remarked upon with wonder. His masterly performances from memory of Beethoven's "Emperor" Concerto and Weber's Konzertstück excited particular admiration. That his musical memory was extraordinary even by present-day standards is demonstrated by several accounts of his memorization—seemingly routinely—of piano accompaniments and even of individual parts in orchestral scores. This outstanding ability also aided him in improvisations, which were a striking feature of his own concerts. Mendelssohn's father mentioned one in which, after Malibran had sung five songs of different nations, his son was dragged to the piano, and improvised upon them all.[42] On another occasion Mendelssohn took three themes from Bach sonatas that had just been performed and astonished an audience of some of the finest musicians in Paris with his inspired spontaneity.[43]

Mendelssohn lived in an age where improvisation itself was hardly unusual—Beethoven and Hummel had been famed for their skills in this regard, while the concerts of Mendelssohn's contemporaries Liszt and Hiller regularly featured improvisations on written themes supplied by the audience (an urn or similar receptacle was placed at the hall entrance for the deposit of suggestions, which could be emptied later with a greater or lesser degree of melodrama). Mendelssohn hardly had the personality to submit himself to this sort of "trial by surprise theme," and one can scarcely imagine him emptying an urn before the public with voluble histrionic pleasure, but improvise he did, and unusually cogently. "It was," said Macfarren, "as fluent and well planned as a written work, and the themes, whether borrowed or invented were not merely brought together but contrapuntally worked."[44]

We can perhaps get some idea of an (admittedly mostly homophonic) Mendelssohn improvisation from his Fantasy on the "Last Rose of Summer," op. 15, a charming if rather uncharacteristic piece in his oeuvre. Although this genre was much cultivated by his virtuoso contemporaries, Mendelssohn once told Schumann that "he had never written occasional pieces, Fantasies on themes from, etc.—only once had he been in danger of this, in the presence of Malibran in London, who gave him the silly notion of writing such a piece."[45] The "Last Rose of Summer" Fantasy is, however, such a piece, though it is unlikely that it bears any relation to Malibran. The theme was a celebrated Irish "national air." The fantasy itself is a rather strange mixture of virtually unadorned statements of the tune interspersed with contrasting stormy episodes in the minor that appear to have little relation to it, rounded off by a coda that makes a glancing and unexpected reference to Beethoven's *An die ferne Geliebte*. There is possibly a hidden programmatic intent here, for to some extent the work seems like a fantasy against the melody rather than on it, and general features even sound compellingly similar to an account of Mendelssohn's boyish improvisation before Goethe in Weimar. Zelter had offered an unknown tune as a basis:

> Felix played it through after him, and the next minute went off into the wildest allegro, transforming the simple melody into a passionate figure, which he took now in the bass, now in the upper part, weaving all manner of new and beautiful thoughts into it in the boldest style. Everyone was in astonishment, as the small childish fingers worked away at the great chords, mastering the most difficult combinations, and evolving the most surprising contrapuntal passages out of a stream of harmonies, though certainly without paying much regard to the melody.[46]

We can hardly recreate a full-scale Mendelssohn improvisation today, and even if "The Last Rose of Summer" Fantasy had its origins in one, Mendelssohn is likely to have made extensive revisions between its first conception in 1827 and its eventual publication around 1831. It is, however, possible to get a little closer to one other improvisatory feature of his performance style—the habit of extemporizing preludes before and between pieces, the latter often constituting a modulating transition when the following work was in a different key. An extempore introductory prelude from the accompanist was especially welcome in the performance of any Lied that in the printed music began immediately with the voice, for it additionally fulfilled the valuable function of helping the singer to pitch the first note. In solo performances of character pieces, etudes, fantasies, and the like, preluding was also the rule. The opening arpeggiated chord of the "Last

Rose of Summer" Fantasy is one of the simplest examples of a prelude actually written into the opening of a solo work, and slightly more extended examples can be found in the *Lieder ohne Worte,* op. 30 no. 3 and op. 38 no. 4. Of course in all these cases, no further prelude needed to be improvised, and in the two *Lieder ohne Worte* Mendelssohn additionally brings back the prelude at the end of the piece as a piquant closing gesture. For a concert in 1846 the composer reportedly improvised an entire slow introduction to the Rondo Brillant in E-flat for Piano and Orchestra, op. 29 (for a general idea of what this might have involved, compare the slow andante introduction—added later—to the Rondo Capriccioso, op. 12). During a charity concert the previous year in the Leipzig Gewandhaus featuring Jenny Lind, Mendelssohn improvised both a prelude and an extensive modulating link between his two solo pieces. William Rockstro left a very detailed account:

> Mendelssohn's own contribution to this performance were his First Concerto in G-minor, and a solo für pianoforte, which consisted of two Lieder ohne Worte—no. 1 Book VI, and No. 6 Book V—both evidently chosen on the spur of the moment, and rendered intensely interesting by a prelude and interlude such as he alone could have improvised. Beginning with a characteristic prelude in E♭, Mendelssohn played, as only he could play it, his own Lied ohne Worte, No 1 book VI. Then, during the course of a long and masterly modulation from the key of E♭ to that of A major he carried on the quiet semiquaver accompaniment of the first Lied for some considerable time, without interruption, treating it with new and unexpected harmonies, so contrived as to permit the continuance of the bell-like B flat in the form of an inverted pedal-point, and always presenting the re-iterated note in some novel and captivating position. As the modulation proceeded, the B flat gave place to other notes, treated in like manner; and presently these were relieved by a new figure, which rapidly developed into the well-known feathery arpeggio of the famous Frühlingslied. Every one thus knew what was coming: but no-one was prepared for the fiery treatment which first worked up this arpeggio-form into a stormy climax carrying all before it, and then as it gradually approached the long-expected chord of A-major, died gently away, in a long-drawn diminuendo, so artfully managed that, when the delicious melody was at last fairly introduced, it sent an electric thrill through every heart in the room.[47]

Although highly, perhaps sadly, unusual nowadays outside cocktail bars and jazz clubs, the practice of improvising a prelude to a piece, or a modulating transition between pieces, remained common up until around the Second World War. A famous recording of Josef Hofmann from the Casimir Hall, Philadelphia, in 1939 strikingly illustrates this practice, and of course many collections of preludes exist by Chopin, Hummel, Kalkbrenner, and others, some of which were certainly intended for use by those unable or unwilling to improvise their own. Written-out transitions are much thinner on the ground, but a fascinating published example of what is effectively a modulatory transition in extempore style (and one that very much recalls Mendelssohn's supposed approach at the Jenny Lind concert mentioned above) can be found in the extensive link between the last two pieces in Charles-Valentin Alkan's Fifth Book of Chants, op. 70.

It could well be that Romantic players' fondness for improvised transitions between pieces in different keys—seemingly so unnecessary to us today—was encouraged by the systems of keyboard tuning then in use. These likely varied from our so-called equal-temperament, even if they did sometimes share the name. Romantic (and earlier) temperaments accentuated the differences between keys to a much greater extent than our standard temperament, and underpinned the frequent references to key "characteristics" made in many treatises. A nineteenth-century player would have been more tempted than we are to mollify the shock of transition from one key to another by extemporizing a short modulating passage.[48]

Despite the upsurge in interest in historical performance practice, present-day players, with a few notable exceptions, have been extremely reluctant to reintroduce the improvised elements that were a normal feature of the concerts of the past. Such diffidence, to be sure, has not merely to do with changing tastes, the standardization of audience expectations after over one hundred years of recordings, and critical concerns for "unity of style" that seem rarely to have troubled musicians of previous eras. Many players in the Classical performance world quite simply lack the training in improvisation that Mendelssohn, Liszt, Alkan, Hiller, and their contemporaries received as a matter of course in their childhood studies. Even when faced with a 6/4 chord and a glaring gap in the score, the first (and certainly understandable) reaction of some modern musicians is to search around to find a stylistically appropriate cadenza printed elsewhere. Yet there is a wealth of material available for those who wish to learn the art of improvisation, not only the collections of specimen preludes by Kalkbrenner and many others mentioned earlier, but extensive treatises such as Czerny's *School of Extemporaneous Performance,* op. 200. This is not a lost art—it is simply one that has been deliberately neglected.

If we try to clean the sentimental varnish of late Romanticism off Mendelssohn performance practice, we find a clearer picture than with many nineteenth-century composers. There is no esoteric rubato to rediscover, of the sort that allowed Chopin's playing of a triple-time mazurka to sound like duple; there were usually no radical adaptations to the score expected in concert, of the sort that could make a Liszt performance sound like a spontaneous recomposition. What we find is an expectation of a certain respectful fidelity to the printed text, and an avoidance of the meretricious. Although von Bülow's "with Mendelssohn you do not need to interpret" is an exaggeration—for every performance necessarily involves acts of interpretation—it does contain a basic truth about Mendelssohn performance practice that is arguably not valid for Chopin and Liszt. In fact, if we wish to be more faithful to the performance practice of Mendelssohn and his times—and, certainly, we may not actually want to be—our greatest challenge is to look not inside the score but around it, and consider how the experience of hearing musical works is changed and refreshed by what might be improvised before them and between them.

NOTES

1. Nathan Dole, *Famous Composers* (New York: Thomas Y. Crowell, 1891; reprint, London: Methuen, 1905), 347 (page citations are to the reprint edition); quoted in Clive Brown, *Portrait of Mendelssohn* (New Haven: Yale University Press, 2003), 489.

2. Carl Lachmund, *Living with Liszt: From the Diary of Carl Lachmund,* an American Pupil of Liszt, 1882–1884, ed. Alan Walker, Franz Liszt Studies (Stuyvesant, N.Y.: Pendragon, 1995), 231.

3. Ibid., 275.

4. Richard Zimdars, *The Piano Masterclasses of Hans von Bülow* (Bloomington: Indiana University Press, 1993), 84.

5. Ibid., 101.

6. Ibid., 84.

7. Richard Zimdars, *The Piano Masterclasses of Franz Liszt* (Bloomington: Indiana University Press, 1996), 47.

8. Ibid., 48.

9. Ibid., 22.

10. Lewis Compton, ed., *The Great Composers: Reviews and Bombardments by George Bernard Shaw* (Berkeley: University of California Press, 1978), 122.

11. Sebastian Hensel, *Die Familie Mendelssohn 1729–1847: Nach Briefen und Tagebüchern* (Berlin: Behr, 1879), 1:360.

12. Christian Lambour, "Fanny Hensel: Die Pianistin," in *Mendelssohn Studien: Beiträge zur neueren deutschen Kultur- und Wirtschaftsgeschichte* 12 (2001): 234.

13. Ibid., 236.

14. Ibid., 239.

15. Larry Todd, *Mendelssohn: A Life in Music* (New York: Oxford University Press, 2003), 207, 254.

16. Ibid., 357. For more information on the development of the piano in the nineteenth century, see Kenneth Hamilton, *After the Golden Age: Romantic Pianism and Modern Performance* (Oxford: Oxford University Press, 2008), 208–18.

17. Zimdars, *The Piano Masterclasses of Hans von Bülow,* 61.

18. *Philadelphia National Gazette,* 20 August 1841.

19. Ibid.

20. Henry Fothergill Chorley, *Music and Manners in France and Germany* (London: Longman, 1841), 274–75.

21. Ibid., 275.

22. May 1837; quoted in Peter Ward Jones, *The Mendelssohns on Honeymoon* (Oxford: Oxford University Press, 1997), 156

23. William Little, "Mendelssohn and Liszt," in *Mendelssohn Studies,* ed. Larry Todd (Cambridge: Cambridge University Press, 1992), 118.

24. Ibid.

25. August Gollerich, *Franz Liszt* (Berlin: Marquardt Verlag, 1908), 20.

26. Sir George Grove, "Mendelssohn," in *Dictionary of Music and Musicians,* ed. Sir George Grove (London: Macmillan, 1880), 2:298.

27. Ibid.

28. Robert Schumann, *Tagebücher, 1836–1854,* ed. Gerd Nauhaus (Leipzig: VEB Deutscher Verlag für Musik, 1987), 2:133; quoted in Brown, 217.

29. Roger Nichols, *Mendelssohn Remembered* (London: Faber, 1997), 64.

30. Grove, 299.

31. Grove, 299.

32. Franz Brendel, *Neue Zeitschrift für Music* no. 24 (1846): 32.

33. Todd, 68.

34. Grove, 398.

35. Nichols, 160.

36. Ibid., 208–209.

37. Ibid., 172.

38. Brown, 223.

39. Little, 122.

40. Nichols, 75.

41. Hans von Bülow, "Felix Mendelssohn" in *Mendelssohn and His World,* ed. Larry Todd (Princeton, N.J.: Princeton University Press, 1991), 392–93.

42. Hensel, 377.

43. Paul Mendelssohn, ed., *Felix Mendelssohn-Barthody: Reisebriefe aus den Jahren 1830 bis 1832* (Leipzig: Hermann Mendelssohn, 1862), 305.

44. Grove, 300.

45. Nichols, 158.

46. Brown, 223–24.

47. Ibid., 228–29. For more information on the improvisation of preludes and transitions during the nineteenth and early twentieth centuries, see Hamilton, *After the Golden Age,* 101–38.

48. See Hamilton, *After the Golden Age,* 21, and Ross W. Duffin, *How Equal Temperament Ruined Harmony, And Why You Should Care* (New York: W. W. Norton, 2006).

3

Mendelssohn and the Organ

PETER WARD JONES

In addition to all his other talents, Mendelssohn was renowned as an organist—especially for his improvisation and Bach performances—although very few of his appearances were in the context of a formal concert. Most of his playing took place on at least nominally private occasions for fellow organists or friends, although news frequently leaked out in advance, with the result that large crowds of admirers assembled to hear him.[1] His lifetime contributions to the published organ repertoire, modest in quantity, but highly influential, consisted of the Three Preludes and Fugues, op. 37 (1837) and the Six Sonatas, op. 65 (1845). He also left seven completed pieces of juvenilia, a few isolated fugues and other pieces composed between 1833 and 1840, and a number of movements written in 1844–45 for possible inclusion in the sonatas, but not in the end used. Most of these remained unpublished until recent years, when three editions incorporating many or all of them have appeared.[2]

Although the surviving documentation on his life and work, including many memoirs by contemporaries, is far greater than for any composer before his time, it has to be admitted that we know frustratingly little about many aspects of Mendelssohn's organ playing, especially as it concerns his own works. Even what evidence we have can at times be contradictory. Reports of his playing all too often consist mainly of admiring generalities and fail to provide useful precise detail. If in the end many questions remain with at best partial answers, some assistance is offered by consideration of early nineteenth-century organ design, published organ methods, and the organ works of his contemporaries.

Mendelssohn's Acquaintance
with the Organ of His Time

Mendelssohn seems to have begun organ lessons with August Wilhelm Bach, organist of the Marienkirche in Berlin, in the latter part of 1820, and continued with them until 1822.[3] At first sight it appears an unlikely instrument for him to have taken up. There was after all no family tradition to call upon, as would have been the case with most young organists at the time. Although Felix and his siblings had been quietly baptized in 1816, regular church attendance was apparently never to form a part of family life, and thus Felix did not have this natural channel for exposure to the instrument. His composition teacher, Carl Friedrich Zelter, may have suggested that Mendelssohn learn the organ; or it is possible that a developing interest in the music of Johann Sebastian Bach, so strong in the family background, may have contributed to the desire. Yet perhaps Mendelssohn was simply attracted by the instrument's sensuality—he would not have been the first youngster to have been inspired by the thrilling sound of a large organ. According to his own recollection, the first organ Mendelssohn played was the small instrument in the pilgrimage Rochuskapelle near Bingen during a visit to the Rhine in the summer of 1820.[4] It is telling that on his youthful travels throughout the next decade he was constantly seeking out organs, and in letters home he frequently commented on their tonal characteristics—he seems to have been particularly attracted by 32' pedal stops, as he reported on finding two organs so equipped in Wittenberg in 1821.[5] He was never to hold any organist's post, but for a musician of his time he had a quite exceptional, perhaps unique, range of experience of many types of organ, especially in Germany and England. Mendelssohn had no close long-term association with any one instrument, and his own compositions are not wedded to any particular organ sound-world. In this way they differ substantially from works such as Liszt's *Prelude and Fugue on BACH* or the Sonata by Julius Reubke, with their close ties to the new Merseberg Cathedral organ in the 1850s.[6]

Mendelssohn's two years of organ lessons from A. W. Bach seem to have been the sum of his tuition on the instrument. He was almost certainly one of those individuals capable of more or less teaching himself, and the lessons with Bach probably only offered a few hints.[7] Of course he was already an accomplished pianist, so it is highly unlikely that he worked from a standard tutor, but instead concentrated on individual pieces selected by Bach, including perhaps compositions of his teacher such as may be found in the three volumes of his *Orgelstücke*.[8] Felix's greatest initial difficulty as an eleven-year-old was probably in reaching the pedals—even as an adult he reached a height of only about five feet, four inches. It may be that he made comparatively little use of his feet at this time, although he was certainly to develop his pedal technique by the end of the decade.[9] It was to be a "modern" technique, making use of heel and toe, as Johann Friedrich Kühnau noted.[10]

The Marienkirche organ was the first one Mendelssohn played at any length. A three-manual instrument originally built by Joachim Wagner in 1720–23, it had undergone radical transformation in 1800 by Abbé Vogler in accordance with his "Simplification System" complete with multiple mutation stops. This, however, was quickly deemed unsatisfactory, and between 1814 and 1829 changes were made, which eventually restored it to something approaching the original specification.[11] One innovation of Vogler, however, was retained—the enclosure of the Unterwerk division in a swell box. Thus Mendelssohn from the start was acquainted with an enclosed division, and we know from A. W. Bach's published compositions that his teacher made use of it. So did Mendelssohn himself in his very first organ piece—a Prelude in D minor, dated 28 November 1820 (around the time of his first organ lessons), specifies a crescendo in the opening bars. Although he would seldom encounter it elsewhere in Germany, an enclosed swell division was a standard feature of the English organs that he experienced from 1829 onward. The possible implications for his own music will be considered in due course.

As an organist, Mendelssohn was also perhaps unique in his time in being also, and primarily, a virtuoso pianist. The "universal" keyboard player of the Baroque had gradually yielded to specialization, both through the changing nature of keyboard instruments in the eighteenth century and through musicians' increasing opportunities for purely secular employment. In the case of Mendelssohn, the refined qualities of his piano playing with its varied touch evidently passed into his organ technique. Precise details are sparse, but some revealing comments are provided by the anonymous reviewer of a London organ recital by the enterprising, if technically and musically deficient, Elizabeth Stirling, published in the *Musical World* in 1838. After commenting on the varied touch of Charles Wesley and the legato approach of his brother Samuel, he continues: "Mendelssohn, by the early practice of the fantastic forms of the olden organ writers, has acquired a wiry, crisp, energetic character of delivery, which tells instantaneously, and his command over the pianoforte mechanism gives him a variation and facility of speech, which in a delivery of Bach's works are invaluable."[12] Allied to this is Henry Gauntlett's 1837 description of Mendelssohn's organ touch as being "so even and firm, so delicate and *volant*."[13] This would indicate he used a great variety of articulation, including semi-staccato, and nothing suggests that his performance style of Bach was in any way deliberately different from that of his own works.[14]

Registration

No one was more conscious than Mendelssohn of the many differences to be found between organs, even within national traditions.[15] Those he played in north and central Germany tended to be basically late-Classical in design—more often than not Baroque instruments which had been subjected to modification over the decades, particularly in the direction of providing more 8-foot tone and developing subsidiary manuals noticeably softer than the Hauptwerk. String-tone stops like gambas, although not unknown in J.S. Bach's time, became ubiquitous, and mixtures increasingly distrusted and neglected. The eccentricities of Vogler, influential as he was in certain places, proved short-lived in immediate effect, although they sowed the seeds for the concept of the organ as, in part, an imitation orchestra that took a powerful hold later in the nineteenth century.[16]

As a point of reference, table 3.1 gives the specification of the Berlin Marienkirche organ by 1829 after it had been largely purged of Vogler's experiments.[17] Simple specifications of contemporary organs known to Mendelssohn, however, have very little value on their own, for they convey no information as to how the stops were actually used. An organ such as the Marienkirche may appear to offer the possibility of "clean" Baroque-style choruses, but there is no certainty that such a sound was still commonly heard by the early nineteenth century, and indeed evidence suggests otherwise. Informative sources are the organ methods of the period, such as those by Knecht, Werner, Rinck, Ritter, and Herzog.[18] Such works typically list and describe all the individual registers, and then offer guidance in combining stops. Most striking are the instructions for changes of volume, which offer a contrast to the blocks-of-sound approach of the Baroque period with its clear choruses built up from stops of different pitches. In an age which placed emphasis both on fundamental tone and on smoother gradations of volume, the advocated technique was to add more 8' stops before one or more 4' stops, and only then 16', 2⅔', 2', and mixtures, with perhaps finally the 8' trumpet.[19] There is little objection to combining different families of stops, such as flutes and principals, in such a build-up. The possibility of coupling manuals, while mentioned, is given little attention. Pedal organs are generally assumed to be modest in stop provision, with the use of 16' and 8' tone alone generally being suggested for quieter combinations, and the use of a pedal coupler being recommended for forte combinations and above. The accompanying pieces in these organ methods offer specific examples, sometimes couched in general terms—*mit sanften Stimmen, mit starken Stimmen, mit vollem Werke*—sometimes suggesting particular stops. An example from A. W. Bach's *Orgel-Stücke für das Concert* (Berlin: Trautwein,

Table 3.1. *Hauptwerk, Oberwerk, Unterwerk, Pedal*

Hauptwerk:

Bourdon 16'	Quinte 2⅔'
Prinzipal 8'	Oktave 2'
Rohrflöte 8'	Schaff 5 ranks
Viola da Gamba 8'	Cymbel 3 ranks
Oktave 4'	Kornett 5 ranks
Spitzflöte 4'	Trompete 8'

Oberwerk:

Quintadena 16'	Oktave 2'
Prinzipal 8'	Sifflöte 1'
Gedact 8'	Mixtura major 4 ranks
Oktave 4'	Mixtura minor 4 ranks
Rohrflöte 4'	Fagott—Hautbois 8'
Nassard 2⅔'	

Unterwerk (enclosed):

Prinzipal 4'	Fugara 4'
Salizional 8'	Liebliche Flöte 4'
Gemshorn 8	Nassard 2⅔'
Gedackt 8'	Oktave 2'
Quintadena 8'	

Pedal:

Prinzipal 16'	Baßflöte 8'
Subbaß 16'	Oktave 4'
Violon 16'	Posaune 32'
Groß-Nassard 10⅔'	Posaune 16'
Gemshorn 8'	

[1829]) is typical and instructive, being clearly based on the specification of the Marienkirche organ:

Konzert-Stück für 2 Manuale und Pedal:
Haupt-Manual: Prinzip. 8 F., Rohrfl[öte] 8 F., Spitzflöte 4 F.
Ober-Manual: Gedacht 8 F., Rohrflöte 4 F., und Hautbois und Fagott 8 F.
Pedal: Prinzipal und Violon 16 F., Gemshorn 8 F.

There is no reason to think that Mendelssohn, even with his historical interests, lay apart from these trends.[20] His own comments on organs frequently mention the more sensual aspects of the instrument. Writing to his family from Munich on 6 October 1831, he describes his daily organ playing at the church of St. Peter, whose instrument was one of Vogler's revolutionary designs built in 1806–1809, and where the restricted pedal compass hampered his Bach performances:

But there are wonderfully beautiful stops, with which you can registrate chorales; so I am edified by the heavenly, flowing tone of the instrument. In particular, Fanny, I have discovered here the stops which should be used in Sebastian Bach's *Schmücke dich, O liebe Seele.* They seem actually made for it, and sound so moving, that a feeling of awe runs through me every time I begin to play it. For the flowing parts I have an eight-foot flute stop and a very soft four-foot one, which continually floats above the chorale. You will recognize this from Berlin. But for the chorale there is a keyboard with nothing but reed stops, so I use a soft oboe and a very delicate clarion (four feet) and a viola. These render the chorale in subdued yet penetrating tones, like distant human voices, singing from the depths of the heart.[21]

At this stage in his life at any rate, Mendelssohn was clearly attracted by aspects of modern design. Although he is here discussing Bach, such a sound world is of course equally applicable to his own works. Indeed, what the passage suggests is that Mendelssohn treated Bach exactly as he would contemporary music—a view borne out by his performance markings in the Bach choral and orchestral works he conducted, with their dynamic gradations and "modern" bowing.[22] We have already noted his comments on organs possessing 32' pedal stops. His appreciation of the special effect of such stops can be seen in the organ part he prepared for the 1841 Leipzig performance of Bach's *St. Matthew Passion* in the Thomaskirche. He stipulates its use in the opening bars of the first chorus and again in the final chorus, evidently reserving it for particular moments.[23]

We have to admit we have no information as to how far Mendelssohn coupled manuals together, even in movements *"mit vollem Werke."* Similarly with his use of the pedal coupler—the opening bar of Sonata no. 4 suggests that the pedal was not coupled here, though most organists would instinctively want to couple once the initial B-flats have been negotiated. The organ works provide virtually no instructions for registration, apart from specifying the use of two manuals in various movements of the sonatas. The only exceptions are the injunction to include 16' manual tone in the opening chorale of Sonata no. 5, and the first movement of Sonata no. 6, where, quite exceptionally the pitch (though not timbre) of the stops is prescribed for most of the variations. Otherwise, only dynamic levels are indicated,[24] though the prefatory remarks to the Sonatas give some general guidance as to the sort of tone expected at various levels. In all this he shows himself eminently practical in approach.

The typical English organ of Mendelssohn's time often had a swell organ descending only to tenor C, and pedal organs, where present at all, of very variable compass. New and rebuilt instruments from the 1830s onward gradually adopted the "German system" compasses (descending to CC on all manuals, and with a pedal compass of at least CC-d'). Henry J. Gauntlett, a friend and admirer of Mendelssohn, was the most influential advocate of

EXAMPLE 3.1.   Felix Mendelssohn, Sonata no. 5. Third movement, mm. 1–9 (Bodleian Library, MS M. Deneke Mendelssohn c.48, fol. 18).

reform in English organ design and was responsible, amongst others, for the important rebuild of Christ Church, Newgate Street, London in the mid 1830s. Mendelssohn's own organ performances in England, aided no doubt by comments on the deficiencies of the organs, also lent a powerful impetus to the movement.[25] However, although the Sonatas originated in a request by the English publisher Charles Coventry for a set of "voluntaries," Mendelssohn made no concessions to the limitations of the average English organ. They are all written on the assumption that the full standard compass is available, even though some of the slow movements might be attempted on more restricted instruments.

The comparative paucity of performance indications, however, does not necessarily mean that a player always has to adhere to simple registration. Practical musician that he was, Mendelssohn would have been keen to make the published organ works as accessible to as wide a range of organs and organists as possible. Evidence suggests that he could be rather more elaborate in his own performances. One telling example concerns changes of manual in the Sonatas. At first sight the published first editions stipulate what appear to be all the obvious uses of different manuals. Yet an intermediate draft of the last movement of Sonata no. 5 shows that at one time he envisaged an elaborate interchange of manuals (example 3.1).[26]

This plan was abandoned, and the movement appears in the first editions without any change of manual indicated. It may be that Mendelssohn came to regard the original scheme as too fussy (or too complex to engrave neatly), but it is also possible that he decided it was better to opt for a simpler scheme in print, since not every organ would possess the two forte chorus combinations necessary for a good balance, and the elaborate change of manuals could be off-putting to potential performers. But given suitable conditions, it may be quite legitimate to opt for Mendelssohn's more ambitious scheme.[27]

Similar consideration might be given to use of the swell box. Nowhere in either op. 37 or op. 65 is there any indication for use of the swell. Yet as we have seen, Mendelssohn was acquainted with the device from the Marienkirche organ in Berlin, and he would meet swell organs regularly in England. None of the accounts of his playing there mention his use of the box, so we remain ignorant of his adult views on the matter. Yet if comparisons are made between the slow movements of the Sonatas and similar moments in the *Lieder ohne Worte* for piano, where Mendelssohn shapes the phrases dynamically, then the parallels suggest that discrete use of the swell box might be appropriate. Such movements can of course sound perfectly musical without it, and it continued to be absent on most German organs in Mendelssohn's lifetime, so this fact alone would account for omission of any crescendo and diminuendo markings in the published editions. But contemporary English organists, as they became acquainted with his works and acquired organs capable of dealing with them, would almost certainly have been making use of the swell device. As so often, I believe Mendelssohn would have regarded it as something to be left to the player's own musical good taste.

How far might Mendelssohn have changed stops in the course of a movement? Such a practice was by no means unknown. Knecht's *Vollständige Orgelschule* (1795–98) already illustrates making a crescendo and diminuendo by playing with one hand and pedals and using the free hand to manipulate the stops.[28] Multiple changes of dynamics by manual changes are common amongst the pieces of this book, and the theme of variety of tone continues throughout the period. Seidel in 1843 compares the organ to an orchestra, noting, "Organ tone should not be always strong nor always weak, because this sort of monotony usually tires the listener."[29] Evidence for Mendelssohn's own practice, though not overabundant, certainly suggests that on occasions he favored some changes. In a letter of 23/24 October 1828 to his family, he describes playing in Brandenburg: "Then I improvised on the chorale 'Christe, du Lamm,' which I played first with flutes, then gradually got louder (for I did the registration myself in the absence of the organist), and finally I chose to close again with the gentle chorale."[30] Of course improvisation is not the same as playing set pieces, and more variety of registration might be expected, but it is significant that Mendelssohn remarks here on having to do his own stop changing, implying that it was common to have assistance on hand. Schumann's review of Mendelssohn's famous 1840 recital in the Thomaskirche in Leipzig mentions that Bach's Passacaglia was "also superbly handled by Mendelssohn in the registration."[31] Although this could mean no more than occasional changes of manual, something more elaborate is probably implied. Most explicit is Elizabeth Mounsey, organist of St. Peter's, Cornhill, London, recalling Mendelssohn's recital in her church in 1840, when both she and Henry Gauntlett were in attendance to change the stops, on either side of the composer. In this instance Mendelssohn performed one of his own works, the Fugue in F minor of 1839 (unpublished in Mendelssohn's lifetime), when he wished to have "the swell stops varied as he proceeded—giving varied shades of tone without any striking change."[32] The occasion on which Prince Albert changed stops for Mendelssohn while he played a chorus from *St. Paul* on a one-manual organ at Buckingham Palace in 1842 can perhaps be disregarded in this context, since changes of dynamics were essential to a proper rendition of the piece, which in any case is not an organ work.[33] Of far more interest is Emil Naumann's recollection of Mendelssohn playing the Sonatas in Kronenberg in the Taunus near Frankfurt in the summer of 1845, shortly after their completion. Although vague in detail, it certainly suggests a more colorful approach to registration than is offered by the printed page:

> Particularly wonderful was the wise and continuously changing use of the tone colors of the various stops, as well as their deep inner connection with the spirit of the works performed. Whereas we often encounter either a tiring monotony of tonal effects or alternatively a coarse piling-up of effects produced through sharp contrasts in the change of the tone colours, the organ seemed here, under Mendelssohn's hands, to become a completely new, hitherto unknown instrument. We have never since heard the organ sing in such a manner, never since experienced so harmoniously arranged and agreeable increases of tone by the use of the reeds. The instrument turned itself into a rich full-toned orchestra, above which one thought one was hearing the voice of a single singer, and then the voices of whole choirs![34]

Naumann did not write down this memoir until 1862, so we must make some allowances for the passing years, but the vivid impression rings true.

For the most part Mendelssohn specifically requires changes of registration only at the ends of movements or sections. The generally forte fugue of op. 37 no. 1 does have mezzo-forte manual episodes, which he presumably intended to be achieved by change of manual. Only once in the whole of op. 37 and op. 65 does Mendelssohn actually stipulate that a build-up be made in the course of a section, and that is in the first movement of Sonata no. 3, with the instruction at the beginning of the second part of the fugue,

"Da questa parte fino al Maggiore poco a poco più forte (sino al M.M. ♩= 100)."
Mendelssohn leaves it to the performer to determine where to add stops—
depending of course in part on the instrument—but the nature of the
movement is such that it would not have been possible on the organs of his
time without an assistant. Although combination pistons lay in the future, it
is hard to believe that Mendelssohn would not have welcomed them had
they been available to him.[35]

But there are certainly moments, particularly in the Sonatas, where more
variety in the tonal palette might legitimately be introduced. Slow movements, such as the second movement of Sonata no. 3, lend themselves to subtle changes of color, without demanding it. Even basically "tutti" movements
like the finale of Sonata no. 1 can arguably benefit from some reduction in
volume for the secondary theme at bar 68 and a subsequent build-up over the
dominant pedal at around bar 100. The device, beloved of the French symphonic and late British Romantic schools, of crescendoing with full swell,
though foreign to the sound of Mendelssohn's organs, might not be so to the
spirit of the latter passage, with its clearly implied crescendo in the ascending
sequences. It does no harm to bear in mind Mendelssohn's own sense of orchestral color. Likewise the beginning of the fugal passage of the finale of
Sonata no. 4 seems to invite some contrast of volume to the *fortissimo* of the
opening. As always it is ultimately a matter of *bon goût*—but a player should
not be afraid of being "imaginative" solely on account of the sparseness of
the composer's own directions. Only liberal use of solo tubas, as suggested
by certain early-twentieth-century editors, may be deemed a step too far!

TEMPI

Mendelssohn considered that an appropriate tempo should be obvious to a
true musician, but on occasion he acceded to requests to provide metronome
markings. Thus, while the op. 37 Preludes and Fugues bear no markings, the
op. 65 Sonatas do have them, thanks reputedly to a request from the English
organist Edward J. Hopkins.[36] Mendelssohn would have considered them as
serving only as guidelines, preventing gross miscalculations on the part of
performers. We also need to bear in mind Wilhelm von Wasielewski's recollection that Mendelssohn could be very inconsistent in the tempi he chose
for his own works, far more so than when playing the works of others.[37]
Metronome marks provided en masse need to be treated with particular cau-
tion. Anyone who has experimented with establishing them quickly realizes
that merely taking the opening bars as a guide is likely to prove deceptive—
continuing on into the movement often leads to second thoughts, as does
returning to the matter a day or two later. Having to calculate a whole stream

EXAMPLE 3.2.   Felix Mendelssohn, Sonata no. 3. Second movement, mm. 1–4 (Leipzig: Breitkopf & Härtel, [1845]).

of tempo markings in a short time, as Mendelssohn would have done, can only make the results more fallible, even for such a composer, and we have plenty of examples from twentieth-century composers whose printed metronome markings and recorded performance tempi are at wide variance with each other.[38] Nevertheless, Mendelssohn's markings for the Sonatas are all plausible, though later editors have sometimes replaced them with their own, and performers often seemingly take no account of them. The temptation is often to play fast movements considerably faster than the metronome marking and slow ones much slower. It is worth noting how many of Mendelssohn's faster Italian tempo indications are qualified by "maestoso" or "serioso." Although in the end the player's own sense of musical "rightness" must prevail, it is worth trying movements through at Mendelssohn's own speeds as part of any decision-making process.

MENDELSSOHN'S SLURS

No topic has perhaps provoked more discussion concerning Mendelssohn's organ works than the apparent problems offered by his use of slurs. These have seemed exacerbated by the fact that the German and English first editions of the Sonatas, both "authentic" editions in which the composer was involved, show variance in this regard.[39] The problems have arisen chiefly through the expectation of editors and interpreters from the end of the nineteenth century onward that slurring should correspond to the phrase structure of the music and articulation within it. Yet in Mendelssohn's case it clearly does not usually set out to do this, as example 3.2 suggests.

But this is not an oddity of Mendelssohn's *organ* music. It is found equally in his piano music, and is typical of his general use of slurs, as it is of

EXAMPLE 3.3.   Joseph Rheinberger, Sonata no. 13 in E-flat, op. 161. Second movement, mm. 1–8 (Leipzig: Forberg, 1890).

many of his contemporaries.[40] As the century progressed, however, so did the trend toward using long slurs to outline whole phrases, with shorter ones allied to staccato marks showing smaller-scale articulation—seen at its clearest in César Franck and Max Reger. Yet the older, more ambiguous use of slurs also continued, as in this example from the slow movement of Rheinberger's Sonata no. 13 (example 3.3).

But, despite the lack of uniqueness in his practice, it was Mendelssohn whose organ music was subjected to comment and extensive editorial revision from the end of the nineteenth century onward, particularly in the Anglo-Saxon world. In 1871 the eminent organist W. T. Best had produced a new edition of the Sonatas for Novello, Ewer, and Co., and was quite content, with a few exceptions, to leave Mendelssohn's slurs alone.[41] But in 1899, an anonymous editor (actually Henry Hudson) set out to provide a "Student's edition" for the London firm of Joseph Williams, and noted amongst matters needing attention, "Absence of proper attention to phrasing," adding "Mendelssohn's phrase-marks are most difficult to understand, and can only be put down as 'bowing' marks such as found in violin music. . . . Young students constantly get [it] wrong in trying to follow these directions, the older players disregard them altogether."[42] He then proceeded to supplant Mendelssohn's slurs with "conventional" phrasing. Hudson did not go as far as some subsequent editors, in that he retained the composer's metronome markings and basic dynamics, although Hudson's suggested registration would produce some changes.

A similar approach to the phrasing had already been taken by the editions of both op. 37 and op. 65 by Samuel P. Warren (1896), and was followed by Edwin H. Lemare (1910), Arthur Eaglefield Hull (1914), and Ivor Atkins (1934), with varying degrees of other editorial intervention.[43] Most extreme is Hull, with wholesale replacement of the metronome marks and changes of dynamics (providing registration for a four-manual organ), all without any indication of his editorial role. A notable exception to these highly interventionist editions was the op. 65 edition of Charles Pearce (1900), who boldly declared that "the present edition gives the text exactly as the composer wrote it."[44] The editor merely added fingering and pedaling, and made suggestions for registration.

EXAMPLE 3.4.   Felix Mendelssohn, Sonata no. 6. First movement, mm. 82–87 (Leipzig: Breitkopf & Härtel, [1845]).

All this meant that most twentieth-century organists in the English-
speaking world were likely to have been playing Mendelssohn from highly
misleading editions. Only with the publication of William Little's complete
edition for Novello (1987–90) did a new British Urtext edition make its
appearance. Performers using German editions were more fortunate, since
Breitkopf & Härtel, who first published op. 37 and op. 65, continued to reproduce the original text, while the Peters edition, which first appeared in
1877, prepared by F. A. Roitsch, differed little in its text, as did that of W.
Volckmar (1878) for Litolff. Recent German editions have therefore been less
corrective in this respect. In France, Widor's edition of op. 37 and 65 (1918)
respected the original slurs, while Marcel Dupré in 1948 provided a very
personal idiosyncratic edition in line with his editions of Bach, Handel,
Schumann, and Franck.[45]

What then did Mendelssohn intend to signify by his use of slurs? When
combined with staccato marks as in the pedal part of the second variation
of the first movement of Sonata no. 6, the intention is clear. The rare long
slurs extending beyond two bars in length seem to imply a sustained legato,
as in the opening pedal phrase of the last movement of Sonata no. 4. Elsewhere the use of a succession of bar-long slurs (e.g., Sonata no. 2, 2nd
movement, bars 22–25, 39–42) appears to suggest a general legato approach
to the passage without, however, denying the possibility of breaks of phrasing within it. A similar interpretation may be made of the *sempre legato* mark
in bar 98 of the first movement of Sonata no. 1. It may also in part be a
warning to the player not to compromise on pedaling technique here.

The more problematic area lies with phrases like this from the first
movement of Sonata no. 6 (example 3.4). Here a player's instinct is to play
each chorale phrase as a legato whole, as given in the editions by Hudson
and others. Another example (commonly cited by critics of his phrasing) is
the Fugue of Sonata no. 2 (example 3.5).

Although Mendelssohn's slurring in this case may superficially resemble
string bowing (as various commentators have suggested), I think his purpose was rather to highlight what could be regarded as significant notes in
the phrase, notes which he saw as having an expressive role. By starting slurs
on the F, D, and A at the beginnings of bars 2–4, he calls attention to the

EXAMPLE 3.5.   Felix Mendelssohn, Sonata no. 2. Third movement, mm. 106 (Leipzig: Breit-kopf & Härtel, [1845]).

Allegro moderato

implied appoggiatura-like tensions of these notes. It actually points up the subtlety of the melodic line far more than later editors' conventionally phrased versions (examples 3.6a and 3.6b).

Players are, however, free to interpret them as they will; the one thing they are certainly not obliged to do is to shorten the last note of each slurred group, as might be their first inclination.[46] Although an organist does not have the same range of subtle emphases open to a violinist or pianist, variety of touch and "placing" of notes by slight delay are all part of the armory.[47] A player could also legitimately decide not to make particular notes audibly stressed at all, but merely let the slurs inform his sense of the phrase.[48] "Placing" of a last note of a phrase may lie behind the frequent ending of a slur on the penultimate note of the phrase before the barline—in this case the analogy with bowing may be appropriate, just as a violinist might mark the final note of a cadence with a change of bow. It may, however, reflect a general tradition of engravers preferring to confine slurs within bars. Mendelssohn's slurring above all seems designed to be *suggestive* and not *prescriptive,* and for this reason he seems not to have over-worried about its consistency either within movements or between editions. As Carolyn Haury and others have noted, the original (and simultaneously published) German and English editions of the Sonatas

EXAMPLE 3.6A.   Felix Mendelssohn, Sonata no. 2. Third movement, mm. 1–6, ed. Samuel P. Warren (New York: G. Schirmer, 1896).

EXAMPLE 3.6B.   Felix Mendelssohn, Sonata no. 2. Third movement, mm. 1–6, ed. A. Eaglefield Hull (London: Augener, 1914).

have many variations in the slurs, with the German one having considerably more, and Mendelssohn evidently felt no need for them to correspond.[49]

CONCLUSION

In respect of matters such as registration, tempi, articulation, and phrasing, we would love to know more of Mendelssohn's own practice, yet we may perhaps take comfort in the fact that he himself entrusted the performer with finding appropriate solutions. In terms of organ sound, the present era, under the influence of the revival of the classical organ, has come to transfer the clarity and brilliance of that sound to performances of Mendelssohn's own music. While the contrapuntal essence at the heart of much of his music suits a "classical" sound in many ways, it does not necessarily represent the composer's own sound world, which may have been rather darker and indeed "muddier" to our ears. It is a sign of the strength of the music itself that it can communicate effectively on many different sorts of organ, and if organists are not afraid to experiment on the varied instruments at their disposal, it is difficult to think that Mendelssohn himself would have disapproved, provided that the elusive quality of "musicality," which he so cherished, remains in evidence.

NOTES

1. Useful general surveys of Mendelssohn's organ activities are found in Susanna Großmann-Vendrey, *Felix Mendelssohn Bartholdy und die Musik der Vergangenheit* (Regensburg: Gustav Bosse, 1969), 179–91; Friedhold Bötel, *Mendelssohns Bachrezeption und ihre Konsequenzen, dargestellt an den Präludien und Fugen für Orgel op. 37* (Munich: Emil Katzbichler, 1984), esp. 21–33; and William A. Little, "Felix Mendelssohn and His Place in the Organ World of His Time," in *The Mendelssohns, Their Music in History,* ed. John Michael Cooper and Julie Prandi (Oxford: Oxford University Press, 2002), 291–302.

2. *Complete Organ Works,* ed. William A. Little, 5 vols. (London: Novello, 1987–90); *Neue Ausgabe sämtliche Orgelwerke,* ed. Christoph Albrecht, 2 vols. (Kassel: Bärenreiter, 1993–94); *Orgelwerke,* ed. Christian Martin Schmidt, 3 vols., *Leipziger Ausgabe der Werke von Felix Mendelssohn Bartholdy,* Serie IV, Bd. 6–8 (Wiesbaden: Breitkopf & Härtel, 2004–2005).

3. Andreas Sieling, *August Wilhelm Bach (1796–1869): Kirchenmusik und Seminarmusiklehrerausbildung in Preußen im zweiten Drittel des 19. Jahrhunderts* (Cologne: Studio, [1995]).

4. Peter Ward Jones, trans. and ed., *The Mendelssohns on Honeymoon: The 1837 Diary of Felix and Cécile Mendelssohn Bartholdy* (Oxford: Clarendon Press, 1997), 62.

5. Letter to his family, 27 Sept. 1821 (New York Public Library Mendelssohn family letters), "Die Stadtkirche . . . hat, damit Du es weißt, liebe Fanni, 25 Register und auch 32 Fuß im Pedal. Die Schloßkirche hat 38 Register und auch 32 Fuß im Pedal (Bordun 32 Fuß)"; quoted in Großmann-Vendrey, 179.

6. Hermann J. Busch, "Die Orgeln Mendelssohns, Liszts und Brahms'," in *Proceedings of the Göteborg International Organ Academy 1994*, ed. Hans Davidsson and Sverker Jullander (Göteborg: Göteborgs Universitet, 1995), 235–50.

7. There are also indications that after a while at any rate, there was a certain amount of tension between teacher and pupil. See William A. Little, "Felix Mendelssohn and J.S. Bach's Prelude and Fugue in E Minor (BWV 533)," *American Organist* 39, no. 2 (Feb. 2005): 73–83.

8. August Wilhelm Bach, *Orgelstücke* (Leipzig: Breitkopf & Härtel, [1818?]).

9. Cf. his Swiss letter of 30 Aug.–5 Sept. 1831, written between Rigikulm and Lindau, printed in Peter Sutermeister, ed.: *Felix Mendelssohn Bartholdy: Briefe einer Reise durch Deutschland, Italien und die Schweiz, nebst Lebensbild* (Zurich: M. Niehans, 1958), 232–49.

10. "So wußte er Absatz und Zehenspitze des Fußes so geschickt zur rechten Zeit mit gehöriger Abrundung zu benützen," *Vossische Zeitung*, 1847, no. 246; quoted in Großmann-Vendrey, 190.

11. On Vogler, see Wolfgang Metzler, *Romantischer Orgelbau in Deutschland* (Ludwigsburg: E. F. Walker, [1965?]), 27–32, and for the history of the Marienkirche instrument, see Uwe Pape: *Orgeln in Berlin* (Berlin: Pape, 2003), 18. How far the de-Voglerisation had gone by the time Mendelssohn was receiving lessons remains unclear, and it may be that the major work was not undertaken until 1829.

12. "Metropolitan Concerts," *Musical World* 9 (1838): 208–11.

13. Henry J. Gauntlett, "Mendelssohn as an Organist," *Musical World* 7 (1837): 8–10.

14. For a survey of comments on organ touch in contemporary methods, see Michael Schneider, *Die Orgelspieltechnik des frühen 19. Jahrhunderts in Deutschland* (Regensburg: Gustav Bosse, 1941), 42–49.

15. See the preface to op. 65, reprinted in almost every edition.

16. See Metzler, 26–40.

17. Given after Andreas Sieling, "'Ein Werk von unendlicher Schönheit': zur Überlieferung und Interpretation Johann Sebastian Bachscher Werke im zweiten Drittel des 19. Jahrhunderts in Berlin, dargestellt am Wirken des Berliner Organisten August Wilhelm Bach (1796–1869)," *Organ Yearbook* 29 (2000): 105–26.

18. Justin Heinrich Knecht, *Vollständige Orgelschule* (Leipzig: Breitkopf, [1795–98]); Johann Gottlob Werner, *Orgelschule* (Meissen: Penig, 1807); Johann Christina H. Rinck, *Praktische Orgelschule, Op. 55* (Bonn: N. Simrock, [1819–21]); August Gottfried Ritter, *Die Kunst des Orgel-Spiels,* 3rd. rev. ed. (Erfurt: G. W. Körner, 1846); Johann Georg Herzog, *Orgelschule, Op. 41* (Erlangen: A. Deichert, 1867).

19. Knecht, *Vollständige Orgelschule,* 2.Abteilung, 24–40 (esp. 30); Johann Justus Seidel, *Die Orgel und ihr Bau* (Breslau: F. E. C. Leuckart, 1843; reprint, Amsterdam: F. A. M. Knuf, 1962), 96–105.

20. Douglas Lamar Butler, "The Organ Works of Felix Mendelssohn Bartholdy" (D.M.A. diss., University of Oregon, 1973), 206–209, suggests that Mendelssohn used Baroque *organo pleno* sounds for fantasia/fugal movements, and more "Romantic" registrations for the quieter movements, but without any real evidence.

21. Paul Mendelssohn Bartholdy, ed., *Reisebriefe von Felix Mendelssohn Bartholdy aus den Jahren 1830 bis 1832* (Leipzig: Hermann Mendelssohn, 1861), 277–78 (my translation).

22. According to Andreas Sieling ("'Ein Werk von unendlicher Schönheit'"—see note 17) A. W. Bach was conservative in performing J. S. Bach's music, advocating clarity and no changes of manual or registration. How far Mendelssohn agreed with or reacted against this style of performance is unknown.

23. Bodleian Library, Oxford, MS. M. Deneke Mendelssohn b. 9, fols. 153–56.

24. The first English edition of op. 37 (London: Novello, [1837]) has the instruction "Diapasons" at the beginning of Prelude no. 2, which appears to have been an independent addition by the English publisher.

25. Nicholas Thistlethwaite, *The Making of the Victorian Organ* (Cambridge: Cambridge University Press, 1990), 163–291.

26. Bodleian Library, Oxford, MS. M. Deneke Mendelssohn c. 48, fols. 18–19v.

27. F. G. Edwards, "Mendelssohn's Organ Sonatas," *Proceedings of the Musical Association* 1894–95: 13, first drew attention to this draft.

28. Knecht, *Vollständige Orgelschule,* 2. Abteilung, 132.

29. Seidel, 100 (my translation).

30. New York Public Library Mendelssohn family letters, quoted in Großmann-Vendrey, 181 (my translation).

31. *Neue Zeitschrift für Musik* 13 (1840): 56, quoted in Großmann-Vendrey, 187.

32. Letter of Elizabeth Mounsey to F. G. Edwards, ca. 20 Feb. 1892 (British Library, *Add. MS. 41572,* fols. 10–11), quoted in Christopher Kent, "A Revolution in Registration—Marsh to Mendelssohn: a View of English Organ Music 1788–1847," *BIOS Journal* 13 (1989): 42. The manuscript of the fugue contains no dynamics.

33. Mendelssohn's account is in a letter of 19 July 1842, published in English in Sebastian Hensel, *The Mendelssohn Family (1729–1847),* trans. Carl Klingemann [Jr.] (London: Sampson Low, Maxston, Searle and Rivington, 1881), 2:169. See also Peter Ward Jones, "Felix Mendelssohn Bartholdy and Prince Albert," in *Prinz Albert: Ein Wettiner in Großbritannien—Prince Albert: A Wettin in England,* ed. Franz Bosbach and John R. Davis, Prinz-Albert Studien 22 (Munich: Saur, 2004), 161–71.

34. Emil Naumann, *Nachklänge* (Berlin: R. Oppenheim, 1872), 45–46 (my translation).

35. Hermann J. Busch, " 'Es kommt . . . auf richtige Wahl der Register sehr viel an.' Zur Orgelpraxis Felix Mendelssohn Bartholdys," in *Zur deutschen Orgelmusik des 19. Jahrhunderts,* ed. Hermann J. Busch and Michael Heinemann (Sinzig: Studio, [2000]), 139–46, suggests places in the organ works where an organist might have changed stops himself, but does not consider the use of assistants.

36. The request was actually made by the English publisher, Charles Coventry, in a letter of 14 July 1845, Bodleian Library, *Mendelssohn 'Green Books' XXII,* 19. Hopkins is not named, but his involvement is recalled in [anon.], "Dr. Edward John Hopkins," *Musical Times* 38 (1897): 590.

37. Wilhelm von Wasielewski, *Schumanniana* (Berlin: E. Strauss, 1883).

38. Marcel Dupré is an obvious example in the organ world—see Graham Steed, *The Organ Music of Marcel Dupré* (Hillsdale, N.Y.: Pendragon Press, 1999), 11.

39. The German and English editions of op. 37 have no more than the occasional divergence, as might be expected when different engravers are involved.

40. See, for example, Nicholas Temperley, "Berlioz and the Slur," *Music and Letters* 50 (1969): 388–92, and Hermann Keller, *Phrasing and Articulation,* trans. Leigh Gerdine (London: Peters, 1966), 58–61.

41. *Six Sonatas and Three Preludes and Fugues,* ed. W. T. Best (London: Novello, Ewer, 1871).

42. Preface to *Six Sonatas for the Organ, Op. 65* (London: Joseph Williams, [1899]).

43. *Compositions for the Organ,* ed. Samuel P. Warren (New York: G. Schirmer, 1896); *Compositions for the Organ,* ed. and rev. Edwin H. Lemare (New York: G. Schirmer, 1910); *Complete Organ Works,* ed. A. Eaglefield Hull (London: Augener, 1914); *Three Preludes and Fugues for Organ, Op. 37,* ed. Ivor Atkins (London: Novello, [1934]); *Six Sonatas for Organ, Op. 65,* ed. Ivor Atkins (London: Novello, [1934]).

44. *Six Grand Sonatas for the Organ,* ed. Charles W. Pearce (London: A. Hammond, 1900).

45. *Kompositionen für die Orgel* [ed. F. A. Roitsch] (Leipzig: Peters, [1877]); *Sämmtliche Compositionen fir Orgel,* ed. W. Volckmann (Braunschweig: Litolff, [1878]); *Oeuvres d'orgue,* ed. Ch. M. Widor (Paris: Durand, 1918); *Oeuvres complètes pour orgue,* ed. Marcel Dupré (Paris: Bornemann, 1948).

46. Mendelssohn himself considered that a staccato dot with the last note of a slur was necessary to imply detachment—cf. Temperley, 391.

47. Hans van Nieuwkoop, "Bogen en metronoomcijfers in de orgelmuziek van Felix Mendelssohn Bartholdy," *Het Orgel* 93, no. 9 (Sept. 1997): 21–28, calls attention to the "expressive" purposes of some of Mendelssohn's slurs, though his suggested interpretations may be open to question.

48. For a discussion of similar problems in Beethoven, see Clive Brown's preface to his edition of *Symphonie Nr. 1, C-dur, op. 21* (Wiesbaden: Breitkopf & Härtel, 2004).

49. Carolyn Schott Haury, "Slur Markings in Mendelssohn's Organ Sonatas, Op. 65: A Study of the Earliest Prints and Manuscripts" (D.M.A. thesis, University of Cincinnati, 1984). A discussion of some of the articulation ambiguities in Sonata no. 3 is found in Douglas M. Moorehead, "Mendelssohn's Organ Sonatas: a Look at Number 3," *Music: the AGO and RCCO Magazine* 9, no. 11 (November 1975): 28–33.

4

The Performance of Mendelssohn's Chamber and Solo Music for Violin

CLIVE BROWN

Mendelssohn's extraordinary skills as a pianist and organist were widely recognized by his contemporaries and are vividly conveyed in press reviews, contemporaneous accounts, and reminiscences. His ability as a string player is not so well known or documented, yet during his childhood he received regular instruction in violin playing. In 1816, when the family visited Paris, it seems possible that the eight-year-old boy had a few lessons with the great French violinist and pedagogue Pierre Baillot. In Berlin regular violin tuition was entrusted first to Carl Wilhelm Henning (1784–1867) and then to Eduard Rietz (1802–32). Mendelssohn's progress under these tutors was rapid. In the early 1820s he referred self-deprecatingly to his violin playing in his humorous poem *Paphlëis,* with the following lines delivered by Paphlos (his brother Paul):

> And on certain occasions we strike up a dire caterwauling,
> Mistress Benicke plays the piano, Flix [*sic*] scratches the fiddle,
> And I play on the cello . . .[1]

Ferdinand Hiller's recollection of an occasion in 1822 makes it clear, however, that at thirteen Felix was far from a "scratcher" on the violin; Hiller recalled: "At his second visit he astonished me immensely. I was showing him a violin sonata of Aloys Schmitt's when he at once took up a violin which lay on the piano and asked me to play the sonata with him; he got through his part very cleverly and well, though the brilliant passages were naturally somewhat sketchy."[2] From Zelter's correspondence with Goethe it is clear that within another twelve months or so Mendelssohn was perceived as having almost as great an aptitude for the violin as for the piano. In 1823 Zelter reported: "His wonderful piano playing I may consider as quite a thing apart. He might also become a great violin player."[3] Clearly, Mendelssohn did not choose to realize that potential, but a review of a concert in Stettin in 1827 indicates that when he was a nineteen-year-old his violin playing was still maintained at a very respectable level. In the first half of the concert Mendelssohn had appeared as pianist in Weber's *Konzertstück* and, with Carl Loewe, in his own Double Piano Concerto in A-flat. After reviewing these performances enthusiastically the writer continued: "The second part of the concert comprised Beethoven's newest grand Symphony in D minor, in which Mr Mendelssohn, as a combatant in the first violins, compelled the respect of his neighbors."[4] In later years Mendelssohn seems to have preferred to play viola, which he did in private chamber music until the end of his life. He occasionally appeared in public as a violist in his own Octet; and one of his last documented performances as a violist was in Spohr's Double String Quartet in E minor at a party in honor of Spohr in 1846.[5]

Mendelssohn's lifelong engagement with the violin and viola as a competent performer undoubtedly left its mark on the technical assurance of his compositions for string instruments, but his contact with accomplished string players of the day was equally important. He counted Eduard Rietz and Ferdinand David among his closest friends and colleagues, had the opportunity to hear and admire (or criticize) the playing of many of the most celebrated violinists of the day, such as Pierre Baillot, Charles Phillipe Lafont, Louis Spohr, Nicolo Paganini, Wilhelm Heinrich Ernst, and Ole Bull, and in the last years of his life acted as mentor to the boy who was to become the leading German violinist of the later nineteenth century, Joseph Joachim. The styles and techniques associated with these violinists provide a background against which Mendelssohn's conception of his music for strings may be appraised; their known practices may offer clues to the kind of execution his music received during his lifetime, allowing us to appreciate some of the ways in which the notation was differently perceived by mid-nineteenth-century musicians than it is by musicians of the early twenty-first century.

An investigation of this kind is nevertheless fraught with difficulties. Documentary sources preserve copious information about playing techniques, and the characteristics of mid-nineteenth-century instruments are well understood, but what sounds these techniques were expected to produce from the instruments and in what musical contexts they would have been employed is much more difficult to determine. Not even the most detailed written accounts of performances and practices are able to convey the musical gestures and infinitely subtle nuances that constituted the sound-world of the past. The advent of sound recording at the end of the nineteenth century, however, provides another crucial resource for understanding the practices of the period. The earliest recordings make it absolutely clear that only a century ago musical notation elicited very different responses from musicians than it does now; what was then considered appropriate and beautiful (in other words what the notation was understood to mean) often seems quaint, bizarre, or even tasteless today. We should not dismiss such differences as merely a matter of style and fashion, for they were integral to the way in which composers of that time conceived their music; nor should we fall into the trap of assuming that current performing styles represent an advance in taste. Among the oldest musicians to make recordings were two unquestionably great German musicians, the pianist Carl Reinecke (1824–1910)[6] and the violinist Joseph Joachim (1831–1907),[7] who were personally associated with Mendelssohn. These important sound documents allow us to experience performing practices with which Mendelssohn would have been familiar; they may not provide us with a Rosetta Stone of music, but in conjunction with the documentary evidence they may allow us to rediscover some of the forgotten implications of Mendelssohn's notation.

Around the time of Mendelssohn's birth, there were a number of disparate trends in string playing, which were generally associated with a place, or the style of a particular master. At the end of the eighteenth century the Lolli School (named after the Italian violinist Antonio Lolli) was prominent; its characteristics were described in 1811 as "a preference for pleasant tone, for great facility and dexterity, for elegance, charm and various so-called tricks [Hexereien]."[8] At about the same time many string players were experimenting with a type of springing bow stroke for the performance of fast or moderately fast passagework; this style was explicitly associated with Wilhelm Cramer, who was said to have originated it in the 1770s (evidently in connection with the development of the hatchet-headed bow sometimes described at the time as the "Cramer" bow). For a while this "Cramer" bowing was very popular in Germany; according to the cellist Bernhard Romberg, it "was formerly in great repute with all Artists, who introduced it in passages of every description."[9] By the second decade of the nineteenth century, however, the practices of the Lolli School and Cramer's manner of bowing were being rapidly superseded in Germany by the style of the Viotti School, which was broadly similar to that of later representatives of the Mannheim School (for instance Spohr's teacher, Franz Eck, and Kreutzer's teacher, Anton Stamitz). The writer of the above-mentioned article in 1811 described the principal characteristics of the Viotti School: "first, big powerful, full tone; secondly, the union of this with powerful, impressive, beautifully connected legato; thirdly, variety, charm, light and shade must be incorporated into the playing through the use of the most varied bowing patterns." He considered that "[t]hrough these principles this school differs completely from that of Lolli and the newer Italian School, which until a few years ago was rather dominant in Germany."[10] Spohr disparaged the "Cramer" springing bow stroke in 1802, referring to it as "the old method,"[11] and by 1820 it appears to have become largely discredited because, as Romberg put it, "it was quite incompatible with a fine, broad style of playing."[12] Mendelssohn grew up, therefore, at a time when the Viotti School and its direct heirs (including Spohr and the majority of the newer generation of German violinists) enjoyed virtually undisputed supremacy. All the violinists with whom Mendelssohn had close contact during his youth were directly or indirectly linked with that tendency; indeed, in 1825 it was possible for another German writer to comment that the playing style of the Viotti School was "as is well known, distinguished by a characteristic use of the bow, and almost all present-day celebrated violin virtuosos have more or less adopted it."[13] And, around 1830, William Gardener observed that, with the exception of François Cramer (Wilhelm Cramer's son), all violinists heard in England in recent times had been "of the Viotti School."[14] The three violinists with whom Mendelssohn had the most intimate working relationship were all connected with the Viotti School through its most widely traveled representative, Pierre Rode, and their styles of playing undoubtedly reflected many of its leading characteristics. Rietz studied with Rode himself; David studied with Spohr, who had modeled his style on Rode's after hearing him perform in 1803; and Joachim was taught by Joseph Boehm, another of Rode's pupils.

Although a distinctive approach to bowing was the principal attribute of the Viotti School, there were other important stylistic features, common to all schools of violin playing throughout much of the nineteenth century, which sharply distinguish the performing practices of that time from those of the present day. Prominent among these were the employment of vibrato as an occasional ornament, rather than a continuous element of tone, and the use of portamento as an essential adjunct to a legato, singing style of performance. In addition to these specific string instrument practices, which were shared to a considerable extent by singers and wind players,[15] all musicians of the period treated the written notes in a rhythmically freer manner, generally within a fairly constant pulse, than modern players do, and their sense of phrasing accentuation and articulation differed markedly from that of musicians today, as Joachim's and Reinecke's recordings indicate. There can be little doubt that the rhythmic freedom in Joachim's recorded performances derived directly from Mendelssohn, for Moser reported in Joachim's lifetime that his "inimitable '*rubato*' may be traced to the example of Mendelssohn, who understood perfectly how to blend one subject with another without forcing the passage in the smallest degree."[16] In the case of piano playing, Reinecke's recordings and those of many other pianists of the older generation indicate that these flexibilities would have been accompanied by extensive use of arpeggiation and a very different concept of coordination of the hands. Mendelssohn's violin and piano playing undoubtedly reflected many of these characteristics.

Mendelssohn deeply admired Eduard Rietz's violin playing. In a letter written immediately after hearing of Rietz's tragically early death, he reports that, shortly before he received the news, "I was listening to Baillot on Tuesday, and said to Hiller[17] that I only knew one man who could play the music I loved for me."[18] Fanny Mendelssohn, too, regarded Rietz's playing as exceptional.[19] In later years Ferdinand David described Rietz as "one of Rode's leading pupils,"[20] and it seems that his manner of performance was perceived to reflect that of his master. In particular, he probably possessed a bowing style in which Rode's characteristic breadth and tone were apparent; this supposition is supported by a comment in a curiously supercilious review of Mendelssohn's Violin Sonata op. 4 in 1825, where it was stated that "Herr Rizius, is supposed to be a really first-rate fiddler, a pupil of young Rode [. . .]—in the good old style with a full, broad bow stroke and a fat, juicy tone."[21]

During the time of their close association, Mendelssohn wrote a number of works with Rietz in mind. The D minor Concerto for Violin and String Orchestra of 1822 seems to have been the first compositional fruit of their relationship,[22] and surviving sources suggest that Rietz may have offered advice to his young friend on the content of the solo part. Mendelssohn's violin writing in the first version of the first movement indicates a degree of familiarity with concertos of the Viotti School, as does the character of some of the thematic material, but much of it, consisting of repeated sixteenth notes in sixths and thirds and long passages of broken chords, seems mechanical and not particularly effective. In the second version, whether at his own initiative or at Rietz's prompting, Mendelssohn abandoned all this material and replaced it with passages that are closer to the style of violin writing in works by Viotti, Rode, Kreutzer, and Spohr. In the original version the solo part contained very few bowing or articulation markings. The revised version, however, is much more extensively supplied with such markings; these indicate that the 14-year-old Mendelssohn was thinking as a violinist and that he was familiar with a considerable corpus of contemporary violin music. Particularly noteworthy is the fact that the bowings cross beats and

EXAMPLE 4.1.   Concerto for Violin and String Orchestra in D minor, second version. Allegro molto, mm. 260–63.

measure lines, reflecting, albeit only occasionally, the varied bowing patterns typical of the Viotti School (see example 4.1).

A letter from Mendelssohn's mother, Lea, to her cousin Henriette von Pereira-Arnstein confirms that the Double Concerto for Violin, Piano, and Orchestra, composed the following year, was also written for Rietz and played at one of the family's Sunday concerts on 25 May; she later reported its public performance on 3 July at a concert given by the Italian soprano Nina Cornega.[23] Not only the spirit and technique of the violin writing, which is more extensively and intricately supplied with indications of slurring, articulation, accents, and even the occasional fingering, but also the melodic style suggests a more mature and extensive knowledge of works by contemporary violinist-composers.

There are several occurrences of slurred staccato in the Double Concerto, confirming that this was an aspect of Rietz's technique and perhaps also of Mendelssohn's. It is very likely that Rietz instructed Mendelssohn to practice this kind of bowing in studies by members of the Viotti School, for example Kreutzer's *Etude* no. 4 and Rode's *Caprice* no. 7. Since the time of Tartini and Leopold Mozart, this bow stroke, performed mostly up-bow with very short martelé stokes from the tip to the middle of the bow, had been seen as an indispensable technique for achieving a sharply separated staccato. It occurs in many violin works of the period and was particularly cultivated by Spohr and his pupil David. Mendelssohn's admiration of Spohr's execution of the staccato is recorded in his reaction to it in 1835, when he accompanied Spohr in the latter's new Concertino op. 92. According to Spohr's account Mendelssohn several times asked him to repeat it, exclaiming to his sister Fanny: "See, this is the famous Spohrish staccato, which no violinist can play like him."[24] It is probably not coincidental that Mendelssohn employed this bow stroke in the main theme of the last movement of his Piano Trio op. 66, which is dedicated to Spohr.

The Double Concerto also contains another typical violinist's device of the period: changing fingers on successive notes of the same pitch within a slur. On one occasion Mendelssohn's autograph includes a fingering to specify this practice (see example 4.2). It was favored particularly in the context of ascending or descending passages of triplets; Kreutzer devoted an etude

EXAMPLE 4.2.   Concerto for Violin, Piano, and Orchestra in D minor. Allegro, mm. 137–40.

(no. 10 in E major) to the latter type, while Baillot gave an example of this pattern of fingering, both ascending and descending, in the context of Variation 4 from Tartini's *L'Arte del arco*.[25] Spohr, who illustrated both species in his *Violinschule* and quite often employed similar figurations in his works, classified it, together with vibrato, as an embellishment and commented: "By changing the finger upon a note another property of singing is likewise imitated, *viz.* the separation of two notes on the same degree of the stave, caused by pronouncing a new syllable on the second of them, both being sung in one breath." He explained that the finger stopping the first of the repeated notes must move into the position necessary for another finger to replace it on the second note, warning that "the change of finger must be made so quick, that the ear may scarcely observe when the first note is left."[26] In Mendelssohn's Double Concerto the effect is also implied near the opening of the first solo; and a similar treatment was probably also intended at the beginning of the Recitative section in the first movement, although the autograph contains no slur (see examples 4.3 a and b).

Apart from the fingerings in measures 138–39 and a purely utilitarian position change in 117 of the first movement, all Mendelssohn's fingering instructions in the autograph indicate natural harmonics. There is a similar occurrence of harmonics in Spohr's music and in Spohr's and Ferdinand David's editions of works by Rode, Kreutzer, and Viotti,[27] where many melodic notes are marked to be played as natural harmonics or open strings. In measure 271 of the first movement of the Double Concerto,

EXAMPLE 4.3A.   Concerto for Violin, Piano, and Orchestra in D minor. Allegro, mm. 80–82.

EXAMPLE 4.3B.   Concerto for Violin, Piano, and Orchestra in D minor. Allegro, mm. 244–45.

Mendelssohn indicated a harmonic on the whole-note a²; and in the Adagio he marked harmonics in measures 57, 106–107, and 123.

The inclusion of harmonics in these circumstances must be understood in the light of early nineteenth-century attitudes toward vibrato. During the eighteenth century vibrato effects, often quite dissimilar to modern vibrato, had been used alongside other ornaments in a culture that encouraged extempore embellishment. Toward the end of the century, however, expression became increasingly associated with the dynamic nuancing of longer notes by means of the bow, rather than with the addition of ornaments. Vibrato, along with many other ornaments, became less fashionable; a violin treatise in 1811 even referred to it as "obsolete,"[28] and at least one prominent violinist of the period, Bernhard Molique (1802–69), apparently eschewed it altogether.[29] There can be no doubt that all the string players associated with Mendelssohn regarded vibrato as an occasional ornament, to be used with discretion in the sense described in Spohr's *Violinschule*, Baillot's *L'art du violon*, David's *Violinschule*, and all other treatises of the period that mentioned it. The inessential character of this ornament in the minds of early to mid–nineteenth-century musicians is emphasized by the minor role allotted to it in these treatises and the fact that some substantial treatises ignored it altogether. Spohr left it until near the end of his *Violinschule*, long after the pupil has been required to play pieces of advanced difficulty. He introduced it after the discussion of other ornaments (trills, turns, etc.), with the statement: "To the class of embellishments belong also the *tremolo*, and the changing of the finger on the same note." Spohr described both these devices as imitations of the human voice. The former, he explained occurred when "the singer in the performance of passionate movements, or when forcing his voice to its highest pitch, produces a certain tremulous sound, resembling the vibrations of a powerfully struck bell." He warned that "its employment is left entirely to the player, who however, must guard against using it too often, and in improper places," adding that "it is employed only in an impassioned style of playing and in accenting notes marked with *fz* or >. Long sustained notes may likewise be animated and reinforced by it; and should a swell from *p* to *f* be introduced on such a note, a beautiful effect is produced by commencing the *tremolo* slowly and gradually accelerating the vibrations, in proportion to the increase in power. If a *diminuendo* occur on a sustained note, it likewise produces a good effect to begin the *tremolo* quick and gently decrease in velocity."[30] The persistence of this aesthetic in the German traditions is emphasized by the verbatim quotation of Spohr's instructions in Joachim's *Violinschule* in 1905,[31] long after most younger violinists had begun to use vibrato much more frequently. Both Spohr and Joachim stressed that the undulation should only be slight, so that "the deviation from purity of tone may scarcely be observed by the ear."[32] Baillot also added that, to

EXAMPLE 4.4A.   String Quartet op. 13. Adagio, mm. 1–2.

EXAMPLE 4.4B.   String Quartet op. 13. Presto, mm. 19–20.

EXAMPLE 4.4C.   String Quartet op. 44 no. 1. Andante, espressivo con moto mm. 141–44.

EXAMPLE 4.4D.   String Quartet op. 44 no. 2. Andante, mm. 71–75.

EXAMPLE 4.4E.   String Quartet op. 44 no. 3. Allegro vivace, mm. 171–74.

"console" the ear, "the violinist must begin and end by producing a tone with pure intonation";[33] his musical illustrations show the vibrato occupying only the middle of the note. The Viotti School associated vibrato particularly with the *messa di voce,* and in music of the period the sign <>, often used over quite short notes, invites vibrato, perhaps combined with a degree of expressive lingering, in addition to the obvious dynamic nuance. It seems probable that Mendelssohn, though not necessarily regarding it as a mandatory instruction to use vibrato, understood this implication of the sign, which is linked specifically with vibrato and lingering in Joachim's *Violinschule.*[34] Mendelssohn employed the marking in his string writing from at least the late 1820s (see examples 4.4 a–e; see also later in this chapter example 4.9b, measure 174).

Although only one of the fingerings in the Double Concerto implies portamento (the slurred figure from f,[1] presumably in first position, to the harmonic d[2]) there were undoubtedly many other places where Rietz would have introduced an audible slide for its expressive effect. Rode was particularly noted for his extensive and prominent portamento, as was Spohr, and it seems highly likely that it was also a characteristic of Rietz's style. Portamento, however, will be discussed in greater detail in connection with the more fully fingered sources of some of Mendelssohn's later works.

The Violin Sonata op. 4, composed for Rietz immediately after the Double Concerto (between 21 May and 3 June 1823), probably reflecting Mendelssohn's appreciation of the distinction between the soloistic idiom of the Viotti School and that of the Classical Viennese chamber music tradition, reveals a different approach to violin writing. Features conceived specifically for the instrument include portato in the Poco adagio, slurred staccato in the final Allegro agitato (both notated with dots under a slur but requiring a different technique), and figures that strongly suggest portamento in the Poco Adagio and the short Adagio section for solo violin toward the end of the last movement; on the whole, however, the violin part is idiomatic without depending for its effectiveness on figurations, patterns, or techniques that are peculiar to string instruments. Here the influences of two composers who were not active violinists, Beethoven and Weber, are more apparent. The passages implying portamento in the Finale could just as well have derived from Beethoven's Violin Sonata op. 96 (written for Rode), where there is a very similar effect at measure 159 of the last movement, as from the works of violinist composers; the influence of Weber's *Konzertstück* in F minor (one of Mendelssohn's pianistic warhorses at the time) is evident in some of the thematic material.

Mendelssohn was never able to compare Rietz's playing with that of Rode, for although he met Rode in 1825, during his visit to Paris he evidently did not hear him play, commenting in a letter to Fanny: "Rode persists in his refusal to touch a violin."[35] He had ample opportunity, however, to experience Baillot's playing when he accompanied him in a performance of the B minor Piano Quartet op. 3; and in 1831 he was able to appraise Baillot's style of performance more thoroughly, for he attended several of his soirées, accompanied him in Bach sonatas, and heard him perform the String Quartets op. 12 and op. 13 and the Octet. A notational oddity in the Intermezzo of the A minor String Quartet op. 13, written in 1827, may reflect the influence of Baillot in 1825 (see example 4.5). Although Mendelssohn makes no comment about it in his letters home, it seems possible that he may have heard Baillot using springing bow strokes in, for instance, the third movement of the B minor Piano Quartet. We cannot be certain, but it seems

EXAMPLE 4.5.   String Quartet op. 13. Intermezzo: Allegro di molto, mm. 84–99.

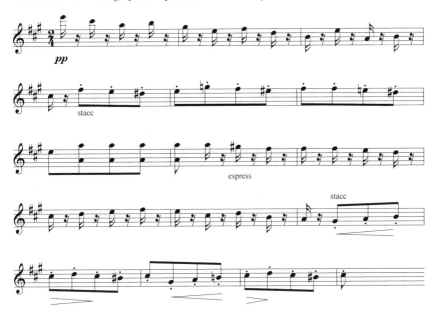

likely that this style of bowing was alien to Rietz's and Mendelssohn's violin playing at that time; in line with the practice of the Viotti School they would probably have used short strokes in the upper half of the bow. Neither the Rode, Kreutzer, and Baillot *Méthode de violon* of 1803, Rode's *Caprices,* Kreutzer's *Etudes,* nor Spohr's *Violinschule* describe or mention a springing bow stroke. The *Méthode* gives the following instructions for the execution of sixteenth notes in a passage marked *maestoso:* "the *détaché* must be given as much length as possible, from about the middle of the stick, so that the sound is full and the string is made to vibrate fully,"[36] Baillot's *L'art du violon* of 1835, on the other hand, gives several examples of springing strokes. His instructions for executing sixteenth notes in a maestoso (quarter note = 108) from Viotti's Violin Concerto no. 24, differ strikingly from those given in the earlier *Méthode;* he states that the notes are to be played in the middle of the bow and "must be separated by the elastic movement of the stick—an imperceptible bouncing of the bow—with slightly lengthened stroke."[37] Curiously, in both the *Méthode de violon* and *L'art du violon,* the effect of the stroke is illustrated by thirty-second notes followed by thirty-second note rests. In a subsequent music example in *L'art du violon* Baillot instructs that in playing the sixteenth notes in the last movement of Haydn, String Quartet op. 64 no. 5, "The same separation is produced by the elasticity of the stick. The bow stroke must be *very* short here because of the fast tempo."[38] He also illustrates a "spiccato" stroke, in which the bow must "bounce lightly in the same place, leaving the string a little."[39] Baillot's description of these strokes in 1835 corresponds closely with bow strokes employed by Paganini, which were regarded by Carl Guhr in 1829 as distinctly different in this respect from the practice of the Viotti School.[40] Mendelssohn's pupil Wasielewski also expressed the view that this type of bowing resulted from Paganini's influence, which he believed "expressed itself most strongly and most enduringly in the French School, whereas Germany was only affected temporarily by it in isolated cases."[41] Springing bowing was scorned by Spohr and seems generally to have been regarded as unidiomatic in the Classical German repertoire. Later in the century Wasielewski commented that "the sharp spiccato [Pointierte], which particularly characterized the French bow stroke, in a word the piquanteries of the bow, remained almost entirely excluded here,"[42] and Hermann Schröder remarked in 1887 that bounced bowing was rarely employed "in the old Italian and particularly in the German School up to L. Spohr."[43] Perhaps, therefore, as a direct result of Baillot's influence, Mendelssohn took a less rigid view of its appropriateness.

It seems likely that in the Allegro di molto section of the Intermezzo in op. 13 Mendelssohn wanted to contrast springing bow strokes (for the sixteenth notes followed by rests) with an on-string stroke in the middle of the bow (for the staccato eighths) and devised this rather unusual notation as a means of conveying his intentions to the players, who might have been expected to play the whole passage on the string in the upper half of the bow if it had all been written with staccato eighths. In the Scherzo of the Octet, too, written shortly after Mendelssohn's 1825 visit to Paris, sixteenth notes and rests are used in contrast to staccato eighths, though not in such obvious juxtaposition as in the quartet. Earlier composers, including Mozart, had notated a succession of notes with rests (e.g., the beginning of the second part of the Menuetto of the String Quartet in E-flat, K. 428) in order to obtain a real separation, which might not have been achieved by simply adding staccato marks to notes of double the value, since these would probably have been played by violinists of that time with a quite extended on-string bow stroke. But this notation had generally been used for passages where there was time for the bow to be lifted, not for rapid notes in a piano dynamic where a springing bow stroke might have been implied. It is important to realize that, in late eighteenth-century and early nineteenth-century string playing, staccato marks were by no means always associated with a distinct shortening of the note. Spohr, for instance, marking a passage of eighth notes with staccato strokes, to be played at half note = 104 (approximately the same speed as Baillot's maestoso, where no staccato is indicated), instructed that "each note . . . is made with a steady back-arm and as long strokes as possible, at the upper part of the bow."[44]

Mendelssohn did not use the notation with alternate notes and rests in his later violin music where an off-string bowing was required, perhaps because by that stage the springing bow stroke was more likely to have been understood as a matter of course in such contexts. Many of Mendelssohn's later scherzo-like movements were certainly envisaged with a springing bowing. Even Spohr, who would have had direct knowledge of practices in Mendelssohn's circle, acknowledged that this bow stroke might occasionally be appropriate "in some passages in some scherzos by Beethoven, Onslow and Mendelssohn."[45] Mendelssohn's openness to the employment of such bowings is confirmed by his advice to the young Joachim. Joachim, as a student of Boehm in Vienna, had studied a range of virtuoso repertoire, including Paganini, but he apparently came to Leipzig in 1844 with the preconception that a springing bow stroke was unidiomatic in Classical compositions. When he consulted Mendelssohn about it, he received the pragmatic response: "Always use it, my boy, where it is suitable, or where it sounds well."[46]

Many of the chamber works of Mendelssohn's early maturity were undoubtedly written with Rietz in mind, but Ferdinand David, too, was associated with their performance. His musical connection with Mendelssohn began during a visit to Berlin in 1825, when he participated in "musical evenings that lived on in the memories of the participants."[47] By the end of the 1820s he and Mendelssohn adopted the intimate *Du* form of address.[48] During his time in Berlin David performed in Mendelssohn's newly written quartets opp. 12 and 13, probably playing second violin to Rietz's first and with Mendelssohn himself on the viola; in a letter from Lea Mendelssohn Bartholdy to Ferdinand David dated 21 February 1832 (after David had left Berlin) she refers to a recent public concert: "There the quartet in A minor was certainly performed very cleanly, with good ensemble, tenderly and delicately; the grandiose tone, the vitality and depth, which Ritz [*sic*] you and Felix brought to it, however, was completely lacking."[49] From 1829 to 1835 David led a private quartet in the house of Karl von Liphart in Dorpat, acquiring an intimate knowledge of the chamber music repertoire, but after Mendelssohn's appointment as director of music in Leipzig, he became leader of the Gewandhaus orchestra, and for the rest of Mendelssohn's life was intimately associated with him as orchestral leader and advisor on string technique, particularly in connection with the Violin Concerto. In private, David continued to play string chamber music with Mendelssohn. This activity is reflected in their correspondence. On 26 January 1844, for instance, David wrote to Mendelssohn, who was in Berlin at the time: "Invite me some time next month to an amateur quartet party at your house: Paul [Mendelssohn Bartholdy], you, [Karl Emil von] Webern (if there is no alternative), I'll certainly come."[50]

While Rietz's style of playing can be surmised only by association with that of Rode, David's can be envisaged in much greater detail as a result of his *Violinschule* of 1863 and the many editions of music for which he provided extensive bowing and fingering, including almost the whole corpus of classic chamber music for strings from Haydn to Schubert. Apart from Mendelssohn's Violin Concerto and arrangements for violin of the two cello sonatas op. 45 and op. 58, David did not publish performing editions of any of his friend's works, but valuable information about his approach to performing them is preserved in his personal copies of the first violin parts of Mendelssohn's string quartets opp. 12, 13, and 44, which are extensively bowed and fingered.[51] David's habit of marking parts in this manner was well established during his Leipzig years. Writing to Mendelssohn in 1844 he commented: "It is a joy to hear young Weissborn play quartets; he plays from Grabau's copies, which I precisely marked up in my first winter here and he imitates every little quirk [Mätzchen] of mine with hair's-breadth precision."[52] David's belief in the utility of bowing and fingering may well have been derived from his studies with Spohr, who was exceptional for the period in his attention to these matters in his own works. Evidence of David's conscientiousness in this respect can be seen in his collaboration with Mendelssohn over the publication of the E minor Violin Concerto. On 2 January 1845, he commented in a letter to the composer:

> I have also revised it [the solo part], striking out many superfluous fingerings and bowings that I had written in and adding many new ones. Just strike out everything that's superfluous. I know from my own experience and with Beethoven and Bach, that it is not good to send forth a violin piece into the uncultivated world of violinists without all the bowings and fingerings. They don't take the trouble to discover the right ones and would rather say that it is ungrateful and unplayable in places. Therefore put up with anything that your composer's conscience can tolerate.[53]

The original edition contains a modest amount of fingering and bowing, but David added many additional markings in a revised edition issued after Mendelssohn's death.

In view of the close relationship between Mendelssohn and David, the following discussion of performance issues will draw upon the evidence of David's markings to elucidate how Mendelssohn's contemporaries may have understood his notation. Reference will also be made to Joachim's editions of the Violin Concerto and the two piano trios, which he studied with Mendelssohn himself, to illustrate similarities and differences.

EXAMPLE 4.6.   Violin Concerto in E minor, op. 64. Allegro molto appassionato, mm. 2–29. (I have added slanting lines in places where portamento would be likely to have been heard.)

David's and Joachim's fingerings provide concrete evidence that they did not envisage vibrato in places where violinists of later generations, who increasingly saw vibrato as an essential element of tone production, would have introduced it. The opening theme of the Violin Concerto, where harmonics abound, is a good example (see example 4.6). In measures 165–69 of the first movement, too, David makes lavish use of harmonics on melodic notes. Joachim avoids the third of these harmonics, but his choice is likely to have been dictated more by his concern to preserve

EXAMPLE 4.7.   Violin Concerto in E minor, op. 64. Allegro molto appassionato, mm. 165–69.
(I have added slanting lines in places where portamento would be likely to have been heard.)

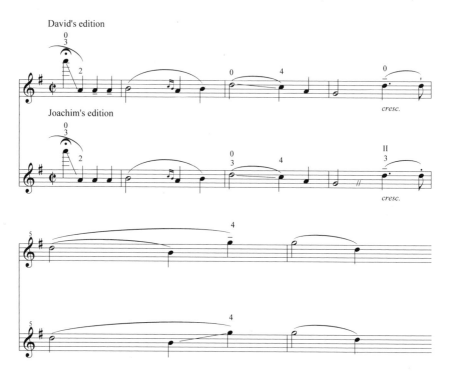

equality of tone, and perhaps to allow portamento in measure 169, than
to permit a vibrato (see example 4.7). Similarly in the Andante, David
uses harmonics more frequently than Joachim. From David's fingering it
is clear that he conceived the whole theme with little if any vibrato.
Joachim, too, who vehemently denounced the late nineteenth-century
trend toward an increasingly continuous vibrato, will almost certainly have
played it mostly with a still left hand (see example 4.8). We might imagine
them executing a vibrato on the first note of the theme, similar to the
delicate finger vibrato in measure 13 of Joachim's *Romance* in his 1903
recording, and on the first notes of measures 12 and 20, but, because of the
diminuendo phrase ending, probably not 26; the fourth notes of measures
15 and 23 might also have invited vibrato. Many passages in String Quartets, as marked by David, show a similar use of harmonics on melody notes
(see examples 4.9 a–b).

Although both violinists played with little vibrato, they clearly employed
a significant amount of portamento. In all the places where position changes
are indicated in examples 4.6–4.8 (marked with my slanting lines), David and

EXAMPLE 4.8.   Violin Concerto in E minor, op. 64. Andante, mm. 9–26. (I have added slanting lines in places where portamento would be likely to have been heard.)

EXAMPLE 4.9A.   String Quartet op. 13. Allegro vivace, mm. 26–34. (Only the staccato marks on mm. 30 n. 8 and 32 nn. 2 and 3 are in the printed edition; the others were added by David, who also changed the printed ones on 33 nn. 3, 4, 7, 8 to lines. David's added bowings are marked as dotted slurs; the up-bow sign in 26 and the fingerings are his.)

EXAMPLE 4.9B.   String Quartet op. 44 no. 2. Allegro assai appassionato, mm. 163–76. (David's added bowing is marked as a dotted slur; the up-bow sign and fingerings are his.)

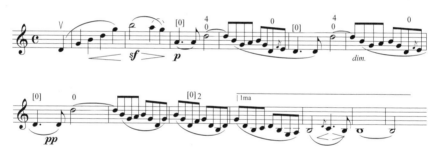

Joachim used a range of more or less audible portamento effects to enhance the cantabile qualities of the theme. From what is known of their back-grounds and attitudes, it seems certain that David employed portamento more frequently and prominently than Joachim, and may have included some types that Joachim would not have favored. Nevertheless, Joachim, though he warned earnestly against the misuse of portamento, regarded it as a more im-portant artistic resource than vibrato. For both violinists, as for Mendelssohn, it would have been one of the principal ways in which the violinist emulated the beauties of singing. Joachim considered that it was a "manner of changing position which, clearly perceptible by the ear, serves to allow expressive singing on the violin."[54] Spohr's technical description of how portamento should be executed was repeated by both David and Joachim in their teach-ing, and these techniques were fundamental to their playing style.[55]

EXAMPLE 4.10.   Spohr: *Violinschule* (trans. Bishop), p. 195: Rode:Violin Concerto no. 7. Adagio, mm. 1–2. (I have added slanting lines in places where Spohr instructs that portamento should occur.)

Joachim's subtle and varied, but frequent, use of portamento as an adjunct to cantabile playing can be heard in his 1903 recordings. In Joachim's *Violinschule* the use of portamento between notes stopped by the same finger is illustrated with measures 21–22 of the Andante of Mendelssohn's Violin Concerto, fingered as in his edition; the commentary merely remarks that in this and other examples from Haydn and Rode, "It will depend entirely on the expressive requirements of the passage in question whether the portamento that is to be used here should be executed quickly or slowly, and should sound tender or passionate."[56] Joachim's restraint in the use of portamento, in comparison with many of his contemporaries, is indicated in the comment that the violinist "should let his artistic understanding be in command, so that what is in itself a useful thing should not degenerate into the unendurable mannerism of whines and slides." Violinists "who are in the habit of connecting a stopped note with the open string by a wiping movement of the hand from the stopped note" are also castigated, and the use of this type of portamento between d^2 and a^1 in measure 11 of the Andante of Mendelssohn's Violin Concerto is condemned as "very ugly."[57] Spohr, however, had recommended just such a type of portamento in his annotation of Rode's A minor Concerto, observing: "The smooth gliding from one note to another must not only take place upward as in the first bar from G to E but also downward, as in the same bar from C to the open E" (see example 4.10).

Although there is no direct evidence, it seems possible that Joachim's condemnation of this practice in Mendelssohn's Andante is an oblique criticism of the manner in which David performed it. Joachim undoubtedly represented a more modern approach to violin playing than David, whose taste he evidently considered questionable in some respects, referring to "certain mannerisms which had crept into his style."[58] A comparison of the two violinists' fingerings in a passage in the first movement of the Violin Concerto clearly illustrates David's greater liking for portamento in general, as well as their rather different approaches to characterizing the phrase through the use of portamento (see example 4.11). David's copy of the string quartets and Joachim's edition of the piano trios provide further instructive examples of the places in which they would have employed portamento (see examples

EXAMPLE 4.11.   Violin Concerto in E minor, op. 64. Allegro molto appassionato, mm. 226–34.
(I have added slanting lines in places where portamento would be likely to have been heard; the
portamento between semitones would have been slight, but no attempt would have been made to
disguise it by releasing the pressure of the bow.)

4.12 a–c). Both violinists would undoubtedly have intended the portamento
to be a clearly audible aspect of their performance.

In contrast to the twentieth century, when the left-hand vibrato became
increasingly associated with the production of a fine and individual tone
quality, nineteenth-century musicians regarded the bow as the principal
means by which a fine tone and characterful delivery was achieved. A writer
in 1835 stated that the skillful use of the bow "is undeniably one of the most
important points in playing or handling string instruments; not only that the
quality and true tonal beauty of the notes themselves is to a large degree dependent on it, but also the whole performance style of a composition derives its life from it; it is the first and most effective means of giving the notes
expression and meaningful tone quality, at the same time embodying the
spirit of the whole composition."[59] David's and Joachim's expectations for
bow stokes in Mendelssohn's violin music can be deduced partly from general information about their relationship to the practices of their day and
partly from their markings in the music itself. David is likely to have used a
far greater proportion of the broad detaché and martelé strokes (including
the slurred staccato) that were characteristic of Spohr; but, perhaps as a direct

EXAMPLE 4.12A.   String Quartet op. 44 no. 3. Allegro vivace, mm. 170–74, with David's markings. (I have added slanting lines in places where portamento would be likely to have been heard; David's added bowing is shown as a dotted slur.)

EXAMPLE 4.12B.   String Quartet op. 44 no. 3. Adagio non troppo, mm. 5–9, with David's markings. (I have added slanting lines in places where portamento would be likely to have been heard; David's added bowings are shown as dotted slurs.)

EXAMPLE 4.12C.   Piano Trio in D minor, op. 49. Allegro assai appasionato, mm. 279–86, with Joachim's markings. (I have added slanting lines in places where portamento would be likely to have been heard.)

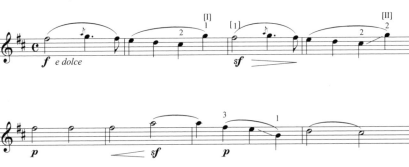

result of Mendelssohn's influence, he probably employed springing strokes, of which he included examples in his *Violinschule,* more frequently than most German violinists of his generation. In fact Mendelssohn's and David's friend Ferdinand Hiller affirmed that "David combined the sterling qualities of Spohr's style with the greater facility and piquancy of a later school."[60] Joachim will nevertheless almost certainly have used springing strokes in the middle and lower half of the bow more often than David. In the Joachim *Violinschule* the change in fashion since Spohr's time is alluded to with the comment that "the spiccato has so triumphantly survived its unmerited condemnation, that it now plays a much more important part than the martelé in the rendering of classical, romantic and modern compositions."[61] The discussion of style in volume 3 of Joachim's *Violinschule* makes clear, however, that martelé was still routinely used in places that would almost invariably be played today with a springing stroke in the lower half of the bow.

As suggested earlier, Mendelssohn clearly intended a number of movements in his violin works to be played with springing bow stokes, executed with various degrees of length in the middle of the bow. His use of the term "leggiero" may be intended to imply this type of bow stroke. Joachim asserted that the last movement of the Violin Concerto "could not be imagined without the use of the spiccato bow."[62] Hermann Schröder quoted measures 8–11 and 17–21, where dots under slurs occur, as an example of the "light staccato-bow," which, unlike the traditional slurred staccato (played near the point), was executed in the middle of the bow and required not only the pressure of the index finger, but also the counterbalancing action of the little finger.[63] Joachim, however, remarked: "the author did not want it played with a 'flying' staccato, although certainly light, but with a pointed note, short and sharp. The flying bow stroke appeared to him to be too soft and flaky."[64]

It is clear, therefore, that Joachim expected spiccato for separate notes, but his description of the appropriate bow stroke for the passages with dots under slurs is ambiguous, leaving it open whether he envisaged the stroke described by Schröder or the firm staccato. David's mastery and frequent employment of the latter stroke, played in the upper half of the bow as a succession of short, sharp, martelé notes, suggests that this may have been what Mendelssohn had in mind. This supposition is strengthened by a comment by Joachim's favored pupil Karl Klingler, who, discussing the use of that kind of staccato, wrote unequivocally: "We know that in the last movement of his Violin Concerto Mendelssohn wanted a firm staccato [festes Staccato]. The technical difficulties, however, and the consideration of an easier ensemble with the orchestra have led to the 'flying staccato' (thrown bow) being generally used."[65] The scherzo of the String Quartet op. 44 no. 2, where the eighth notes at Mendelssohn's metronome mark are somewhat faster than those in the Violin Concerto at Joachim's metronome mark, provides an interesting comparison. Initially, in his own copy, David marked the eighths with slurs over the staccato marks, presumably intending a similar bow stroke to the slurred firm staccato in the Violin Concerto, but he later deleted the slurs, perhaps because of the faster tempo required (see example 4.13). Subsequently David wrote a large capital M under the first measure, evidently indicating the middle *(Mitte, milieu)* of the bow and a springing bow stroke.

Other movements in Mendelssohn's later violin music where he almost certainly envisaged extensive use of a springing stroke include the scherzos (all marked *leggiero*) of the two piano trios and the String Quartet op. 44 no. 3. Some movements are ambiguous, such as the Andante scherzando of the

EXAMPLE 4.13.   String Quartet op. 44 no. 2. Allegro di molto (dotted half=72), mm. 1–9. (The M in m. 1 and the fingering in m. 4 are in the blue crayon of David's second version; the dotted slurs represent the deleted pencil markings of his earlier version. Everything else is in the original printed edition.)

String Quintet op. 87, where a rather more lengthened stroke may have been envisaged, and the last movement of the F major Violin Sonata (1838), which may have required a springing stroke for the sixteenths and a martelé stroke for the eighths. It is interesting, however, that in the *piu mosso* middle section of the Allegretto Canzonetta of the String Quartet op. 12 (marked *stacc.*), where the sixteenth notes might have been expected to elicit a springing bow stroke (and where modern players would almost certainly use one), Karl Klingler used a rather firm stroke, with no apparent spring, in the Klingler Quartet's 1922 recording.[66] It must not be forgotten that even in the first decades of the twentieth century players in the German tradition used the upper half of the bow for many passages that are now routinely played in the lower half; the passage in example 4.14, as marked by David, in which the eighths would certainly have been played in the upper half of the bow with detaché or martelé bow strokes, provides a good instance.

It is abundantly clear that the manner in which this repertoire is generally performed today would have seemed alien to nineteenth-century musicians. Because the notation looks the same as it did to Mendelssohn, it is all too easy to assume that it means the same. This is a fallacy. In many fundamental respects the notes and signs had a different range of meanings and implications. Mendelssohn might have been impressed by the technical proficiency of a modern professional performance, but he would have been surprised by the absence of many techniques and practices that were taken for granted by performers of his time, and the modern continuous vibrato would probably have horrified him. Above all he would have been astonished and puzzled by the rhythmic literalness with which modern musicians play what he wrote. In our concern to be faithful to the composer's notation we have certainly been unfaithful to his expectations.

EXAMPLE 4.14.   String Quartet op. 44 no. 3. Allegro vivace, mm. 67–81. (David's added bow-ings are given as dotted slurs; the up-bow signs and fingerings are David's, as are the two staccato marks on m. 72 nn. 7–8.)

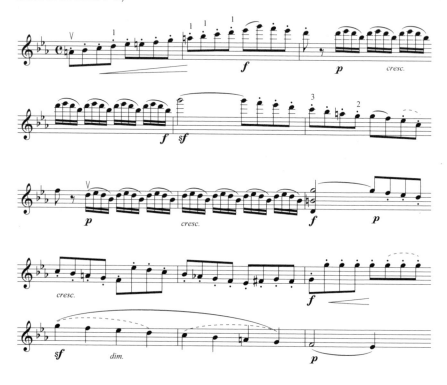

NOTES

1. Felix Mendelssohn, *Paphlëis,* trans. Clive Brown; quoted in Clive Brown, *A Portrait of Mendelssohn* (New Haven: Yale University Press, 2003), 69. The poem, in hexameters, is a parody of Goethe's *Achillëis* of 1808.

2. Ferdinand Hiller, *Mendelssohn, Letters and Recollections,* trans. M. E. von Glehn (London: Macmillan, 1874), 4.

3. Letter from Zelter to Goethe, 11 March 1823; quoted in Karl Mendelssohn Bartholdy, *Goethe and Mendelssohn,* trans. M. E. von Glehn (London: Macmillan, 1872), 35.

4. Anon., "Felix Mendelssohn-Bartholdy, in Stettin," *Berliner allgemeine musikalische Zeitung* 4 (1827): 84.

5. Louis Spohr, *Selbstbiographie* (Cassel and Göttingen: George H. Wigand, 1860) 2:308.

6. Reinecke's recordings were made on Welte-Mignon piano rolls in 1905 and on Triphonola. Two of the Welte rolls have been issued on CD along with rolls by Saint-Saëns and Leschetizky (Archiphon-106: *The Closest Approach to 19th-Century Piano Interpretation*), but in a rather inadequate transcription; more satisfactory transcriptions have been made privately by Denis Hall, who kindly supplied me with recordings.

7. Issued on CD by Opal-9851.

8. Anon., "Bemerkungen über Musik in Warschau," *Allgemeine musikalische Zeitung* 13, (1811): 453.

9. Bernhard Romberg, *A Complete Theoretical and Practical School for the Violoncello* (London: T. Boosey, 1840), 109.

10. Anon., "Bemerkungen über Musik in Warschau," *Allgemeine musikalische Zeitung* 13 (1811): 452–53.

11. Louis Spohr, *Lebenserinnerungen,* ed. Folker Göthel (Tutzing: H. Schneider, 1968), 1:43.

12. Romberg, 109.

13. G. C. F. Lobedanz, "Gibt es in der Musik, wie in der Malerey, verschiedene Schulen, und wie wären solche wohl zu bestimmen?" *Cäcilia* 2 (1825): 267.

14. William Gardiner, *The Music of Nature* (London: Longman, 1832), 216.

15. For information about the use of vibrato and portamento in wind playing, see Clive Brown, *Classical and Romantic Performing Practice* (Oxford: Oxford University Press, 1999), especially 542–45 and 573–75.

16. Andreas Moser, *Joseph Joachim ein Lebensbild* (Berlin: B. Behr's, 1898); trans. Lilla Durham as *Joseph Joachim, A Biography* (London: P. Welby, 1902), 46. See also Clive Brown, "Joachim's Violin Playing and the Performance of Brahms's String Music," in *Performing Brahms,* ed. M. Musgrave and B. D. Sherman (Cambridge: Cambridge University Press, 2003), 87–90.

17. His friend, the pianist and composer Ferdinand Hiller.

18. Mendelssohn to his family, 16 June 1831, in Felix Mendelssohn, *Letters from Italy and Switzerland,* trans. Lady Wallace, 2nd ed. (London: Longman, Green, Longman, Roberts and Green, 1862), 333.

19. For instance, Marcia J. Citron, *The Letters of Fanny Hensel to Felix Mendelssohn* (New York: Pendragon Press, 1987), 29.

20. *Concert-Studien für die Violine,* vol. 2: Rode Violin Concertos nos. 5, 6, 7, 8 (Leipzig: Senff, c. 1860), 20 and 29. The full text of the footnotes at the beginning of the 7th and 8th concertos is: "The markings and embellishments are precisely those the composer used to employ in performing this concerto and the editor owes the transmission of them to his deceased friend Eduard Rietz, one of Rode's leading pupils."

21. Lukas van Leyden (pseud.), "Recensionen," *Berliner allgemeine musikalische Zeitung* 2 (1825): 367.

22. The first page of the incomplete autograph of the first version, which was given to Ferdinand David by Mendelssohn's widow in 1853, contains the remark "Composed for E. Rietz in 1822," perhaps in the hand of David's son Peter Julius Paul David, who spent the latter part of his life in Oxford.

23. Christoph Hellmundt, *Leipziger Ausgabe der Werke Felix Mendelssohn Bartholdys,* II/8 (Leipzig: Internationale Felix-Mendelssohn-Gesellschaft, 1999), xvi.

24. Spohr, *Selbstbiographie,* 2:203.

25. Pierre Marie François de Sales Baillot, *L'art du violon* (Paris: Heugel, [1835]), 155; trans. Louise Goldberg as *The Art of the Violin* (Evanston, Ill.: Northwestern University Press, 1996), 271, Ex. 16.20.

26. Louis Spohr, *Violinschule;* trans. John Bishop as *Louis Spohr's Celebrated Violin School* (London: Gould and Boltler, [c. 1843]), 163–64.

27. Pierre Rode, Violin Concerto No. 7 in A minor, in Louis Spohr, *Violinschule,* trans. Bishop, 184–203; Ferdinand David, *Concert-Studien für die Violine,* vols. 1–3 (Leipzig: Senff, c. 1860) (see note 20).

28. John Jousse, *The Theory and Practice of the Violin* (London: R. Birchall, [1811]), 48.

29. Joachim remarked that Molique, whom he considered "a very distinguished musician" played "without any vibrato whatsoever"; quoted in Samuel B. Grimson and Cecil Forsyth, *Modern Violin Playing* (New York: H. W. Gray, 1920), 34.

30. Spohr, *Violinschule,* 163.

31. Joseph Joachim and Andreas Moser, *Violinschule* (Berlin: N. Simrock, 1905), 2:96.

Although Moser wrote most of the text, it is clear from the Vorwort that it was Joachim's ideas that were embodied in it.

32. Spohr, *Violinschule,* 163; quoted in Joachim, *Violinschule,* 2:96.

33. Baillot, *L'art du violon,* 240.

34. See Clive Brown, "Bowing Styles, Vibrato and Portamento in Nineteenth-Century Violin Playing," *Journal of the Royal Musical Association* 113, no. 1 (1988): 118–21, and Brown, *Classical and Romantic Performance Practice,* ch. 14, "Vibrato."

35. Felix Mendelssohn to his family, Paris, 20 April 1825, in Sebastian Hensel, *The Mendelssohn Family,* 3rd ed., trans. Carl Klingemann (London: Samson Low, Marston, Searle, and Rivington, 1882), 1:127.

36. Pierre Rode, Rudolf Kreutzer, and Pierre Baillot, *Méthode de violon* (Paris: Magazine de Musique, 1803), 129; translation from Robin Stowell, *Violin Technique and Performance Practice in the Late Eighteenth and Early Nineteenth Centuries* (Cambridge: Cambridge University Press, 1985), 301.

37. Baillot, *L'art du violon,* 162.

38. Ibid., 163.

39. Ibid., 187.

40. See Brown, *Classical and Romantic Performance Practice,* 279.

41. Wilhelm Joseph von Wasielewski, *Die Violine und ihre Meister,* 3rd ed. (Leipzig: Breitkopf & Härtel, 1893), 391.

42. Ibid., 421.

43. Hermann Schröder, *Die Kunst des Violinspiels* (Köln: Tonger, 1887), 72.

44. Spohr, *Violinschule,* 118.

45. Alexandre Malibran, *Louis Spohr* (Frankfurt-am-Main: J. D. Sauerländer's Verlag, 1860), 208.

46. Moser, *Joseph Joachim ein Lebensbild,* 46.

47. Julius Eckardt, *Ferdinand David und die Familie Mendelssohn-Bartholdy* (Leipzig: Duncker und Humblot, 1888), 8.

48. In a letter of August 1826 Mendelssohn still wrote to David as *Sie,* while in a letter of 13 April 1830 he used *Du;* Eckardt, *Ferdinand David und die Familie Mendelssohn-Bartholdy,* 9 and 32.

49. Eckardt, 45.

50. Ibid., 204.

51. In the Bodleian Library, Oxford.

52. Eckardt, 204.

53. Ibid., 229.

54. Joachim, *Violinschule,* 2:92.

55. For further technical details, see Brown, *Classical and Romantic Performance Practice,* 558–87.

56. Joachim, *Violinschule,* 2:92.

57. Ibid., 3:9.

58. Moser, *Joseph Joachim ein Lebensbild;* trans. Durham, *Joseph Joachim: A Biography,* 45.

59. Gustav Schilling, ed., *Encyclopädie der gesammten musikalischen Wissenschaften.* s. v. "Bogenstrich" (Stuttgart: Franz Heinrich Köhler, 1835), 1:694.

60. Ferdinand Hiller, s. v. "David, Ferdinand," in Sir George Grove, ed. *A Dictionary of Music and Musicians* (London: Macmillan, 1879–89).

61. Joachim, *Violinschule,* 1:126.

62. Ibid.

63. Schröder, 75.

64. Joachim, *Violinschule,* 3:230.

65. Karl Klingler, *"Über die Grundlagen des Violinspiels" und nachgelassene Schriften* (Hildesheim: Georg Olms Verlag, 1990), 246.

66. CD transcription: Testament SBT 2136.

5

Mendelssohn and the Orchestra

DAVID MILSOM

In discussion of musical life in England, Mendelssohn commented to Moscheles:

> Our inner life it is all that is worth living; but then that is a very different thing to our outer doings,—something much better. Conducting and getting up public performances is all very well . . . but the result, even for the public, does not go far. A little better, a little worse, what does it matter? How soon it is forgotten![1]

This famous passage underlines the chief difficulty in any study of performance. Music is an ephemeral act. In the absence of preserved sounds from Mendelssohn's lifetime, one is compelled to undertake a process of archaeological synthesis, drawing together various indirect forms of evidence, all of which are filtered through biased contemporary commentary.

Moreover, the performing practice of an orchestra is not the result of the actions of any one performer. One can speak of a "Nikitsch orchestra" or a "Mendelssohn orchestra," but the extent to which conductors can influence sound is a contentious matter. Mendelssohn frequently encountered ensembles that were unable to comply with his wishes. Commenting upon the standard of ensemble he was compelled to work with in Düsseldorf, he remarked to Hiller in 1833: "I assure you that at the beat, they all come in separately, not one with any decision, and in the pianos the flute is always too high, and not a single Düsseldorfer can play a triplet clearly, but all play a quaver and two semiquavers instead, and every Allegro leaves off twice as fast as it began, and the oboe plays E natural in C minor."[2] Knowing what constituted Mendelssohn's aesthetic ideals is also somewhat elusive. Unlike Wagner and Berlioz, Mendelssohn did not write extensively on the subject of performing practice, and Wehner points out the incomplete state of the evidence: "[M]any contemporary performing materials probably are lost. Owing to their intended purpose, they continued to be reused until they were worn out. . . . This is unfortunate since they might have provided information about many details of the musical text as well as phrasings, dynamics, and other indications that Mendelssohn gave during rehearsals but failed to enter into his score."[3] Mendelssohn's reputation in the hands of both critics and admirers affects the matter of his relationship with the orchestra as much as his other areas of activity. This problem is inherent in the reception history of all composers of course, but in Mendelssohn's case the problems are more noticeable. Unlike Spohr, whose reputation gradually ebbed away with changing performance tastes, only to be revived in more recent times (in many respects because of his importance in terms of performing practice), Mendelssohn commentary has veered from the views of unctuous admirers to Wagner's acrimonious criticism. Dispassionate evidence in the sphere of Mendelssohn's practical activities as a musician is as hard a matter to grasp as it is with respect to his compositions.

Mendelssohn's supporters attracted attention to his versatility—Lampadius describing him as being "as great a conductor as he was as virtuoso and composer," with the "electric fire of Mendelssohn's nature."[4] Such unbridled enthusiasm characterizes older documents and is rarely found in modern writings. By contrast, Wagner's denunciations have fed into generations of scholarship. The conventional view of Mendelssohn as a "polite man writing polite music"[5] is echoed in even quite recent studies. Whittall, in 1987, thus remarked that "[i]t could be that too much was expected of the prodigy . . . and that, for fear of failure, Mendelssohn dissipated—or dammed—his energies; alternatively, he never matured emotionally to a sufficient extent to sustain, still less to consolidate, his adolescent genius."[6] Such a view can be seen as a direct result of Wagner's remarks. It is perhaps rather more surprising than Stratton's 1901 evaluation: "As a conductor Mendelssohn was among the first of his time. He brought discipline into the role . . . yet, judged by modern standards, his conducting would leave something to be desired. It was like himself, bright and sunny; but not penetrating deeply below the surface."[7] This comment is interesting. It is couched in deterministic language, asserting an automatic assumption of procedural superiority by modern performers. It also alludes to the nature of Wagner's criticism, which is summed up in his famous tirade against Mendelssohn's supposed attitude to tempo in a Dresden performance of Beethoven's F Major Symphony:

I told Mendelssohn that I believed I had convinced Reisinger who had promised that he would take the tempo slower than usual. Mendelssohn perfectly
agreed with me. We listened. The third movement began and I was terrified on
hearing precisely the old Ländler tempo; but before I could give vent to my
annoyance, Mendelssohn smiled and pleasantly nodded his head. . . . So my
terror changed to astonishment. . . . I fancied myself standing before an abyss
of superficiality, a veritable void.[8]

The purpose of this short essay is to answer one fundamental research
question—what were the essential practical and aesthetic features of
Mendelssohn's orchestra? The purpose in so doing is to provide some insight
into the issues inherent in reawakening his style and practice. In view of the
often difficult experiences Mendelssohn had with orchestras in Berlin and
Düsseldorf, this essay will focus on the Leipzig Gewandhaus orchestra from
1835.

MENDELSSOHN'S CONDUCTING STYLE

Regarding Mendelssohn's actions as a conductor, Wasielewski gives us a
vivid portrayal of his presence on the podium: "Mendelssohn's fiery eye
surveyed and dominated the entire orchestra. And the reverse: every glance
clung to the tip of his baton. He was therefore able to move the mass just as
he wished. . . . Whenever during a performance he allowed himself to
make occasional small alterations in tempo by means of improvised ritardandos or accelerandos, these were realised in such a way that one would
have believed they had been prepared in rehearsal."[9] In addition, Chorley
relates how "the fortes and crescendos he accompanied with an energetic
play of features and the most forcible action; while the decrescendos and pianos he used to modulate with a motion of both hands, till they slowly sank
to almost perfect silence."[10]

These remarks suggest that Mendelssohn's success as a conductor lay in
his inspirational directorship. Wasielewski's comment in particular might
well describe the practice of Arthur Nikisch, a later Gewandhaus conductor, who conducted in front of his face as a way of ensuring the attention of
all of the players.[11] Mendelssohn's main achievement was thus his control
over the orchestra. Friedrich Schmidt commented with regard to the
Gewandhaus concerts: "Right from the first concert[12] Mendelssohn introduced a most useful innovation. Up to this time, the concertmaster sometimes beating time, sometimes playing, directed instrumental works from
his desk. But as soon as singing occurred, the music director beat time.
Now Mendelssohn directed all instrumental performances . . . and also
conducted all rehearsals."[13] This implies rigorous rehearsal by the standards

of the time. Louis Spohr's activities as Kapellmeister in Frankfurt in 1817–20 acted as a model for Mendelssohn's aspirations, including strict discipline, careful rehearsing, and baton conducting (or at least, comparatively unambiguous direction with the violin bow from the front desk of violins.)[14] Many of these practices seem unremarkable to today's permanent ensembles, but they represented high standards at the time.

That Mendelssohn employed a baton when conducting, standing with his left side to the orchestra as a mark of respect to his audience, is sufficiently well known as to require little comment in this essay. It is, however, useful to outline the circumstances of ensemble directing as Spohr experienced it in London in 1820 as an example of the methods of direction extant in the first decades of the nineteenth century. Spohr's experiences in London show how his (and Mendelssohn's) approach was comparatively progressive. In London, the custom was for a "conductor" to sit at the piano and fulfill a supporting role, while the leader might direct from the first desk of the violins, using his violin bow to beat time where necessary (or possible). This seems to have been the established practice in London and was laid down by what Bowen describes as a set of "fiercely democratic laws,"[15] which involved the piano "conductor" and violin "leader" changing places regularly. Hogarth described the procedure in 1813, the year the society was formed: "The duty of the leader was not only to execute his own part with exemplary accuracy and firmness, but to attend to all other performers. . . . His coadjutor, at the pianoforte, and with the full score before him, was to watch the performance and to be ready to correct any mistake."[16] Spohr's attitude to this manner of direction can be gauged from his comments to Wilhelm Speyer: "The manner of conducting at the theatres and concerts here [London] is the most preposterous which can be imagined. With two conductors figuring away, there is really not even one. He who is styled 'conductor' in the bills, sits at the piano and plays from the score, but neither marks time nor gives the tempi; this the 'leader' or first violinist ought to do. As he has however, merely a violin part before him, he cannot help the orchestra."[17]

The Leipzig Gewandhaus orchestra also lacked coordinated direction, as Wagner relates from his experiences of c. 1830: "[I]nstrumental works were not led by any conductor but rather by the first violinist from his desk; but as soon as any singing began . . . Pohlenz would appear at the conductor's stand."[18] Ironically perhaps, it is this very form of loose and (to a modern perspective) archaic direction that Wagner seems to reflect upon with fond reminiscence. Thus he writes: "In the days of my youth, orchestral pieces at the celebrated Leipzig Gewandhaus concerts were not conducted at all; they were simply played through under the leadership of the Concertmeister Mattai, like overtures or entr'acts at the theatre. At least there was no 'disturbing individualism' in the shape of a conductor."[19] The passage is typically contradictory. Mendelssohn is berated for his genial superficiality elsewhere; here, by implication, he is criticized for the very "disturbing individualism" Wagner was to make a feature of his own conducting. Moreover, Wagner attempted to discredit Mendelssohn's rehearsal technique, as in this account of his rehearsals for Beethoven's Eighth Symphony: "I noticed that he chose a detail here and there—almost at random—and worked at it with a certain obstinacy, until it stood forth clearly. This was so manifestly to the advantage of the detail that I could not but wonder why he did not take similar pains with other nuances."[20]

While Wagner's comments are conspicuously untrustworthy, they color our perception of Mendelssohn's stature as a musician. The idealized picture by Mendelssohn's admirers is equally unhelpful. Spohr's work as a pioneering baton conductor and disciplinarian laid foundations upon which Mendelssohn built his reputation. It is neither possible nor useful to judge Mendelssohn's conducting by the standards of the present. It is clear, however, that Mendelssohn, along with Spohr, represented an important phase of innovation at a time when the topography of the modern orchestral concert was being formed.

MENDELSSOHN'S ORCHESTRA

The Leipzig Gewandhaus orchestra rarely elicited Mendelssohn's criticism. Upon his arrival in 1835, he remarked: "The orchestra is very good, and thoroughly musical; and I think that six months hence it will be much improved, for the sympathy and attention with which these people receive my suggestions, and instantly adopt them, were really touching in both the rehearsals we have hitherto had; there was as great a difference as if another orchestra had been playing."[21] The orchestra was a permanent one of paid members, with what Schumann described as a family atmosphere: "[E]ven . . . [Paris and London] can scarcely boast such fine, united symphony playing. . . . Our musicians here form a family; they see each other and practice together daily; they are always the same, so that they are able to play a Beethoven Symphony without notes [music]."[22]

The Gewandhaus concert-room, replaced in 1894, also gained praise. It seated 400 in 1842, and this was extended to 570 after balconies were added. Precise dimensions are hard to ascertain clearly; Koury proposes that it was somewhat smaller than London's Hanover Square rooms.[23] Table 5.1 shows the numbers of the Gewandhaus orchestra in the period of Mendelssohn's directorship: it shows a noticeable strengthening of forces in 1839.

Table 5.1. Size and Strength of the Leipzig Gewandhaus Orchestra 1802–39

Date	Vln 1	Vln 2	Vla	Cel	DB	Fl.	Cl.	Ob.	Bsn.	Hn.	Trp.	Trb.	Other	Total	Source
1802	6	6	?	3	3	?	?	?	?	?	?	?	?	33	Allgemeine Musikalische Zeitung 3 (1802): 783; quoted in Carse, 51.
1830	6	6	2	2	3	2	2	2	2	4	?	?	1 Picc. 1 Timp.	39	Hans-Joachim Nosselt, Das Gewandhausorchester: Erstehung und Entwicklang eines Orchesters (Leipzig: Koehler and Amelang, 1943), 269; quoted in Koury, 324.
1831	8	8	4	3	3	2	2	2	2	2	2	?	Timpani	39	Alfred Dorffel, Geschichte der Gewandhausconcerte zu Leipzig vom 25 November 1781 bis 25 November 1881 (Leipzig Concert-Direction, 1884), 90; quoted in Koury, 324.
1833	5	5	4	2	2	2	2	2	2	2	2	2	1 Timp.	34	Nosselt, 118–19; quoted in Koury, 324.
1839	9	8	5	5	4	2	2	2	2	2	2	2	Timpani	47	Eberhard Creuzberg, Die Gewandhaus-Konzerte zu Leipzig 1871–1931 (Leipzig: Breitkopf and Härtel, 1931), 85; quoted in Carse, 51.

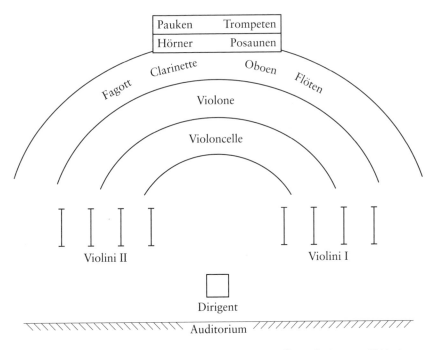

FIGURE 5.1.   Seating/Standing Positions—Leipzig Gewandhaus Orchestra c.1844. August Schmidt, *Musikalische Reise-Momente auf einer Wanderung durch Norddeutschland* (Hamburg: Schuberth, 1846), 46; duplicated in Koury, 207.

It was not until 1850 that the orchestra reached a regular number of fifty-six men,[24] and Koury suggests that the orchestra "must have been the basis of the inner-aural image Mendelssohn, Schumann and even the young Wagner experienced when thinking in orchestral forces."[25] Certainly, these numbers in a moderately sized hall suggest a more transparent, chamber-like sonority. Indeed, Berlioz remarked to this effect in 1843 in a passage that also suggests the close affinity between Mendelssohn and his leader, Ferdinand David: "The orchestral arrangement in this admirable hall is so good, communication between the conductor and each member of the orchestra is so easy, and the players, besides being capital musicians, have been trained by Mendelssohn and David to such a pitch of discipline and concentration that two rehearsals sufficed for putting together a long programme."[26]

Figure 5.1 represents the positioning of the Gewandhaus orchestra in 1844 (or 1846, according to Zlotnik);[27] it would make a suitable model for a Mendelssohn orchestral performance in modern times, given that Mendelssohn's tenure as conductor extended to 1843 and there is little evidence to suggest a dramatic change at Leipzig during his lifetime. Attention might be drawn to the encircling of the ensemble by double basses and the rather peripheral nature of the violas. For instrumental concerts, musicians who could do so would stand, in a tradition that persisted until 1905, during Arthur Nikisch's directorship.

The membership of the ensemble during Mendelssohn's time suggests a few important musicians and a larger number of dutiful but not outstanding ones. Noteworthy performers included C. T. Quiesser,[28] a trombonist in the orchestra from 1825 (originally engaged as a viola player) and described by Schumann as a "god of the trombone," for whom Ferdinand David wrote a number of concerti.

Joseph Joachim (1831–1907), one of the most important violinists of the German tradition in the nineteenth century, took part in Gewandhaus concerts and, shortly after Mendelssohn's death, became an "Extrageiger" and, by 1850, second *Concertmeister* to David.[29] Joachim's artistic outlook was fashioned in Leipzig, and his puritanical stance upon matters of style (which made him one of the most revered exponents of German "Classicism") is likely to have been congruent with Mendelssohn's. Excellent as the Leipzig situation was, he left to join Liszt in Weimar. This somewhat qualifies Leipzig's credentials, since he obviously felt it necessary to change posts. One of the possible reasons for this was the humble status of the Gewandhaus musicians. The poor remuneration they received is well known; when Mendelssohn arrived in Leipzig in 1835, the members of the orchestra were obliged to provide musical entertainment in coffee-and-cake gardens during the summer season, such was their impecuniousness.[30]

The orchestra was led by Mendelssohn's childhood friend Ferdinand David. As Chorley commented in 1839: "I have met with no one at the executive head of an orchestra to compare with Herr David. Spirit, delicacy, and consummate intelligence . . . are combined in no ordinary measure."[31] Mendelssohn's high opinion of David can be seen in his praise in a letter to Ignaz Moscheles, with the intention of securing a London debut for David. Thus he writes that "he is a sympathetic, straightforward, and honest a man as ever was, a first rate artist and one of the few who love Art for its own sake."[32]

David studied with Spohr in Cassel in 1823 and 1824, and first appeared at the Gewandhaus in 1825. Ferdinand Hiller, in the first edition of Sir George Grove's *A Dictionary of Music and Musicians,* describes him thus: "As a virtuoso David combined the sterling qualities of Spohr's style, with the greater facility and piquancy of the modern school; as a leader he had a rare power of holding together and animating the band; while as a quartet-player his intelligence and tact enabled him to do justice to the masterpieces of the most different periods and schools."[33] Otto Jahn, however, wrote as follows in *Der Grenzbote* in 1855: "Unfortunately he developed an ever-forced manner . . . he introduced all sort of cheap [effects] to give piquancy to the works of Haydn and Mozart."[34] This viewpoint perhaps implies the changing tastes of the nineteenth century. It is revealing that Joachim's biographer, Andreas Moser, perpetuated such criticism of David: "He doctored up the old masters to suit the taste of certain contemporaries, by shameless alterations, adding superfluous ornamentations, far-fetched marks of expression, and introducing cadenzas quite opposed to the character of the music, and the insinuation of a host of vulgar and exaggerated nuances, thereby robbing these works of their charm and simplicity."[35]

In spite of Joachim's connections to David he did re-edit many of the works David published, often in a lighter way and in such fashion as to provide fascinating insights into changing performing practices.[36] It serves to remind us that Mendelssohn's attitude was refracted through the prism of contemporary ideals, which saw little difficulty in pragmatic modernizations.[37] Whilst David's strong leadership might be seen as a universal attribute, many aspects of his performing practice departed very significantly from modern tastes, and any attempt to recapture the sonorities of the Leipzig orchestra as a symbol of Mendelssohn's orchestral directing would necessitate careful consideration of such stylistic matters.[38]

The musicianship of the orchestra is hinted at by Chorley, who describes its handling of problems in accompanying a "Mademoiselle List": "I cannot conceive how it could ever have been brought to an end with an orchestra less admirably under conduct; and, after counting 5 notes in 1 bar and 9 in another, in the vain hope of ascertaining what was the real tempo of the movement in which she was engaged, I went home penetrated with admiration at the courtesy of my Leipzig friends in playing out of time when 'a lady was in the case.' "[39]

PROGRAMMING

The nature of concert programming in Mendelssohn's lifetime creates a stark contrast to current practice. Today, programming is an esoteric affair. Works are usually performed complete, and organizers consider subtle relationships between items to ensure a coherent program. In Mendelssohn's time, concerts were a heterogeneous collection of comparatively arbitrarily chosen items. Large-scale compositions, such as symphonies, were summarily carved up. In a culture of new music, compositions from the past were often seen as curiosities.

Something of the context of such programming can be seen in Miltitz's recommendations of 1837. As Mintz relates: "A concert should begin, [Miltitz] maintained, with a powerful overture or the first movement of a symphony. A vocal number, solo or ensemble should follow. Lieder and light songs, however, are not appropriate. The second part of the concert should begin with two of the remaining movements of the symphony or an ensemble for wind or strings."[40] A correspondent in the Berlin *Allgemeine Musicalische Zeitung,* as early as 1824, saw the dangers and limitations of this approach, however:

> Putting together a mass of pieces of various genres and by various masters, a process by which a botched piece may well slip in, and the arbitrary cutting up that a large and honourable work is often subjected to in order to make room for this or that bravura aria necessarily also cuts up the listener's perceptions. . . . A clever concert giver . . . must therefore be very careful in choosing pieces and arranging the order in which they will be performed.[41]

Mendelssohn's position here was as a reformer who promoted the cause of historical music and sought to program material with care and discernment. His programs could be comparatively learned, as the examples from Leipzig (table 5.2) show.[42]

Chorley depicts Mendelssohn's programming as intelligent, balancing old and new repertoire and thus "taking good care . . . in cases of experiment, to assure the interest of the evening's performance by the repetition of some favourite and well-known production."[43] This implies that Mendelssohn knew that he needed a gentle tide of reformation. At the same time, Chorley praises Mendelssohn not only for "an admirable selection of the music to be performed at the concerts," but also for his prowess in "awakening, through his superb direction of the orchestra, a taste on the part of the public for the works of the later great masters; as for example the 'Ninth Symphony' of Beethoven." Chorley goes on: "He not only cultivated a relish for the historical development of music, but he summoned the mighty spirits of the past to the help and delight of the present age."[44] As Lampadius observes upon examination of the 1839 Gewandhaus series, "Handel, Gluck, Haydn, Beethoven, Mozart, Cherubini, Weber, Spohr, Rossini alternate in the list, yet not to the exclusion of the later and the latest masters in music. For example, new symphonies by Kalliwoda, Lachner, Mohring and Dobrycinski were given, and the newly discovered symphony by Franz Schubert."[45]

Mendelssohn's advocacy of Bach's music is shown by his letter to the directors of the Lower Rhine Festival on January 18, 1838: "I consider it absolutely necessary to have the name of Sebastian Bach in the programme, if only for one short piece; for it is certainly high time that at these festivals, on which the name of Handel has shed such lustre, another immortal

Table 5.2. Examples of Mendelssohn's Concert Programming

4 October 1835, Leipzig Gewandhaus

Mendelssohn:	Overture *Calm Sea & Prosperous Voyage*
Weber:	Scene and Aria from *Der Freischütz*
	(Mme Grabon)
Spohr:	Violin Concerto No. 8 (Gehrke, violin)
Cherubini:	Overture and Introduction to *Ali Baba*
	(with the Leipzig Singakademie and
	St. Thomas Choir)
Beethoven:	Fourth Symphony

[Source: George Marek, *Gentle Genius—The Story of Felix Mendelssohn* (London: Hale, 1977), 229.]

15 February 1838, Leipzig Gewandhaus (first of 1837–38 season historical concerts)

Bach:	D major Suite BWV 1068
	E major Violin Sonata BWV 1006
Handel:	"Groß ist der Herr" from *Zadok the Priest*
Gluck:	*Iphigenia in Aulis* Overture
Viotti:	unspecified violin concerto

[Source: Donald Mintz, "Mendelssohn as Performer and Teacher," in *The Mendelssohn Companion,* ed. Douglass Seaton (Westport, Conn.: Greenwood, 2001), 102.]

2 November 1840, Leipzig Gewandhaus

Beethoven:	unspecified overture aria from
	Fidelio (sung by Louise Schlegel)
Prume:	*La Melancolia* (sung by Uhlrich)
Bellini:	duet from *Il Pirata* (sung by Wild and
	Schlegel)
Cherubini:	Overture to *Les deux jounées*
Bellini:	duet from *Romeo und Julie* (sung by
	Schloss and Schlegel)
Wild:	unspecified aria
Crusell:	Andante pastorale for clarinet (played by
	Heinze Jr, member of the orchestra)
A. Pohlenz:	*The Farewell* (sung by Schlegel)

[Source: Marek, 231.]

master, who is in no one point inferior to any master, and in many points superior to all, should no longer be forgotten."[46] It is, however, a mistake to assume that Mendelssohn's historical practice took a modern form. In a very different critical culture, Lampadius praises Mendelssohn for his updating of classical works: "It is to be said about the performance of the symphonies of Haydn and Mozart that for all his piety towards those old masters of the tonal art, Mendelssohn, through his spirited conception and occasionally somewhat accelerated tempos, and the subtlest nuancing by means of Piano, Decrescendo and Crescendo understood how to reconcile those works with modern demands and taste in the most apt way."[47]

Mendelssohn's programming proved prophetic, but how such works were treated in performance qualifies his progressive tendencies from a modern viewpoint. Many of the more contemporary works he programmed have, moreover, become unfamiliar to modern audiences.[48] While examples of his programming contain elements familiar to a modern observer, it was to be a further seventy years or so before programs resembled present-day arrangements. Nonetheless, Mendelssohn's reforming contribution was substantial and has proved one of the more enduring parts of his legacy as a performing musician.

"HISTORICALLY AWARE" MENDELSSOHN ORCHESTRAL PERFORMANCE: RE-ENACTING HIS PERFORMING PRACTICES

While many of the physical features of a "Mendelssohn orchestra" can be enacted relatively easily, performance style is arguably more fundamental to the activity of "historically aware" performance.

One of the most conspicuous aspects of a Mendelssohn orchestra is the need for a predominantly non-vibrato tone. This affected all instruments capable of the device. Vibrato was seen as an ornament, to be applied sparingly, as a way of emulating the practices of contemporary singers. The evidence of early recordings shows clearly how singers and instrumentalists steeped in earlier nineteenth-century traditions (that is to say, the oldest to make recordings, such as Adelina Patti, Sir Charles Santley, or Joseph Joachim)[49] used a more discreet vibrato, and much less frequently than the modern so-called continuous device. Early recordings of orchestras give some idea of this "purer" sound. The characteristically "raw" senza vibrato oboe tone can be heard in countless performances of the 1920s, while ensembles under the influence of conservative figures, such as the Vienna Philharmonic at the time of Arnold Rosé's leadership, are worthy of close study.[50]

Louis Spohr's recommendations at the close of his *Violinschule* are likely to have been shared by Mendelssohn. Spohr cautions the violinist against "soloistic" mannerisms in an orchestral context. Thus he states that the orchestral violinist should "avoid every addition of turns, doubleturns, shakes &c. likewise all artificial shiftings, the sliding from one tone to another, the changing of the fingers on one tone, in short, every embellishment properly belonging to the Solo."[51] Accordingly, the orchestral player is exhorted to agree upon shadings, dynamics, and accentuation, and tempo rubato is to be avoided: "The Solo performer must neither be hurried nor retarded by the accompaniment: he should be instantly followed wherever he deviates a little from the time. This latter deviation, however, does not apply to the *Tempo rubato* of the Solo performer; the accompaniment continuing its quiet, regular movement."[52] This passage indicates temporal dislocation of melody from accompaniment in concerto performance. There are a few extant examples of this in practice, such as the solo piano rolls of pianists such as Carl Reinecke (1824–1910), in which it is manifest in tempo dislocation between the hands.[53] Ensemble examples are more difficult to find, although the Klingler String Quartet, formed with the intention of carrying on the ideals and practices of the Joachim Quartet, do provide some instances of this.[54]

In a general sense our knowledge of nineteenth-century performing practices suggests a degree of restraint in playing style, favoring detailed phrasing but avoiding a more sensuous means of expression. This might suggest a more puritanical realization in line with Mendelssohn's "Classical" status, where neatness and precision was the desideratum pro quo, rather than Wagner's epic and egocentric subjectivism. Indeed, Leon Botstein's essay comparing Wagner and Mendelssohn suggests that their music was perhaps more similar than we might be drawn to suppose and that the disparities between them are underlined rather more by differences in performing practice. Thus Botstein posits, with regard to a performance of *Tristan und Isolde:* "Imagine that it would be performed at a brisker tempo than commonly anticipated. Perhaps the string fingerings would favour lower positions and a thinner sound. Bow use would be lighter, more flautando and vibrato would be sparing. A smaller string section would result in a less thick orchestral texture . . . making Wagner Mendelssohnian, we can discover shared attributes of music and meaning."[55] This is an intriguing prospect, suggesting that the differences Wagner had with Mendelssohn were chiefly presentational.

All of this confirms the importance of the performing practice conditions of a work and the need to experiment with a "Mendelssohn orchestra." Modern performing practices run in diametric opposition to many aspects of Mendelssohn's envisaged performance style. The string sound, inevitably the dominant characteristic of an orchestra's character, would be radically different from that of today's ensembles. Such sonority and approach are not beyond our grasp, for Ferdinand David edited solo and chamber music copiously and wrote a two-volume violin treatise which gives a vivid insight into the style of playing Mendelssohn would have found familiar.[56] At present, however, commercial "historically informed" performance is motivated only to re-create known and well-documented practices selectively, borrowing aspects of style and creating a fusion of modern practice with elements of nineteenth-century performance. To attempt to replicate the sounds of an orchestra led by David and conducted by Mendelssohn would demand better training in historical matters, more difficult en masse than in smaller ensembles, given that only relatively few performer-scholars have sufficient in-depth knowledge for this to be a credible and successful enterprise. Certainly, it would necessitate players laying down many aspects of modern approaches considered sacred (such as ensemble togetherness and "continuous vibrato") which evidently had little or no place in Mendelssohn's aural experience.

Accordingly, this essay ends with a challenge. While there is much about Mendelssohn and the orchestra we will never know, we have not, as yet, acted upon such knowledge as does exist in the interests of performing his music in the manner he envisaged. Issues concerning intention and attainment in historical performing practice are complex, but the aim to act upon available evidence in order to attempt to perform as the Leipzig Gewandhaus orchestra did is worthy of serious attention. Wagner's antagonism toward Mendelssohn casts a shadow over the latter's reputation. Whatever the validity of Botstein's view, making attempts to recreate original performing conditions can do little other than improve our understanding of the material in question, and in Mendelssohn's case might aid further rehabilitation of his reputation.

NOTES

1. Felix Mendelssohn Bartholdy, *Letters of Felix Mendelssohn to Ignaz and Charlotte Moscheles,* trans. and ed. Felix Moscheles (London: Trübner, 1888), 248.

2. Ferdinand Hiller, *Mendelssohn's Letters and Recollections,* trans. M. E. von Glehn (London: Macmillan, 1874), 47.

3. Ralf Wehner, "On Mendelssohn Sources," in *The Mendelssohns: Their Music in History,* ed. John M. Cooper and Julie D. Prandi (Oxford: Oxford University Press, 2004), 12.

4. Wilhelm A. Lampadius, *Life of Felix Mendelssohn Bartholdy,* trans. and ed. William L. Gage (London: William Reeves, 1877), 155.

5. George Marek, *Gentle Genius: The Story of Felix Mendelssohn* (London: Hale, 1977), 91.

6. Arnold Whittall, *Romantic Music: A Concise History from Schubert to Sibelius* (London: Thames and Hudson, 1987), 35–36.

7. Stephen Stratton, *Mendelssohn* (London: J. M. Dent, 1901), 213–14.

8. Richard Wagner, *On Conducting: A Treatise on Style in the Execution of Classical Music,* trans. E. Dannreuther (London: William Reeves, 1887), 28.

9. Wilhelm J. von Wasielewski, *Aus siebzig Jahren: Lebenserinnerungen* (Stuttgart: Deutsche Verlags-Anstalt, 1897), 59; quoted in Donald Mintz, "Mendelssohn as Performer and Teacher," in *The Mendelssohn Companion,* ed. Douglass Seaton (Westport, Conn.: Greenwood Press, 2001), 99.

10. *Life of Felix Mendelssohn Bartholdy from the German of W. A. Lampadius with Supplementary Sketches by Sir Julius Benedict, Henry F. Chorley, Ludwig Rellstab, Bayard Taylor, R. S. Willis and J. S. Dwight,* trans. and ed. William L. Gage (London: William Reeves, 1877), 159.

11. See Raymond Holden, "The Technique of Conducting," in José A. Bowen, *The Cambridge Companion to Conducting* (Cambridge: Cambridge University Press, 2003), 12.

12. October 4, 1835.

13. Friedrich Schmidt, "Das Musikleben der bürgerlichen Gesellschaft Leipzigs im Vormärz (1815–1848)," *Musikalisches Magazin* 47 (Langensalza: Hermann Beyer and Söhne, 1912), in Seaton, 97.

14. See Clive Brown, *Louis Spohr: A Critical Biography* (Cambridge: Cambridge University Press, 1984), 116.

15. José Antonio Bowen, "The Rise of Conducting," in Bowen, 99.

16. George Hogarth, *The Philharmonic Society of London* (London: Bradbury and Evans 1862), 6; quoted in Miles B. Foster, *The History of the Philharmonic Society of London, 1813–1912* (London: John Lane, 1912), 6.

17. Spohr's letter to Wilhelm Speyer in E. Speyer, *Wilhelm Speyer die Liederkomponist* (Munich, 1925), quoted in Brown, *Louis Spohr,* 131.

18. Richard Wagner, *My Life,* trans. A. Gray, ed. M. Whittall (Cambridge: Cambridge University Press, 1983), 56–57.

19. Richard Wagner, *On Conducting (Über das Dirigieren): A Treatise on Style in the Execution of Classical Music* (London: William Reeves, 1887), 14.

20. Ibid., 22.

21. *Letters of Felix Mendelssohn Bartholdy from 1833 to 1847 edited by Paul Mendelssohn Bartholdy and Dr Carl Mendelssohn Bartholdy with a Catalogue of All His Musical Compositions Compiled by Dr Julius Rietz,* trans. Lady Wallace (London: Longman Green, 1863), 91.

22. Robert Schumann, *Music and Musicians,* trans. Fanny R. Ritter (London: William Reeves, 1891), 1:364.

23. Daniel J. Koury, *Orchestral Performance Practices in the Nineteenth Century: Size, Proportions and Seating* (Ann Arbor: UMI Research Press, 1986), 328.

24. Ibid., 324.

25. Ibid., 325.

26. Hector Berlioz, *The Memoirs of Hector Berlioz, Member of the French Institute, Including His Travels in Italy, Germany, Russia and England 1803–65,* trans. David Cairns (New York: Norton, 1975), 296.

27. Asher G. Zlotnik, "Orchestration Revisions in the Symphonies of Robert Schumann" (Ph.D. diss., Indiana University, 1972), 46–47; quoted in Koury, 206.

28. Schumann, 1:365.

29. Eberhard Creutzberg, *Die Gewandhaus-konzerte zu Leipzig* (Leipzig: Breitkopf and Härtel, 1931), 85; quoted in Adam Carse, *The Orchestra from Beethoven to Berlioz* (Cambridge: Heffer, 1948), 141.

30. Carl Loewe, *Selstbiographie* (Berlin, 1870), 191; quoted in Clive Brown, *Portrait of Mendelssohn* (London: Yale, 1996), 151. Mendelssohn thus wrote to Moscheles in 1839, "My present hobby is the improvement of our poor orchestra. After no end of letter-writing, soliciting, and importuning, I have succeeded in getting their salaries raised by five hundred thalers; and before I leave them I mean to get them double that amount"; Mendelssohn, 197–98.

31. Henry F. Chorley, *Music and Manners in France and Germany* (London: Longmans, 1841), 3:103.

32. Mendelssohn, 27 February 1839, 186.

33. Sir Charles Grove, ed., *A Dictionary of Music and Musicians 1400–1889,* 1894 edition, s.v. "Ferdinand David."

34. Otto Jahn, quoted in Edward van der Straeten, *The History of the Violin* (London: Cassell, 1933), 3:204.

35. Andreas Moser, *Joseph Joachim: A Biography,* trans. L. Durham (London: Wellby, 1901), 44.

36. Compare, for example, David's edition of Beethoven's violin sonatas (Peters,

plate 6531) with Joachim's edition (Peters, plate 8762). Joachim's edition is more lightly edited, maintaining more of the original notation especially as regards bowing, and abandoning some of the slurred staccati and portamento-inviting fingerings David's edition encourages.

37. Mendelssohn's historicism was quite distinct from modern notions and did not extend far beyond the matter of repertoire itself. Ignaz Moscheles, in *Felix Mendelssohn Bartholdy, Letters of Felix Mendelssohn to Ignaz and Charlotte Moscheles,* 152–53, thus hints at contemporary attitudes when describing retouching J. S. Bach's orchestration on the grounds that "it seemed to me that one might give it a kind of new varnish, by doing for it what Mozart had done with such perfect taste for the 'Messiah' when he added wind instruments to the score."

38. A comprehensive review of nineteenth-century style and practice can be found in Clive Brown, *Classical and Romantic Performing Practice 1750–1900* (Oxford: Oxford University Press, 1999); while a stylistic study of "schools" of violin playing style (and selected singers) can be found in David Milsom, *Theory and Practice in Late-Nineteenth-Century Violin Performance* (Aldershot: Ashgate, 2003).

39. Henry F. Chorley, *Modern German Music: Recollections and Criticisms* (London: Smith Elder), 2:35.

40. "Korrespondenz. Berlin, den 2. April," *Berliner allgemeine musikalische Zeitung* 1, no. 15 (14 April 1824): 137–38; quoted in Donald Mintz, "Mendelssohn as Performer and Teacher," in Seaton, 100.

41. Carl B. von Miltitz, *Berliner allgemeine musikalische Zeitung* 39, no. 8 (22 February 1837), in Seaton, 100.

42. See also Item 964 in Peter Ward Jones, *Catalogue of the Mendelssohn Papers in the Bodleian Library, Oxford,* vol. 3, *Printed Music and Books* (Tutzing: Hans Schneider, 1989), 269. This item lists programs nine programs from 4 October 1835 to 2 December 1847.

43. Chorley, *Modern German Music,* 30.

44. *Life of Felix Mendelssohn Bartholdy,* trans. and ed. William L. Gage, 29.

45. Ibid., 58.

46. *Letters of Felix Mendelssohn Bartholdy from 1833 to 1847,* 146.

47. Wilhelm A. Lampadius, *Felix Mendelssohn Bartholdy: Ein Denkmal für seine Freunde* (Leipzig, Hinrichs, 1848), 51–52; quoted in Donald Mintz, "Mendelssohn as Performer and Teacher," in Seaton, 95.

48. Marek (229) alleges that "[a]mong the contemporary he preferred the less problematical, polite stuff which has been washed through the sieve of history." See also table 5.2.

49. See note 37.

50. Mahler Symphony no. 9 (Vienna Philharmonic Orchestra; conductor: Bruno Walter), 1938 (CDEA 5005 Dutton).

51. Louis Spohr, *Violinschule* (Vienna 1832), trans. C. Rudolphus as *Grand Violin School* (London: Edwin Ashdown, 1843), 232.

52. Spohr, 232.

53. Published Reinecke rolls can be heard on *Nineteenth-Century Pianists on Welte-Mignon,* Archiphon, ARC 106.

54. Bars 105–22 of the fifth movement of their Beethoven op. 130 quartet performance of 1912 are a good example; reissued on *The Great Recordings of German and Austrian String Quartets,* vol. 6 (Japanese HMV, SGR 8506).

55. Leon Botstein, "Wagner as Mendelssohn," in *The Cambridge Companion to Mendelssohn,* ed. Peter Mercer-Taylor (Cambridge: Cambridge University Press, 2004), 262.

56. Ferdinand David, *Violinschule/Violin-school* (Leipzig, 1864; English trans. London, 1874).

6

Mendelssohn as Composer/Conductor: Early Performances of *Paulus*

SIEGWART REICHWALD

Felix Mendelssohn's dual role as composer and conductor placed him in a position of seemingly complete control to present his large-scale works in an ideal fashion. In 1835, at the age of twenty-six, Mendelssohn became the music director of the Gewandhaus orchestra in Leipzig, after having established himself as one of the most prominent conductors and composers during his tenure in Düsseldorf. Mendelssohn raised the performance level of the orchestra dramatically and turned it into one of the most highly regarded ensembles in Europe.

His innovative approach to orchestral performance became apparent at his first concert with the Gewandhaus orchestra, on 4 October 1835. Robert Schumann wrote about Mendelssohn's conducting of his *Calm Sea and Prosperous Voyage:*

> F. Meritis stepped out. A hundred eyes flew towards him in the first moment. . . . F. Meritis conducted as though he had composed the overture himself and the orchestra played accordingly. . . . For my part, the baton disturbed me, and I agreed with Florestan, who thought that in the symphony the orchestra should be a republic . . . but it was a pleasure to see how F. Meritis foreshadowed with his eye every spiritual nuance of the composition, from the most distant to the strongest, and how he, the blessed one, swam far ahead of the common herd.[1]

Hans von Bülow also remarked on the interpretative qualities of Mendelssohn's conducting:

> I recall the impression—never again so powerful in subsequent performances—which was made on me by Schubert's C major Symphony under Mendelssohn's direction. At that time it was not yet fashionable to install Schubert on the

heights of Mt. Olympus; he was loved, admired, and enjoyed as *minorum gentium,* but there were complaints about the expansiveness of his forms and the monotony of rhythms. But, under Mendelssohn's baton, one was not aware of these faults. Without using the blue pencil—simply through his elastic sensitivity and the magnetic eloquence of his gestures—the brilliant leader was able completely to conceal the abovementioned deficiencies. What wonderful nuances of color, what intelligently thought-out shadings of tempo he used! How easily he caused us to glide over the varied steppes of the "endless" Allegretto, so that, at the end, the hearer had no conception of the duration of the acoustical phenomenon! For we had just dwelt in eternity, in a timeless world.[2]

Mendelssohn had established himself especially well at the Lower Rhine Music Festivals as conductor. His father, Abraham Mendelssohn, wrote to his wife about Felix's initial rehearsal at his first festival in Düsseldorf in 1833:

> As new musicians from all directions were arriving continuously, it had become fashionable for orchestra members, who just met their friends again, to use the orchestra as their parlor; there was much talking, the rehearsals went badly, the conductor had to scream his lungs out and was still not heard; and since until the hour of the performance new players were still arriving, the disturbances were unbearable. After all this had happened as always on the first day of rehearsals, Felix proclaimed, that he would not tolerate it; that he would not and could not scream all the time, that they would need to hear him, and that he demanded total silence and order in the orchestra when he was talking. After he repeated it sternly, I assure you, I had never seen a better obedience; it had become apparent to them, that this was necessary, so whenever he was getting ready to say something, a general "Sshh" was heard and then there was deep silence.
>
> As a result, there were, for the first time, as I was assured, nuances evident in the chorus and orchestra, which pleased everybody, as they were able to feel proud of their achievements.[3]

During his preparations for the premiere of *Paulus* at the 1836 Lower Rhine Festival in Düsseldorf, Mendelssohn viewed this oratorio as the most important composition of his career. He had labored intensely over *Paulus* for four years. Felix's father expressed high expectations for *Paulus* as a revolutionary, neo-classical type of work in a letter to his son:

> The question, however, ought to be put in a different form,—not whether Handel would compose his oratorios now as he did a century since, but rather, whether he would compose any oratorios whatever; hardly—if they only could be written in the styles of those of the present day.
>
> From my saying this you may gather with what eager anticipation and confidence I look forward to your oratorio, which will, I trust, solve the problem of combining ancient conceptions with modern appliances; otherwise the result would be as great a failure as that of the painters of the nineteenth century, who only make themselves ridiculous by attempting to revive the reli-

gious elements of the fifteenth, with its long arms and legs, and topsy-turvy perspective.[4]

Mendelssohn eagerly wanted to meet his father's high expectations, especially since Abraham had died six months (November 1835) before the premiere:

> I work now with double zeal on the completion of *Paulus,* since father's last letter urged me on, and since he impatiently awaited the finishing of this work; I feel that I must do everything possible to make it as good as possible, and then imagine that he took part in it.[5]

The composer clearly saw the Lower Rhine Music Festival as the perfect platform for his mission, as can be gathered from a letter to his father, written over a year before the premiere:

> My oratorio is to be performed in Frankfort in November, so Schelble writes to me; and much as I should like you to hear it soon, still I should prefer your hearing it first next year, at the Musical Festival. Before decidedly accepting the proposal, I have stipulated to wait till after the performance at Frankfort, that I may judge whether it be suitable for the festival; but prove this to be the case, as I hope and wish it may, it will have a much finer effect there.[6]

Mendelssohn wanted to make sure that *Paulus* would be a finished, polished product, representing his very best effort. The composer's high hopes of the perfect performance were dashed, however. Schelble, the director the Frankfurter Cäcilienverein, became ill, which erased the possibility of an early trial run. With extra time until the first performance, Mendelssohn embarked on more extensive revisions of his composition. He realized soon, however, that he would not be able to finish the revised score in time for the festival performance and made the necessary arrangements with the publisher.

> Since it is important to me to have heard the oratorio before the engraving of the piano-vocal score, I wish to wait with it until after the performance, since I will probably want to change more things, for which it would be too late otherwise. I ask you therefore to make for now only engravings of the choral parts, in which I will definitely not have to make any changes. The engravings of the solo parts, if you intend to make them, I would also like to postpone until after the first performance. While I fear that you do not like this, and that you would like to have the piano-vocal score finished for the first performance, it is also in your interest to publish the work in as polished and complete a form as I am able to make it, and I have to admit that it is too important to me to have heard the work first, rather than handing it to the public in definitive form with some things in it that are hurried.[7]

While the premiere was a huge success, it was not at all the performance of a completed work. Mendelssohn wrote in a letter to his friend Schleinitz:

During the whole of the rehearsals and the performance I thought little enough about directing, but listened eagerly to the general effect, and whether it went according to my idea, without thinking of anything else. When the people gave me a flourish of trumpets or applauded, it was welcome for a moment, but then my father came back to my mind, and I strove once more to recall my thoughts to my work. Thus, during the entire performance I was almost in the position of a listener, and tried to retain an impression of the whole. Many parts caused me much pleasure, others not so; but I learnt a lesson from it all, and hope to succeed the next time I write an oratorio.[8]

The highly anticipated 22 May 1836 premiere at the Lower Rhine Music Festival, although extremely successful, had turned into a test run. Mendelssohn revised *Paulus* extensively, including the already printed choruses.

There is also evidence in the same letter quoted above that the performance itself was not of the highest quality:

You would assuredly have been delighted by the love and goodwill with which the whole affair was carried on, and the marvelous fire with which the chorus and orchestra burst forth, though there were individual passages, especially in the solos, which might have annoyed you. I think I see it in your face, could you have heard St. Paul's aria sung in an indifferent, mechanical manner, and I think I hear you breaking loose on the Apostle of the Gentiles in a dressing-gown.[9]

Maybe the scariest moment of the premiere happened early in the performance in the duet of the false witnesses. One of the soloists lost her place and dropped out. Fanny Hensel, who sang in the alto section, quickly jumped in, helping the soloist to recover.[10]

According to Abraham Mendelssohn, the performance hall in Düsseldorf held 1,200 people.[11] The printed program lists 106 sopranos, 60 altos, 90 tenors, 108 basses (364 singers), 73 violins, 24 violas, 24 cellos, 12 basses, 6 flutes, 4 oboes, 6 clarinets, 4 bassoons, and 1 contrabassoon; a total of 515 performers, which filled up more than a third of the hall. Ferdinand Hiller commented on this bombastic performance setting:

The concert was held at the Becker-Garden (now the so-called "Rittersaal" belonging to the town music hall), but the room was too small for the large audience and orchestra, and in the "Sleepers, wake" chorus, the blast of the trumpets and trombones from the gallery down into the low hall was quite overpowering. I had arrived too late for the rehearsal, and, sitting there all alone, listening to an entirely new work, in a frightfully hot and close room, I was naturally not so deeply impressed as I expected to be. But the audience, who had already heard it three or four times, were delighted; the performers were thoroughly inspired; and on the third day, when, among other things, the chorus "Rise up, arise" was repeated, I listened with very different ears, and was as enthusiastic as anybody.[12]

Despite this less-than-perfect performance of a "draft" of *Paulus,* its success was so astounding that the organizers of the Manchester festival asked to perform a selection of the work that same summer. After that project fell through, the Liverpool festival included a performance of *Paulus* on 7 October 1836. It is not quite clear which version of *Paulus* was performed there. It was presumably much closer to the revised version, which would in some sense make it the "premiere" of *Paulus* as we know the work today.

Since the work was sung in English, however, the text had to be translated quickly. This was done without any input from the composer. While Mendelssohn spent the summer in Frankfurt, revising *Paulus,* which took until the end of July, Ignaz Moscheles told him about the progress of the preparations for the performance:

> I am glad to find that all promises well for your oratorio in England. Novello, Sir George Smart, and the whole profession are looking forward to its production with sympathy and interest. Like Hercules, you have throttled Envy while still in the cradle.
>
> Klingemann, Smart, and Novello are busy directing Mr. Ball, the translator. I have offered to correct the proofs, but have not yet received them.[13]

There is more specific evidence, however, that this premiere was not an accurate performance of Mendelssohn's *Paulus.* Henri Phillips (1801–76), the bass for the first and subsequent performances, remembered: "In this first performance of 'St. Paul' I sang my part, which was rendered extremely difficult in being in manuscript, and in a very cramped, illegible hand, a few printed sheets only were interspersed with English words written over the German; altogether the part was anything but agreeable to take into the orchestra."[14] Mr. Phillips then went on to explain that he had decided to change some passages in his vocal lines to better fit his range.[15]

The *Musical Times* reported that the performance was overshadowed by the death of Mrs. Malibran, who was supposed to have sung the principal soprano parts. Madame Caradori-Allen filled in on short notice.[16] Maria Malibran (1808–36) had been a good friend of the Mendelssohns, and Felix had thought very highly of her abilities as a singer. Obviously, this performance was not anywhere close to Mendelssohn's ideals, since he had no influence over either the translation or performance.

The actual "premiere" of the revised, printed *Paulus* was a semi-private "chamber performance" in the Mendelssohns' Gartensaal in Berlin on 19 January 1837 under Fanny Hensel's direction. Felix was not present, nor had he been involved in that performance. Fanny wrote in her diary over two years later:

On January 22 [1837] I gave an as complete as possible performance of *St. Paul;* the soloists performed superbly, the choruses had been reasonably well rehearsed. There were over 100 people present.[17]

Fanny had been more critical, however, of the soloists in a letter to Felix the day after the performance:

> *St. Paul* was launched yesterday. Friday evening there was a rehearsal, Saturday the room had to be turned upside-down, and then I couldn't get back to it. . . . All the singers derived great pleasure from it, especially Bader who sang splendidly. Even Stürmer, with what little voice he has left, sounded very nice. Decker excellent, and Bötticher exerted every possible effort. He has a wonderful, rich voice and is uncommonly musical, but his singing is still somewhat crude and stiff, and consequently nothing is more difficult for him than a piano.[18]

There were probably at most 50 chorus members and only a small chamber orchestra with players from the Royal Chapel orchestra.[19] There is no record about how much Fanny actually conducted and how much she might have led the performance from the piano. It seems ironic that *Paulus* had its first "trial run" at a music festival with 515 performers in front a very large audience, while the printed, final version was premiered with maybe 80 performers in front of a few listeners.

While the number of performers seems almost ridiculously small, the quality and care of the rehearsals and performance were probably unequaled. Fanny had played an important part in the compositional process, since Felix relied on her as his most honest critic. In January 1836—three months before the premiere in Düsseldorf—Fanny had organized informal performances of parts of *Paulus.*[20] For Felix's birthday (3 February), Fanny had planned yet another small house performance.[21] In June 1836, only one month after her participation in the Düsseldorf performance, Fanny's interest in *Paulus* was still strong:

> I recently held a performance of the first part of *St. Paul* and will undertake the 2nd part shortly. But let me know how things stand with respect to its publication, and when it will appear. In addition, please send me the metronome markings for "siehe wir preisen selig," and Paul's aria, "Herr, sey mir gnädig." Paul and I have been arguing about the tempos. I'm truly sorry that I didn't know the entire oratorio before Düsseldorf. There exists a special charm in first becoming acquainted with a work when it's finished, but it's even more enjoyable if one knows every note in advance. But I wish you could hear Decker sing the soprano arias sometime—she did a splendid job.[22]

Only the "little brother" knew *Paulus* better than Fanny, who had been in constant contact with the composer throughout the compositional process, as he had sent her most of his drafts of *Paulus* (with the exception of the final changes immediately before the Düsseldorf premiere). In July

Fanny mentioned more rehearsals of *Paulus*.[23] In November she was one of the first to receive the published piano vocal score; she was the first person—including the composer—to rehearse the revised version.[24]

The date set for the great "public premiere" of the printed, revised version of *Paulus* was 13 March 1837 at the Paulinerkirche in Leipzig. Mendelssohn presumably had complete control over the size and quality of the performance ensembles, and he should have had more rehearsal time than anywhere else. The choir was made up of about 190 sopranos and altos, and 120 tenors and basses [310]; the orchestra was 65 members strong, bringing the number of performers to 375, which made for a much better balance between choir and orchestra than at the Lower Rhine music festival performance.[25] The people of Leipzig were ready to celebrate their much-loved musical giant. Several of Felix's family members would come to the performance to join the excitement. Only six weeks before the performance, however, Felix wrote to his sister Fanny:

> I am thinking to leave for Frankfurt on March 17, and for the 13th we propose the church performance. Unfortunately, that date seems set, and I feel completely unmotivated for this performance, and I don't like it, that I have such a hectic schedule right before my honeymoon. I curse the whole concert and music scene here, and yet I have to bless them, because they are so kind.[26]

Felix's thoughts were obviously more on his wedding on March 28 and his honeymoon than the "premiere" of *Paulus*. In many letters from that time Mendelssohn expressed a change of focus in his life. He was much less interested in performing, as he looked forward to a life centered around building a home and composing quietly at his own pace.[27]

The preparations for the "premiere" turned out to be even more stressful than already anticipated, however:

> Yesterday, Schleinitz told me, that Nauenburg wants to arrive only in time for the dress rehearsal; since I don't know him enough as a singer to give him my complete trust, and since Lehmann had nothing good to say about his pitch accuracy, I find it absolutely necessary to have Nauenburg here at least one day before the dress rehearsal. If he cannot be here then, I would prefer to have Richter try, if he receives permission.[28]

Mendelssohn ended up moving the "premiere" of *Paulus* from 13 to 16 March, less than two weeks before his wedding. Since the original plan was for *Paulus* to be performed as the last subscription concert of the 1836–37 season, Mendelssohn still had to play a concert on 13 March, which meant that he had to plan, rehearse, and perform an extra concert. The program consisted of Weber's *Freischütz* Overture, an aria by Rossini, a concertino by C. G. Müller, a *Salve regina* by Carl Gottlieb Reißiger, and Beethoven's Ninth Symphony![29] Mendelssohn's correspondence following the performance does not even mention *Paulus*. Besides writing about his travels with his new bride, Mendelssohn discussed the composition of new works, including the idea of *Peter* as a new oratorio.

The most intriguing of the early performances of *Paulus* took place in Berlin on 18 January 1838 by the Singakademie, under the direction of Mendelssohn's former rival Rungenhagen. Despite the open hostility between the Mendelssohns and some members of the Singakademie, Rungenhagen had asked Fanny for help in the preparations for the performance. Fanny described her struggle in dealing with this delicate situation to her brother Felix:

> By the way, the story concerning *St. Paul* is really fascinating. If nothing else, in my role as advisor I was able to avert great disaster for the noble apostle. Mother seems to have written you that Rungenhagen asked me in writing to attend the rehearsals and enlighten him with my opinions. So I went there last Tuesday and was quite appalled, just as you have described it. I was suffering and champing at the bit, just like you, as I heard the whining and Grell's dirty fingers on the piano. I thought to myself, "If you were only up there, everything would be fine." Lichtenstein sat next to me and heard my sighs.[30]

Fanny decided to place her interest in a good performance of her brother's most important work above her anger and frustration with the Singakademie. After all, this was her chance to show to all of Berlin that Felix should have been the obvious choice for the directorship of the Berlin Singakademie:

> They started "Mache dich auf" at half the right tempo, and then I instinctively called out, "My God, it must go twice as fast!" Lichtenstein invited me to show them the way but told me that Schneider, the music director, had assured them that one cannot be ruled by a metronome marking. Then I assured them that they could be ruled by my word, and they had better do it, for God's sake. I went back on Friday, this time to the small hall in the Academy. I hadn't been there since Zelter's death and encountered all sorts of living and deceased ghosts. Then Rungenhagen came up to me after each chorus and asked me whether it was correct, and I told him honestly yes or no. But, overall, I was pleasantly surprised to find such an improvement, and started to become hopeful.[31]

Encouraged by the positive response of Rungenhagen, Fanny became more involved in the preparations than anybody could have imagined:

> On Saturday Rungenhagen was here for over an hour and had me listen to all the solo numbers. Friday I also spoke to Ries, who asked, among other things,

how I would feel about adding a tuba to the organ part, as has been done in churches. Now, said tuba is a monstrosity; it transforms all passages in which it appears into drunken beer brewers. Thus I fell on my knees and asked them to spare me and leave the tuba at home. Rungenhagen lifted me up and granted my plea.[32]

Fanny's patience, poise, and humor throughout the process seem to have had a tremendous impact on the interpretation of the work, as well as the overall performance quality:

Yesterday was the first large rehearsal, which far exceeded my expectations. To my great satisfaction, I can tell you that I was totally delighted with everything. The choruses, now taken with the correct tempo (a few perhaps too fast), were performed with fire and power, and enunciated as well as one could wish. The good old blockhead really went all out, and everyone was astonished at his liveliness.[33]

In her mind Fanny had been able to greatly influence the performance without sacrificing her integrity as a member of the Mendelssohn family:

Many people realized from which direction the wind was blowing. But I've calmly restrained myself so as not to seem like Don Quixote of your *St. Paul,* and I hope I haven't made any enemies—unless you count the tuba player. Ries was here again today, and I dispensed all the good advice that I had in my arsenal. Now I am silent. First I must get together with you and learn some more. It's a shame, however, that you aren't conducting this performance; it would have been splendid and required only a minimum of effort on your part.[34]

In her performance review Fanny focused on the positives to show the success of her somewhat revengeful quest for her brother:

I want to send you a summary report of *St. Paul,* dear Felix, because since I was satisfied overall, you won't ask me to go into details and mention the mistakes. It was by far the best performance that has taken place here since Zelter's death. Every possible effort was expended, and one couldn't ask for more from anyone. It would have become a historic performance had you been here. The public was delighted, and here I'm declaring that I'm more satisfied after the fact than I had been, because such good impressions shouldn't be weakened by fault-finding, even if justified. I never heard the soprano part sung as beautifully as Fassmann did it on this occasion. She is perfectly suited to this music, with a simple, noble, clear interpretation, transmitted by a beautiful bright voice. I know you would like her.[35]

Felix's response to Fanny's report was cautious, which perhaps shows his own struggle in his dual role as composer and performer:

Your report on *St. Paul* in the Singakademie was also very gratifying, but forgive me if I attribute your pleasure more to your feelings for me and my music than to the performance.[36]

A few days earlier Felix expressed more clearly his frustration with handing of his composition to somebody else:

> You, meanwhile are sentenced to attend the rehearsals of the Singakademie as punishment, which to be sure must be hard for you, since I know from experience what an unspeakable feeling it is to sit there, champing at the bit, but nonetheless being unable to help at all with the nicest words, because only the stick can help (I mean, of course, only the conductor's stick).[37]

While the public "Berlin premiere" would seem least likely to have succeeded, it might arguably have been the truest early performances of *Paulus.* The sound of the Singakademie had shaped Felix's ideals of choral performance, and Fanny, who had played a part in the compositional process of *Paulus,* had played a major part in shaping all aspects of the performance. Thus Fanny Hensel—not Felix—was responsible for the first performance of the revised version, as well as the best early performance of *Paulus.*

It could be argued then that, as a conductor, Mendelssohn was able to aid other composers more than himself, as his historic performance of Bach's *St. Matthew Passion* and Schubert's "Great" C major Symphony illustrate. His concert programming showed a careful balance between upholding the treasures of the past—as can be seen in his historical concert series—and showcasing the new music of lesser-known, young composers. Mendelssohn's work as composer and as conductor intersected less than one might anticipate. He was as much or more a proponent of the works of other composers—dead or alive—as he was of his own compositions.

There seems never to have been an ideal performance of *Paulus* under Mendelssohn's baton. Felix never pointed out more than one soloist as truly outstanding for any particular performance. In August 1844, for example, he wrote about a performance in Zweibrücken:

> As to the performances themselves—now, I must of course resume my usual sober style, for the other forms to great a contrast to my *métier*—but no! I think I must continue my tipsy tone, and tell you amid a great many deficiencies, we had the best St. Paul and Druid Priest whom I have ever met with in Germany, namely, a Herr Oberhofer, a singer from Carlsruhe, who was formerly in the capital. I do not know what he may be on stage, but it is impossible for any one to sing, or to deliver the music which I heard better, with more intelligence, or more impressively, than he did.[38]

Mendelssohn nevertheless seems to have striven continuously for bigger and better performances of *Paulus,* as this letter to Carl Klingemann exemplifies:

The number of friends that "St. Paul" has gained me is really quite remarkable. I could never have anticipated it. It was performed twice at Vienna in the spring, and they want to have a festival there in November, with one thousand performers ("St. Paul" is to be given), which I shall probably go to conduct. This has surprised me the more, because no other work of mine has ever made its way to Vienna. I must be in Brunswick for the Musical Festival the end of this month, in order to conduct "St. Paul"; and it is always a source of twofold pleasure to me when I have no personal acquaintances in a place, which will be the case there.[39]

CONCLUSION

A look at early performances of *Paulus* shows that Mendelssohn was able to use his dual role as composer and conductor to his advantage. Despite the "flawed" early performances, *Paulus* was always received enthusiastically—partly because of this ability as a conductor to make the most of the premiere of an unpolished draft of *Paulus*. More importantly, however, as a composer Mendelssohn did not let the success as a conductor of his own works get in the way of his goal to create the best possible final product. In fact, he used his role as conductor to further his development as a composer, seemingly placing his career as composer above that of a performer. Not only was he able to work on *Paulus* up to the very last minute, having the luxury of making changes even after the initial rehearsals; he also could use the information gained from "working in the trenches" to revise and polish his compositions after a premiere.

Mendelssohn nevertheless had to work within the limitations of everyday performing. In the process, he learned that the composer ceases to have much control over the "fate" of his compositions by the time they reach the concert hall. Just as Mendelssohn the conductor was able to promote other composers effectively, so Mendelssohn the composer seems to have been equally dependent on the success of enthusiastic performances by others.

NOTES

1. Robert Schumann, *Schriften über Musik und Musiker,* vol. 1, *Schwärmbriefe* (Leipzig: Wiegand, 1854); quoted in Eric Werner, *Mendelssohn: A New Image of the Composer and His Age* (Westport, Conn.: Greenwood, 1978), 264.

2. Hans von Bülow, *Ausgewählte Schriften* (Leipzig, 1896), 335–36; quoted in Werner, 314.

3. Sebastian Hensel, *Die Familie Mendelssohn: 1729–1847* (Berlin: B. Behr's Verlag, 1884), 320–21; unless otherwise noted, all translations of German quotations are by the author: "Ferner war es hier, bei dem successiven Eintreffen Fremder von allen Punkten, die sich im Orchester meist zum ersten Mal treffen und dort mit den hiesigen Freunden zusammenkommen, früher zur Mode geworden, das Orchester zu-

gleich als parloir zu benützen; es wurde ungeheuer viel geschwatzt, die Proben gingen schlecht, der Dirigent musste sich die Lunge ausschreien und wurde nicht gehört; und da bis zur Stunde der Aufführung immer neue hinzukamen, so wurde die Störung unleidlich. Nachdem Alles dies am ersten Probetage sich wieder zugetragen hatte, stellte ihnen Felix vor, dass er sich da nicht gefallen lassen könne, dass er weder schreien könne noch wolle, dass sie ihn hören müssten, und dass er auf die unbedingteste Stille und Ruhe im Orchester, während er spräche, rechnen und halten müsste. Nachdem er auch dieses ein zweites Mal sehr Ernst und bestimmt wiederholt hatte, versichere ich Dich, dass ich eine pünktlichere Befolgung einer Anordnung nicht gesehen; es leuchtete ihnen ein, dass es nothwending und richtig sei, und sowie er nun aufklopft und etwas sagen will, hört man ein allgemeines 'Pst' und es ist tiefe Stille. Dadurch hat man es nun bewirkt, dass, zum ersten Mal, wie man mich allgemein versichert, Nuancen im Chor und Orchester hineinkommen, was sie wieder Alle erfreut und ihren Leistungen in ihren eigenen Augen und Ohren einen höheren Werth beilegt."

4. Letter from 10 March 1835, Abraham Mendelssohn, *Letters of Felix Mendelssohn Bartholdy: From 1833 to 1847*, ed. Paul Mendelssohn, trans. Lady Wallace (London: Longman, 1863), 72.

5. Letter from 6 December 1835, Felix Mendelssohn, *Briefwechsel zwischen Felix Mendelssohn und J. Schubring zugleich ein Beitrag zur Geschichte des Oratoriums,* ed. Julius Schubring (Leipzig: Duncker and Humblot, 1892), 99–100: "Überhaupt mache ich mich nun mit doppeltem Eifer an die Vollendung des Paulus, da der letzte Brief des Vaters mich dazu trieb, und er in der letzten Zeit sehr ungeduldig die Beendigung dieser Arbeit erwartete; mir ists, als müßte ich nun alles anwenden, um Paulus so gut als möglich zu vollenden, und mir dann denken, er nähme Theil daran. Fallen dir noch gute Stellen auf, so schicke sie mir noch, Du kennst ja den Gang des Ganzen; ich habe heute wieder zum erstenmale wieder daran geschrieben, und will es nun täglich thun."

6. Letter from 3 April 1835, Felix Mendelssohn, *Letters of Felix Mendelssohn Bartholdy: from 1833 to 1847,* 84.

7. Letter from 27 February 1836, Felix Mendelssohn, *Briefe an deutsche Verleger,* ed. Rudolf Elvers (Berlin: Walter de Gruyter, 1968), 200–201: "Da es mir sehr darum zu thun wäre, das Oratorium erst einmal gehört zu haben, ehe der Stich des Clavierauszugs vorgenommen würde, so wünsche ich, daß derselbe bis *nach* der Aufführung verschoben würde, da ich doch wahrscheinlich noch manches würde ändern wollen, wozu es hernach zu spät wäre. Ich bitte sie also für jetzt nur die Chorstimmen stechen zu lassen, in den auf keinen Fall später noch Abänderungen zu machen sein werden. Den Stich der Solostimmen, wenn Sie ihn beabsichtigen, wünsche ich aber ebenfalls bis nach der ersten Aufführung verschoben zu haben. Obwohl ich fürchten muß, daß die Ihnen nicht ganz recht ist, und daß Sie bei den ersten Aufführungen lieber schon den Clavierauszug fertig hätten, so wird doch auch Ihnen daran liegen, das Werk so abgerundet und vollendet, als ich es vermag, erscheinen zu sehen, und ich gestehe Ihnen daß es mir zu wichtig ist als daß ich nicht wünschen sollte es erst selbst gehört zu haben, ehe ich es der Öffentlichkeit definitiv übergeben möchte, und etwas dabei übereilte."

8. Letter from 5 July 1836, Felix Mendelssohn, *Letters of Felix Mendelssohn Bartholdy: from 1833 to 1847,* 105.

9. Ibid., 105.

10. F. G. Edwards, "First Performances. I. Mendelssohn's 'St. Paul,' " *Musical Times,* 1 March 1891, 138.

11. Sebastian Hensel, 320.

12. Ferdinand Hiller, *Mendelssohn. Letters and Recollections* (London: MacMillan, 1874), 51–52.

13. Letter from 14 August 1836, Felix Mendelssohn, *Letters of Felix Mendelssohn to Ignaz and Charlotte Moscheles,* trans. Felix Moscheles (Freeport, N.Y.: Books for Libraries Press, 1970), 154–55.

14. Roger Nichols, *Mendelssohn Remembered* (London: Faber and Faber, 1997), 224.

15. Ibid., 226.

16. Edwards, 138.

17. Fanny Mendelssohn Hensel, *Tagebücher* (Leipzig: Breitkopf & Härtel, 2002), 8 July 1839, 84: "Im Januar [am 22.1] veranstaltete ich eine möglichst vollständige Aufführung des Paulus, worin die Soli vortrefflich augeführt, die Chöre möglichst gut einstudirt worden waren. Es waren über 100 Pers. zugegen."

18. Letter from 20 January 1837, Fanny Mendelssohn Hensel, *The Letters of Fanny Hensel to Felix Mendelssohn,* ed. and trans. by Marcia J. Citron (Stuyvesant, N.Y.: Pendragon, 1987), 227.

19. Ibid., 19 June 1837, 239: "Yesterday I held a brilliant rehearsal of *Paulus* in the garden hall, with a chorus of 40 that will swell to about 50 next Sunday. That probably seems rather ridiculous to you, but we're very happy about it." [Felix writes that he would love to hear a performance "and also see my dear Cantor at the piano; that will sound fuller than many of the renowned public performances that the newspapers drivel about." Felix had claimed that a performance of *Paulus* in Berlin had been ridiculous, for it included only eleven numbers, presented out of order (24 June 1837, NYpl). Felix thanks Fanny for her efforts on behalf of his oratorio (to Fanny 24 June 1837; D-B, 21)]

20. Letter from 5 January 1836, Fanny Mendelssohn Hensel, *The Letters of Fanny Hensel to Felix Mendelssohn,* 194–95.

21. Ibid., letter from 26 January 1836, 196.

22. Ibid., letter from 28 June 1836, 205–206.

23. Ibid., letter from 30 July 1836, 208.

24. Ibid., letter from 11 December 1836, 223.

25. Alfred Dörffel, *Geschichte der Gewandhausconcerte zu Leipzig* (Leipzig, 1884), 90.

26. Sebastian Hensel, 32: "Ich denke am 17ten März abzureisen nach Frankfurt, und für den 13then ist die Kirchenaufführung bestimmt. Ich möchte fast sagen leider bestimmt, denn ich habe doch auch gar keinen Animus jetzt dazu, und es gefällt mir nicht, dass ich so kurz vor meiner Hochzeitsreise solch einer entsetzlichen Hatze entgegengehe. Ich fluche auf die ganze Concert- und Musikwirthschaft hier und muss sie doch mitunter segnen, denn sie ist wirklich liebenswürdig."

27. Ibid., 40.

28. Letter from 6 January 1837, Felix Mendelssohn, *Briefe aus Leipziger Archiven,* ed. Hans-Joachim Rothe and Reinhard Szeskus (Leipzig: Deutscher Verleger für Musik, 1972), 51: "Gestern sagte mir Herr Adv.[ocat] *Schleinitz* daß der Herr *Nauenburg* erst am Freitag zur Generalprobe kommen wolle; da ich ihn aber als Sänger zu wenig kenne um so unbedingtes Vertrauen in ihn zu setzen, und da Hr. *v. Lehmann* im Gegentheil seine Sicherheit im Treffen nicht gelobt hat, so finde ich es durchaus nothwending, daß Hr. *Nauenburg* wenigstens einen Tag vor der Probe hier sei.—Kann er das wirklich nicht, so würde ichs doch lieber mit dem hiesigen Herrn Richter versuchen, wenn er die Erlaubniß dazu bekommt."

29. Ibid., 51–52.

30. Letter from 15 January 1838, Fanny Mendelssohn Hensel, *The Letters of Fanny Hensel to Felix Mendelssohn,* 248.

31. Ibid., 248.

32. Ibid.

33. Ibid.

34. Ibid., 248–49.

35. Ibid., letter from 19 January 1838, 251.

36. Letter from 3 February 1838, Felix Mendelssohn, *The Letters of Fanny Hensel to Felix Mendelssohn*, 253.

37. Ibid., letter from 13 January 1838, 246.

38. Letter from 15 August 1844, Felix Mendelssohn, *Letters of Felix Mendelssohn Bartholdy: from 1833 to 1847*, 192.

39. Ibid., letter from 1 August 1839, 173–74.

7

From Drawing Room to Theater: Performance
Traditions of Mendelssohn's Stage Works

MONIKA HENNEMANN

Mendelssohn's stage works have had a remarkably uneven performance and reception history. One—the *Midsummer Night's Dream* music—has been produced in a multiplicity of guises. The other incidental music, however, is relatively little-known, and the early operas have scarcely had a performance history at all. Many relatively cultivated members of the concert-going public have not even heard of the existence of his five youthful Singspiele and Liederspiele, let alone the fragments of the unfinished opera *Lorelei,* whereas the "Wedding March" from *A Midsummer Night's Dream* is familiar to almost everybody in the West who has ever attended a marriage ceremony. This chapter will address the reasons for this anomalous situation through a discussion of the first productions of these works and a mapping of their subsequent divergent fates. It will emerge that no matter how easy it is to document Mendelssohn's general performance intentions for his dramatic works, much of this information is more than usually difficult to utilize today. The few pieces that did receive professional production during the composer's lifetime were often not performed to his satisfaction, while those intended for intimate family gatherings were originally performed in circumstances hardly reproducible in subsequent eras.

MENDELSSOHN'S OPERAS: PRIVATE VERSUS PUBLIC PERFORMANCES

The intended performance context of Mendelssohn's early dramatic works vanished with the Mendelssohn family and their social milieu. Four operas (or operettas) were composed by the prodigy between the ages of twelve and fifteen, intended for production only in the—admittedly large and lavish—family home in Berlin. Although these were followed by a publicly performed stage work, *Die Hochzeit des Camacho* (1827), the subsequent Liederspiel *Die Heimkehr aus der Fremde* (1829) reverted to type in being both inspired by family circumstances and duly performed before the family circle. Birthdays and anniversaries were taken very seriously in the Mendelssohn household, and the operas were the direct result of a hardworking attitude to their celebration as part of a varied program of activities for the family and their guests.

It is difficult nowadays for many of us to picture the atmosphere of wealth, commerce, and culture that surrounded the young Mendelssohn as he grew up in Berlin. However, only by setting Mendelssohn's early operas in their original performance context can we begin to understand the unusual nature of the pieces themselves, and also the psychological hurdles their composer faced when he later assayed an opera for the general public.

The Mendelssohns' vast and lavish mansion in Leipziger Straße and their two previous Berlin residences are no longer with us, but enough survives in the surrounding area to give a vague hint of what growing up there in the early nineteenth century might have been like. This truly is an elegant location. Even a superficial glance at the map shows us that we are bang in downtown Berlin, only a short walk or even shorter carriage ride from the Brandenburger Tor, from no fewer than four cathedrals, from the Hofoper (now Staatsoper), from the now nonexistent Stadtschloß (replaced by the dilapidated communist Palast der Republik) to the still-surviving Schauspielhaus (1821—contemporary with Mendelssohn's early opera attempts). If we stroll today from the elegant and highly fashionable Gendarmenmarkt, where the Schauspielhaus stands, down Jägerstraße, we quickly pass the former home of Rahel Varnhagen von Ense, site of a celebrated literary salon in Mendelssohn's day, to reach no. 51, the splendid building that once held the Mendelssohn family banking house. Almost directly opposite (no. 22) is the birthplace of Alexander von Humbolt, philosopher, founder of the University of Berlin, and a close friend of the Mendelssohns.

The Mendelssohns, therefore, not only lived richly in the heart of Berlin—like living in central Manhattan, or near London's Regent's Park—but were intimately bound up with the heart of its cultural and commercial life. When Mendelssohn attended the University of Berlin in the late 1820s he was therefore a student at the local university up the road from his father's bank, one that moreover had been founded by a friend of the family. The famous premier of Weber's *Der Freischütz* in 1821 took place virtually round the corner at the Schauspielhaus, allowing the young Mendelssohn time to greet the startled older composer both on leaving his hotel and also–after a quick sprint–on alighting from his carriage at the performance venue. Growing up as Mendelssohn did in this hard-working, but well-heeled and well-educated, circle, coming from this cushioned background, it is perhaps not so surprising that the lukewarm public reception given to *Die Hochzeit des Camacho* at the Schauspielhaus seems to have somewhat wounded the youthful prodigy. He was used to the warmth, at times adulation, of private performance in a quite exceptional family circle.

Four of Mendelssohn's early dramatic works, *Die Soldatenliebschaft* (1820), *Die beiden Pädagogen* (1821), *Die wandernden Komödianten* (1821), and *Die beiden Neffen, oder Der Onkel aus Boston* (1822–23) were based on texts of Johann Ludwig Casper, a family friend who later made a name for himself as a forensic pathologist. His participation, however, was not merely creative—he also participated in the operas as a tenor buffo. The libretti steered clear of forensic pathology in favor of plots taken from contemporary French "vaudevilles"—humorous, if sometimes harmlessly radical, stage pieces promoting progressive bourgeois viewpoints. In the case of *Die Soldatenliebschaft* (The Soldiers' Love Affair) for example, the slender plot—set during the French siege of a city in Spain—deals with two soldiers of opposing nationalities in love with two girls predictably also of opposing nationalities. At the end, the motto "make love, not war" is triumphantly affirmed, when all concerned realize that passion is more important than politics. The work was premiered on Abraham Mendelssohn's birthday, 11 December 1820—albeit only with piano accompaniment, which was the commonly accepted procedure. Only after its success had been secured was Felix granted the privilege of the performance of an orchestrated version. This took place on his own birthday a few weeks later as one constituent of the musical program, which also included a farce titled "L'homme automate" with a specially written overture by Felix built around a medley of popular folk tunes. Two things are clear from this: firstly, the operatic pieces were not expected to fill an entire evening and remained comfortably within modest limits with regard to resources and time; secondly, an—in this case mostly professional—orchestra was a desirable but not essential constituent of these home performances.

With his first small opera Mendelssohn set the pattern for the ones to follow, although we can detect an increase in scope. It is very obvious that his parents wanted to support his operatic endeavors in order to prepare for an anticipated career as a stage composer, and they therefore informed him immediately after the performance of *Die Soldatenliebschaft* that Casper would prepare a second libretto for him, to be composed for his mother's birthday on 15 March 1821. This gave the young composer less than two months to complete the task. The libretto to *Die beiden Pädagogen,* based on Scribe's 1817 comedy *Les deux Précepteurs ou asinus asinum fricat,* turned out

to be "very lively, light, and musical."[1] As planned, the premiere took place
again at the piano, with an orchestrated performance (in versions for string
quartet and full orchestra) soon after, both using friends as members of the
cast—in this instance, for example, Mendelssohn's violin teacher Henning
took three of the six roles in the first performance. A third one-act opera
was to follow soon, *Die wandernden Komödianten,* scheduled to be first performed in March 1822. It was—owing to a thumb injury of the young
composer—postponed until April, when it was programmed in conjunction with a repeat performance of *Die beiden Pädagogen.*

  After successfully producing these three domestic one-acters,
Mendelssohn was given a more challenging task: his fourth work, *Die beiden
Neffen* (or *Der Onkel aus Boston,* 1824), again based on a text by Casper,
contained three acts of a much wider ambit, including two ballets. As it fills
about 150 minutes, it is no surprise that it took Mendelssohn not merely a
few weeks, but around eighteen months to complete—he began the composition on 1 May 1822 and finished on 21 November 1823. A leisurely
three months were reserved for rehearsals, and the work was premiered directly with an orchestra on 7 February 1824, like the follow-up performance on 9 February in front of a full house seating 150 guests. This
marked the end of his training period in the eyes of his composition
teacher Carl Friedrich Zelter, who on the occasion of the first full rehearsal
on Felix's fifteenth birthday famously proclaimed him "a journeyman in
the name of Mozart, Haydn, and the old Bach."[2] The successful performances also saw the enforced retirement of "house librettist" Casper, whose
capabilities could not keep up with the increasing level of sophistication
and complexity of the young composer's development.

  Mendelssohn's most ambitious youthful opera project—the first stage
work designed for public performance—was *Die Hochzeit des Camacho* (op.
10, 1824–25). He composed it very much with audience comprehensibility
in mind, rejecting the opportunity to experiment with increasingly popular
through-composed forms, as we know from a letter to his librettist, Friedrich
Voigts: "Do not make the dialogue between the musical numbers too short.
Singers, orchestra and listeners must be able to draw breath. I consider a few
words between the songs to be absolutely necessary."[3] The possibility of cen-
sorship in public theaters also troubled him, for he obviously had hopes that
if the opera were a success in Berlin, international performances might follow: "It would be good to allow the *priest* to appear, although this is not accepted on most German stages. . . . If that is the case here, how much worse
will it be in Austria?"[4] He eventually submitted the composition to the
Königliche Schauspiele in Berlin, where the Generalintendant Graf Brühl
approved a performance. The notorious Generalmusikdirektor Spontini,

however, delayed it for a while owing to other, supposedly more important, undertakings. The premiere, which took place on the smaller stage of the Schauspielhaus on 29 April 1827, was a moderate success, but the fastidious and sensitive composer was disappointed—probably with both the performance (apparently, the chorus had been unsteady) and the audience reaction. He left the theater before the end. The rigors of public opera production were a baptism of fire that the nurturing atmosphere of birthday parties in his own home had not fully prepared him for, and when a repeat performance was first postponed owing to an illness of baritone Heinrich Blume (Don Quixote), then seemingly forgotten, Mendelssohn did not push the matter. In the eyes of his experienced friend Devrient, "the music was essentially of the same character as all of Felix's boyish works. The hearer was at once struck by the admirable musicianship, command of form, and intelligent declamation of the vocal parts; these qualities were indisputable and claimed esteem for the young composer of sixteen, but they alone would not command success with the public."[5] Although the opera was published in piano-vocal score in 1828 by Laue in Berlin, the moderate reception put a distinct psychological damper on Mendelssohn's operatic aspirations—it would not be until the final years of his life that he managed to begin composing another work in the genre, his unfinished opera *Die Lorelei*.

Next on his agenda, however, was another work designed for the home stage in his parents' house, the Liederspiel *Die Heimkehr aus der Fremde* ("Son and Stranger," 1829, op. 89), on a text by his close friend Carl Klingemann. It was designed for the occasion of his parents' silver wedding anniversary and mostly composed in the three weeks between Mendelssohn's return from London and the premiere. A typical "Gelegenheitskomposition," the first production on 26 December 1829—prefaced, among other contributions, by a chorus from Cherubini's *Les deux journées*—included Mendelssohn's brother Paul at the cello, his sisters Fanny and Rebecka as singers, and Devrient as director. Even the truly unmusical future brother-in-law, Wilhelm Hensel, was given a part—consisting of a single repeated note that the overly nervous performer duly failed to hit, much to the audience's delight. The reception of the opera was so positive that one of the 120 guests, Meyerbeer's brother Heinrich Beer, extraordinarily requested a performance in his own home (which was denied by the composer).[6] Even a printed libretto seems to have been prepared for the occasion.[7]

In many ways, the work is one of the last highlights of the Liederspiel genre. It is substantially more developed than its typical predecessors through the use of an orchestra and the inclusion of ensemble numbers. It represents not only Mendelssohn's own return home "from foreign lands" (in this case Britain), but also a musical homecoming in terms of genre, scope, and resources after a time of compositional experimentation. He himself was convinced of the high quality of this Liederspiel: "Klingemann has told you the details about the 'Festspiel'; it has become one of our most cherished memories, and I think it is my best composition."[8] Nevertheless, he declined the opportunity of further productions, despite pressure from friends and family. Devrient reported:

> It was urged upon him to consent to a public performance of the operetta; his mother especially wished it, but the filial piety of Felix shrank from exposing to the public the work which to him was associated with a solemn occasion; there was much in the music which had a purely personal significance. . . . Moreover, he argued, the whole work was not suited for the dimensions of the theatre, for which the instrumentation would have to be entirely remodeled. I also hinted that the slender interest of the action would barely satisfy an exacting public. Finally, I thought it would have been unwise to let this delicate little work follow upon the quasi-failure of "Camacho's Wedding."[9]

Mendelssohn's and Devrient's concerns were insurmountable, and the work was never produced publicly during Mendelssohn's lifetime, although excerpts were frequently performed by friends and family members: "We often sang pieces from the operetta; . . . and when she [Devrient's wife Theresa] begged him to let her have a few of the pieces with piano accompaniment, having already given the air of the Evening Bells to Mantius,—one day he brought her the pianoforte score of the entire work in his own writing."[10] Only after the composer's death was *Die Heimkehr aus der Fremde* put on various national and international stages (with a text adaptation by Eduard Devrient[11]), then later also performed in English, French, Swedish, and Hungarian translations in the respective countries.[12] Such performances, however, would obviously have been against not only the intention, but also the expressed wish, of the composer. On the other hand, he would have appreciated the continued tradition of private performances of the Liederspiel, such as the one documented by his biographer W. A. Lampadius, who claims to have declaimed the narrative text himself at such a performance in Leipzig.[13]

Mendelssohn would no doubt have equally strongly disapproved of the publication and performance of fragments from his later opera, *Die Lorelei,* left unfinished at his death. The finale to Act 1, an "Ave Maria" for female chorus, and a "Vintner's Song" had been given a hasty premiere under Julius Rietz at the Gewandhaus as early as 1848 and appeared in piano score soon afterwards (as op. 98 in 1852). Numerous follow-up performances, both on the stage (for example, 1852 in Leipzig, 1853 in Prague, and 1854 in Basel) and in the concert hall (including 1851 in Berlin and Leipzig, 1852 in London, in a translation of William Bartholomew, and 1860 in Vienna)[14] cemented the impression that this had been the only music composed, despite

Mendelssohn's statement that he had almost completed the first act.[15] Recent studies have rediscovered further manuscript sources, such as a love duet for Lenore and Otto for Scene 2 and a large number of drafts for Scene 7 (including a March for Choir and a vocal quartet, plus music for the end of this scene).[16] Larry Todd has concluded: "Though some of this material was probably viewed as too fragmentary to warrant publication, the festive march and the quartet are fully scored in Mendelssohn's hand, and it is difficult to understand why they were neglected."[17] The shock of the composer's early death, however, stimulated a temporary rescue from oblivion of at least the published *Lorelei* fragments, along with Mendelssohn's Liederspiel, but such interest as there was soon burnt itself out.

If the later nineteenth and early twentieth centuries showed little interest in Mendelssohn's actual operas—completed or otherwise—they did nevertheless feature attempts to turn his most celebrated oratorio into one. As genre distinctions became more fluid and new performance options were experimented with—in a bizarre echo of Liszt's intended dramatization of sacred music proclaimed in his essay "Religious Music of the Future" of 1834"[18]—scenic performances of oratorios became popular. These included Liszt's own *Die Legende der heiligen Elisabeth* in a Weimar stage production of 1881 (ironically against the composer's wishes) and Mendelssohn's *Elijah*. Just as Mendelssohn himself had taken the liberty to move Bach's *St. Matthew Passion* from the church to the concert hall in his epoch-making revival performance of 1829, others decided to move *Elijah* into the theater. This was perhaps not so surprising, given that the work has been often compared to an opera. Donald Mintz, among others, stated that "Elijah is largely a dramatic work, indeed in some ways it is Mendelssohn's opera."[19] Scenic performances were tried in various contexts, for example in New York during the 1912–13 season by the Majestic Grand Opera Company, where *Elijah* was advertised as appearing for the "first time in America as music drama" in a theatrical version by W. de Wagstaffe (cf. figure 7.1). This too proved to be—perhaps fortunately—a passing fashion.

Despite their limited dissemination as a whole, Mendelssohn's operas had an intermittently lively second strand of performance history. The composer often prepared (or had prepared for him) several copies of individual arias and numbers as gifts for friends and acquaintances—in the case of *Die Heimkehr aus der Fremde* it was even the original that was promised to Klingemann by Lea Mendelssohn.[20] The cavatina "Still und freundlich ist die Nacht" (extant in a copy dedicated to Adele Schopenhauer in 1882) and the tercet "Alles schwelgt in süßen Träumen" (jotted down in part as late as 1822 into an album for Heinrich Beer, who had participated in a performance of the work) seem to have been the circulating numbers of *Die Soldatenliebschaft*.[21]

FIGURE 7.1.   Announcement of the first dramatic performance of Elijah during the 1912–13 season in New York, in *The Musical Courier,* New York, n.d.

For *Die Hochzeit des Camacho* the published edition of 1828 promised that "the overture and all numbers from this work are individually available."[22] We must therefore assume that excerpts at least from these works were sung in the salons and drawing rooms of Berlin (and London), and were possibly more widely known there than it might seem at first glance. An even more extensive distribution is manifested in the actual publication of individual vocal numbers (in addition to piano reductions of the overtures), particularly in England and France, starting during Mendelssohn's lifetime and continuing well into the twentieth century. Certain excerpts even attained a genuine popularity, such as the so-called Nuptial Chorus ("Nun zündet an geweihte Kerzen") from *Die Hochzeit des Camacho*,[23] a duet ("Beglücktes Jugendleben") from the same source, translated as "Fond Hours,"[24] and especially the positively Rossinian number beloved of British audiences as "I Am a Roamer Bold and Gay." This last number turns up in an amazing variety of editions: no doubt many of those who perused a choral part-song (TTB) with this title arranged by W. Gillies Whittaker (with added sol-fa notation), and humbly dedicated to the St. Anne's Music Festival Committee of 1938, would be unaware that its (secret) origin was actually "Ich bin ein vielgereister Mann" from *Die Heimkehr aus der Fremde* (cf. figure 7.2)[25]

In recent decades, Mendelssohn's operatic endeavors have undergone occasional small-scale localized revivals, none of them providing a convincing replacement for their original performance context. Some were put back onto the stage or dragged into the concert hall. These attempts included John Warrack and Clive Brown's staging of *Die Hochzeit des Camacho* in Oxford in 1986, and most recently performances and a recording of *Der Onkel aus Boston* under the baton of Helmuth Rilling in 2005. The latter cleverly (but perhaps not so dramatically) circumvented the problem of the missing dialogue to Act 3 by simply replacing all of the opera's spoken texts with a summary of the action delivered by two speakers. Several others of Mendelssohn's stage works have been issued as CDs, and *Die beiden Pädagogen* was produced in 1989 by the Saarländischer Rundfunk to be shown on German television. However, none of these undertakings has forced the operas into the consciousness of the general concert-going audience.

MENDELSSOHN AS CONDUCTOR OF STAGE WORKS

Mendelssohn's own experiences as a conductor of opera during his tenure as music director of the Düsseldorf theater not surprisingly bear little direct relationship to the originally amateur performance traditions of his own early operatic compositions, but they do give a good idea of the sort of repertoire and stage productions he would have become familiar with, and are

FIGURE 7.2.   "I Am a Roamer by Mendelssohn," arranged as a part-song for T.T.B.B. by H. Noble, translated by H. F. Chorley (London: Oxford University Press, 1939), 1–4. © Oxford University Press 1938. Reproduced by permission.

FIGURE 7.2. *continued*

FIGURE 7.2.   *continued*

FIGURE 7.2.   *continued*

important for understanding his increasing involvement with theater incidental music. Three works were staged under his baton before he left the position and town on 10 November 1834 after a series of unpleasant quarrels with his superior, Generaldirektor Immermann.

The first piece Mendelssohn chose for performance was Mozart's *Don Giovanni* (November 1833), followed by Cherubini's *Der Wasserträger* (March 1834), and finally Weber's *Oberon* (November 1834).[26] This was, amazingly, his last active contact with the world of professional operatic production, although opera continued to play an important role in his life as a composer and concert conductor. A second tranche of his duties at the theater was the provision of incidental music. Mendelssohn here gathered practical experience that would turn out to be very valuable for his famous Berlin commissions in the early 1840s. Immermann's first request was that he should provide music for the production of Calderón de la Barca's *The Steadfast Prince*. Although the commission came at a rather inconvenient time—and actually long before he had officially been offered the position at the theater—Mendelssohn seemed delighted about its possibilities, and even more so about the prospect of participating in the performance.

An important issue here, and one that casts light on contemporary theater practice, was that of an overture. Often, unrelated music was played as a curtain-opener for dramatic performances, which in this case would have meant a break in style with the specially composed incidental music—a procedure Mendelssohn deprecated. He therefore considered composing an overture himself in addition to the commissioned pieces. That an overture would be necessary in any case was beyond doubt: "I would rather like to compose an overture myself because any foreign one would remain alien to the piece; however, I am afraid my time may not allow this, much as I would wish to do it. Alternatively, I would send you the overture they have used here, or—in case they have played a very jolly one, as they like to do for tragedies— I would attempt to find another one. However, I won't totally give up the idea of creating one myself—the task is too appealing for me!"[27] In the end, Mendelssohn did not get around to composing the overture—what was used instead is not known. Even the actual incidental music, based on A. W. Schlegel's translation, which differed drastically from Immermann's version used for the production, although performed on 9 April 1833 in Düsseldorf, has remained unpublished.[28] It is clear, however, that in addition to gaining experience with incidental music, Mendelssohn also had hopes that his new position would allow him to get his own operas written and performed: first of all his *Pervonte,* a project that was in the works with Klingemann at the time, and secondly, *Der Zaubermantel in Caligans Händen* based on *The Tempest,* for which Immermann had written the libretto. Both projects never got beyond the planning stage, hindered by Mendelssohn's dissatisfaction with the respective libretti and his increasing difficulties with the mundane administrative duties related to his job.

Despite his complaints, Mendelssohn had a rather privileged position in Düsseldorf. In conception, the theater management's plans were based on Goethe's idea of "Mustervorstellungen," applied to musical theater for the first time. In contrast to the contemporary practice of surprisingly few rehearsals even for large-scale pieces, Mendelssohn had his debut as opera conductor after no less than twenty. A similar approach was applied to the subsequent two productions, when he began to complain that he was "obliged to undertake the regulation of everything—the acting, scenery, and the dialogue"[29] during an average of nine to ten hours of daily rehearsals. Other projects Mendelssohn participated in as the theater's music director were performances of Goethe's *Egmont* with Beethoven's incidental music, Immermann's own tragedy *Andreas Hofer* (for which he supplied two musical numbers), and Calderón's aforementioned *El principe constante*.

However serious Mendelssohn's difficulties in Düsseldorf were, his work there no doubt prepared him for his more enduring achievements as a theater composer in Berlin. On the Prussian monarch Friedrich Wilhelm IV's ascension to the throne in 1840, he sought to surround himself with Germany's leading intellectuals, and took pains to promote what he regarded as the finest works of culture of both ancient and modern periods, including, of course, Greek drama and Shakespeare. Among the leading intellectuals was the now aged poet Ludwig Tieck, soon appointed as the king's resident reader, and the relatively young Mendelssohn, only reluctantly answering the summons to Berlin from his position in Leipzig. In collaboration, they were commissioned to prepare a series of "model" performances for the king's theater, starting with Sophocles's *Antigone* (1841), followed by Shakespeare's *A Midsummer Night's Dream* (1843), Sophocles's *Oedipus at Colonos,* and Racine's *Athalie* (1844–45). A few other commissioned projects, such as Aeschylus's *Eumenides* and Sophocles's *Oedipus Rex,* quietly fell by the wayside, although Mendelssohn at one point claimed he had composed the music for the latter.[30] The resulting productions were all hybrids between opera and spoken drama in an attempt to revive the great masterpieces of literature with the help of music.

The production of *Antigone,* prepared in consultation with the Classical philologist August Boeckh and based on the faithful translation of Donner, posed novel challenges for the composer, who also took the liberty to insert text changes whenever musically required. Owing to the lack of evidence, a reconstruction of the original Greek music was impossible, so the only similarity to the performance practice of Sophocles's time was the employment of a male choir consisting of sixteen voices, albeit accompanied by a Romantic symphonic orchestra. Mendelssohn's solution was to "conjure the spirit of antiquity using modern means of expression,"[31] and in consequence he decided against continuous choral recitation and the use of ancient instruments. Potential problems of composing music to a relatively faithful translation from the Greek did not affect Mendelssohn, who had a good knowledge of the ancient language and its poetic meters. The composition took place between 14 and 25 September 1841, followed by a period of intense preparation for the performance: "We have two rehearsals of it daily, and the choruses are executed with such precision that it is a real delight to listen to them."[32] Devrient, who had been appointed as choral leader for the performance, reports in his diaries of rehearsal strategies that differed significantly from normal contemporary ones: At a production meeting on 14 September 1841, for example, Tieck read the piece aloud to everyone as an introduction, apparently with moderate success.[33] He also took a pedantic approach to correcting the actors at later stages, causing frustration for Mendelssohn.[34] Nevertheless, Tieck had, according to Devrient, a positive overall effect on the rehearsals: "Tieck's presence awakened in the performers so much attention, accuracy, interest in the tiniest details and subordination of everything to the basic idea of the piece that I myself was really galvanized into action. How wonderful it would be if it were always like that."[35]

The first scenic rehearsal took place on 21 October, followed by the premiere on the proscenium arch stage at the Neue Palais in Potsdam a week later. After a repeat performance on 6 November, the work became available to the public in a performance at the Berlin Hoftheater almost half a year later, on 13 April 1842. The audience reacted with bafflement to this unusual event, not knowing which genre the work belonged to: "At the exits of the actors, a few attempts were made at applauding, but not for any of the musical numbers, and at the end of the performance was a big silence. Possibly, the people regarded the performance as some sort of oratorio where applause is unsuitable, although this is rather stupid—why did they try to applaud the actors? And not the music!"[36]

We know some of the staging details of the first production of *Antigone* through Boeckh's essay "Über die Darstellung der Antigone." He commented that

> the scenic arrangements were highly practical in view of the limited space. In order to provide clear sight lines of the ground-level performance space (orchestra), seating must, wherever possible, be tiered and in the round, which was an advantage already present in the little theater that housed the performance. The stage is more than five feet higher than the ground-level performance-space; this relationship is rather appropriate, for it allows the protagonists, especially the king, to be sufficiently elevated in comparison with the choir.[37]

While generally approving of Mendelssohn's musical decisions, Boeckh regretted that the chorus did not also dance, as they would have in the ancient theater. He conceded, however, that exact adherence to the choreographic elements of ancient Greek performances would have seemed too "stiff and pedantic" for modern audiences.[38]

Despite Mendelssohn's avoidance of experiments with choral dancing, *Antigone* marked a stylistically new orientation not only for his oeuvre, but for the genre of incidental music as a whole. Contemporary critics recognized this: "German music has been enriched by a new genre: The choruses of Greek tragedy have found their composer in Mendelssohn, as the psalms once did in Marcello."[39] The performances initiated a lively, sometimes even vehemently controversial discussion among composers and Classical philologists, and an amateurishly uncritical adoration of Greek antiquity amongst the uneducated members of the public, which Lortzing subsequently ridiculed in his opera *Der Wildschütz*.

Antigone was, like the other dramas for the king's stage, designed with a unique performance context in mind (Mendelssohn referred to it as a "private amusement"),[40] which made it almost impossible for these works to enter the standard repertoire in their original form. Critical voices, such as Robert Schumann's, claimed that the work had "much too much music, but not deep and significant enough. . . . The whole does not offer pure artistic pleasure—it is half opera, half tragedy."[41] Nevertheless, the music seemed perfectly suited for the occasion and the purpose, which made it doubly difficult to apply it to other contexts. This, however, did not stop several theaters trying, most swiftly in Leipzig (on 5 March 1842, even before the public premiere in Berlin), most oddly with the original Greek text under Carl Loewe in Stettin, and most prominently and successfully in London (with forty-five sold-out performances between 2 January and 21 February alone). In the last production there was the attraction of the girls from the ballet featuring some distinctly non-Greek choreography, as well as the "celebrated Music by Dr. Felix Mendelssohn Bartholdy executed by sixty male voices"[42] (see figure 7.3). From a letter of the composer to George Macfarren we know not only that he wholeheartedly approved of the increased vocal resources, but also that he supplied detailed instructions particularly on the transitions between speaking and singing and on what he called the "*acting* of the chorus."[43]

In terms of printed dissemination, the fate of the incidental works paralleled that of the operas: After the initial publication of the choruses of *Antigone* (in piano score) by Kistner in 1843, a steady stream of reissues and excerpted individual numbers kept appearing in print, not only in Germany, but also in England. In the case of *Athalie* the publication of the piano score (1848) and of the most favored numbers (the "War March of

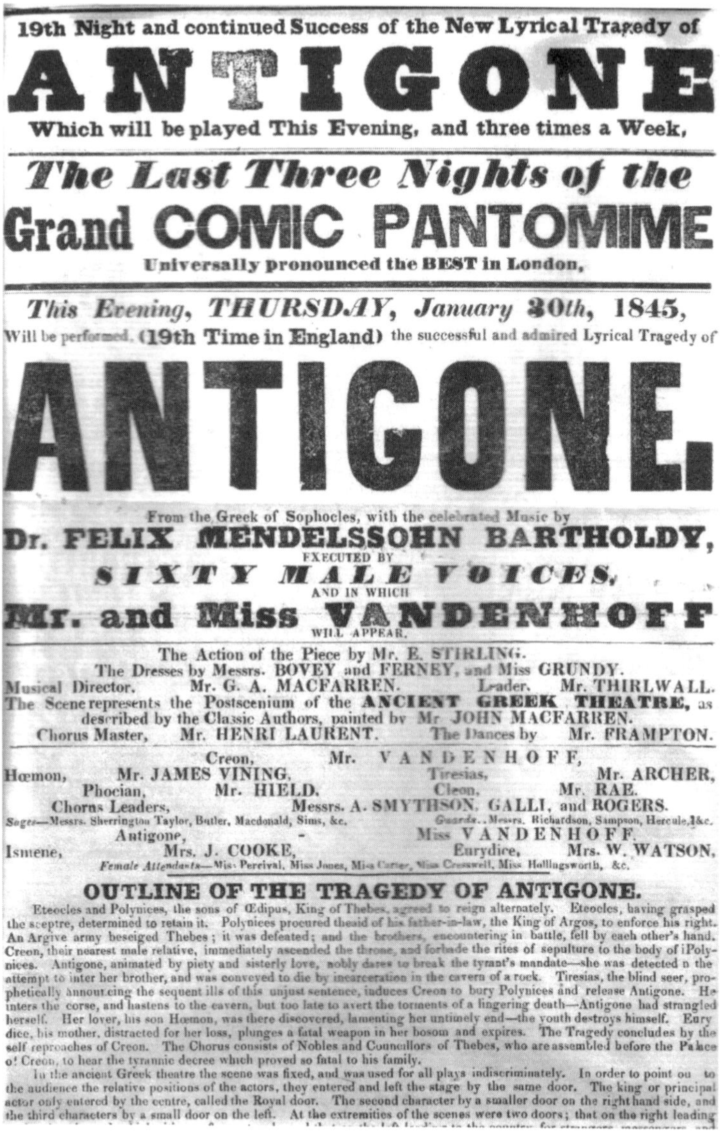

19th Night and continued Success of the New Lyrical Tragedy of

ANTIGONE

Which will be played This Evening, and three times a Week,

The Last Three Nights of the

Grand COMIC PANTOMIME

Universally pronounced the BEST in London,

This Evening, THURSDAY, January 30th, 1845,

Will be performed. (19th Time in England) the successful and admired Lyrical Tragedy of

ANTIGONE.

From the Greek of Sophocles, with the celebrated Music by

Dr. FELIX MENDELSSOHN BARTHOLDY,

EXECUTED BY

SIXTY MALE VOICES,

AND IN WHICH

Mr. and Miss VANDENHOFF

WILL APPEAR.

The Action of the Piece by Mr. E. STIRLING.
The Dresses by Messrs. BOVEY and FERNEY, and Miss GRUNDY.
Musical Director,   Mr. G. A. MACFARREN.   Leader,   Mr. THIRLWALL.
The Scene represents the Postscenium of the ANCIENT GREEK THEATRE, as
described by the Classic Authors, painted by Mr JOHN MACFARREN.
Chorus Master,   Mr. HENRI LAURENT.   The Dances by   Mr. FRAMPTON.

Creon,   Mr. VANDENHOFF,
Hœmon,   Mr. JAMES VINING,   Tiresias,   Mr. ARCHER,
Phocian,   Mr. HIELD,   Cleon,   Mr. RAE,
Chorus Leaders,   Messrs. A. SMYTHSON, GALLI, and ROGERS.
Sages—Messrs. Sherrington Taylor, Butler, Macdonald, Sims, &c.   Guards—Messrs. Richardson, Sampson, Hercule, &c.
Antigone,   -   Miss VANDENHOFF,
Ismene,   Mrs. J. COOKE,   Eurydice,   Mrs. W. WATSON,
Female Attendants—Miss Percival, Miss Jones, Miss Carter, Miss Cresswell, Miss Hollingsworth, &c.

OUTLINE OF THE TRAGEDY OF ANTIGONE.

Eteocles and Polynices, the sons of Œdipus, King of Thebes, agreed to reign alternately. Eteocles, having grasped the sceptre, determined to retain it. Polynices procured the aid of his father-in-law, the King of Argos, to enforce his right. An Argive army besieged Thebes; it was defeated; and the brothers, encountering in battle, fell by each other's hand. Creon, their nearest male relative, immediately ascended the throne, and forbade the rites of sepulture to the body of Poly-nices. Antigone, animated by piety and sisterly love, nobly dares to break the tyrant's mandate—she was detected in the attempt to inter her brother, and was conveyed to die by incarceration in the cavern of a rock. Tiresias, the blind seer, pro-phetically announcing the sequent ills of this unjust sentence, induces Creon to bury Polynices and release Antigone. He enters the corse, and hastens to the cavern, but too late to avert the torments of a lingering death—Antigone had strangled herself. Her lover, his son Hœmon, was there discovered, lamenting her untimely end—the youth destroys himself. Eury-dice, his mother, distracted for her loss, plunges a fatal weapon in her bosom and expires. The Tragedy concludes by the self reproaches of Creon. The Chorus consists of Nobles and Councillors of Thebes, who are assembled before the Palace of Creon, to hear the tyrannic decree which proved so fatal to his family.
In the ancient Greek theatre the scene was fixed, and was used for all plays indiscriminately. In order to point out to the audience the relative positions of the actors, they entered and left the stage by the same door. The king or principal actor only entered by the centre, called the Royal door. The second character by a smaller door on the right hand side, and the third characters by a small door on the left. At the extremities of the scenes were two doors; that on the right leading

FIGURE 7.3.   Public poster announcing the nineteenth performance of the London *Antigone* production on 30 January 1830.

the Priests"—including such monstrosities as an arrangement for two pianos and eight hands[44]—and the trio for female voices) took place only after Mendelssohn's death.

One last aspect of Mendelssohn's relationship to stage works concerns his concert programming. The official release from his Berlin obligations also marked the end of his career as a theater conductor, and for the rest of his life he performed stage works only in the concert hall, that is, not within their originally intended performance context. This was normal contemporary practice. Although operas were usually heard in their entirety in the opera house, they often had a much more vivid afterlife in excerpts, most often in the form of arias, overtures, and lieder. Many never became available in full score, but were published in piano reductions for two or four hands. This was true for overtures in particular. Such excerpts had always been highly appreciated by Mendelssohn as a resource for more relaxed musical activities. According to Johann Gustav Droysen's report on the intense semi-private choir rehearsals led by the composer: "In the winters of 1827 and 1828, Mendelssohn formed a small, reliable choir consisting of his and his sister's friends that met on Sunday nights—modelled after Zelter's Friday rehearsals—in order to rehearse rare music under his direction. However, they also sang, as a reward, the odd piece from a popular opera."[45]

From 1835 onward, Mendelssohn's most significant performance outlet for stage compositions was the Gewandhaus, where programs more often than not included instrumental and vocal excerpts of operas. Beethoven's posthumously published *Leonore Overture,* for example, was given in the season's first subscription concert on 2 December 1836. As a supplement, and in combination with the *Emperor Concerto* with Mendelssohn as soloist, the finale from *Leonore* (Fidelio) was performed, after which Mendelssohn improvised on its melodies on the piano—concerts were indeed different in those days. An equally noteworthy event was the (spontaneous) performance of all three *Leonore* overtures and that for *Fidelio* in a single concert on 9 January 1840—Mendelssohn decided to add the three later versions, two of which were totally unrehearsed, to the program when the violinist Stör refused to return to the stage for a scheduled solo piece after the intermission.[46]

Another very important ingredient of the subscription concerts was of course freshly composed works, such as for example two (unspecified) overtures by Ferdinand Hiller, and one each by Lindpaintner, Spohr, and Rosenhain in the 1836–37 season. Operatic ensemble numbers in this season included again excerpts from *Leonore,* the finales of Cherubini's *Wasserträger,* Lindpaintner's *Die Macht des Liedes,* Mozart's *La Clemenza di Tito,* and Weber's *Freischütz,* as well as choral numbers, vocal ensembles, and introductions from

Rossini's *Semiramis* and *Tell,* and Spohr's *Faust* and *Jessonda.* During the following season, the programs of the "historical concerts"—another emphasis of Mendelssohn's activities in Leipzig—alone contained, in chronological order, excerpts from Gluck's *Iphigenia in Aulis, Iphigenia in Tauris,* Cimarosa's *Il Matrimonio segreto,* Righini's *Tigranes* and *Armida,* Mozart's *Zauberflöte* and *Zaide,* Salieri's *Palmira,* Méhul's *Uthal,* Vogler's *Samori,* Weber's *Euryanthe,* and Beethoven's *Fidelio*—all in all an eclectic mixture in terms of national origins, familiarity, and quality. In addition, it was only to be expected that the concerts of vocal stars—either contracted singers or traveling divas such as Elise Vogel and Jenny Lind—strongly relied on opera. Relatively few of Mendelssohn's own stage compositions, however, were included in these concert series, with the exception of *Antigone* (on 5 March 1842) and *A Midsummer Night's Dream* (on 22 January 1846). The multifaceted performance history of this famous latter work forms our last topic of investigation.

A CASE STUDY: MENDELSSOHN'S INCIDENTAL MUSIC TO *A MIDSUMMER NIGHT'S DREAM*

The only one of Mendelssohn's stage works that allows us to study a truly rich and uninterrupted history of performance and reception from the composer's time to our own is the incidental music to Shakespeare's *A Midsummer Night's Dream.* Unlike the early operas, this both was composed for professional production and has had an extensive performance history since its first successful appearance under the baton of the composer. Unlike Mendelssohn's other incidental theater music, it also remains in the active repertoire to this day, and has maintained an almost unique position as a staple of theater, concert hall, and latterly cinema. In fact, Mendelssohn's music is now so inextricably linked with Shakespeare's play that it has become a frequent object of parody—whether affectionate or otherwise—in several self-consciously "postmodern" productions. This is particularly noteworthy considering the fact that several hundreds of pieces of incidental music have been (and are still being) composed by other hands for individual productions of the comedy, and that dozens of operas have made use of the subject, some as famous as Henry Purcell's semi-opera *The Fairy Queen* (1692–93) and Benjamin Britten's *A Midsummer Night's Dream* (premiered 1960), but most of them as unsuccessful as *The Fairies* by Handel's pupil J. C. Smith (1755).[47]

In the following paragraphs, the genesis of the work is outlined, followed by a discussion of its original performance circumstances and subsequent adaptations. Ironically, despite the fully professional nature of the first stage performances of the *Dream's* music, they can hardly be held up as a model for modern productions even for those who might wish, as an experiment, to recreate Shakespeare as it was performed in the nineteenth century. Mendelssohn's artistic intentions were often in conflict with those of the original director, and there was no ideal performance during his lifetime from which we could even superficially derive a chimerical "authentic" performance practice.

Mendelssohn's incidental music to the *Dream* owes its origin to the Romantic Shakespeare-mania in late eighteenth- and early nineteenth-century Germany. A. W. Schlegel's famous translation of 1795–96 was the medium through which Mendelssohn, and many others, became acquainted with the play. Schlegel's wonderfully melodious iambic pentameter does indeed seem to capture some of the flavor and versatility of Shakespeare's verse, as here in Puck's celebrated closing address to the audience: "So verheißt auf Kobolds Ehren/Puck, daß wir Euch Dank gewähren; /Ist ein Schelm zu heißen willig,/Wenn dieß nicht geschieht, wie billig./Nun gute Nacht! Das Spiel zu enden, Begrüßt uns mit gewognen Händen!"[48] Among the people under Schlegel and Shakespeare's spell was the Prussian king, Friedrich Wilhelm IV, which caused him to commission the incidental music. For this second joint project with Tieck, the compositional challenges were rather different from the ones Mendelssohn had faced in composing music for *Antigone*. Shakespeare offered much more freedom and flexibility, for there was no impetus to restrain his own style in order to capture a historical period—it was not necessary to set the play to either pseudo-antique or faked-up Elizabethan music. Rather, Mendelssohn was allowed to employ to the full the expressive means of his natural Romantic idiom to represent the play's magical and elfin, sylvan and comic aspects. It required songs and dances, but also offered room for much more music even than a Greek play.

Mendelssohn's incidental music was not, of course, his first musical encounter with Shakespeare's work—in 1826 he had already composed his Overture (op. 21) to the *Dream,* one of the first examples of the new genre of the concert overture and one of the earliest masterpieces of the adolescent genius. Understandably, he picked up where he had left off sixteen years earlier—there was no reason not to reuse the concert overture as an overture to the play itself, and then to further develop themes from it. Although the overture had been conceived in concise sonata form, Mendelssohn had also captured in characteristic music the leading personages—Oberon, Puck and the other fairies, Theseus and his court, the lovers, the rustics (especially Bottom as an ass)—as well as the overall mood of the play. Thirteen newly composed instrumental and vocal numbers were then added, including four intermezzi designed to entertain the audience between the acts and set the tone for upcoming events, the latter exemplifying serious differences of dramatic vision between Mendelssohn and Tieck.

Whereas the composer had envisioned that the play should be performed in five acts (as originally published), the entr'actes filled with the four aforementioned musical intermezzi, the poet decided unilaterally to partition the play into three acts in order not to interrupt the scene of the night in the forest. The highly unsatisfactory consequence for the composer was that two of the intermezzi, the frantic Allegro in A minor and the "Nocturne," had to be played with the curtain up. Despite this conflict of artistic views the premiere on 14 October 1841 was a tremendous success, and three public performances in Berlin (on 18–21 October) followed immediately upon those for the court. As Mendelssohn's sister Fanny put it: "The Midsummer Night's Dream has been dreamt in the Neue Palais. . . . It was wonderfully beautiful, and the music especially is the most magical thing you will ever hear. . . . All children of Berlin will truly enjoy the piece."[49] Many performances of the score, both in conjunction with the play as incidental music (the Berlin production was performed a total of 169 times and abandoned only in 1885) and in excerpt for concert use, were to follow in the succeeding decades.

One indicator of success that had tremendous consequences for the establishment of the work in the repertoire was the speedy availability of the score, which first appeared (in 1844) in both Germany and England in an abridged version for piano four-hands prepared by the composer (with German and English words, respectively); a complete solo piano score was issued in 1845 (without text). A full score was published by Breitkopf & Härtel as early as 1848, which was highly unusual, but had in fact also been the case with the overture, which appeared in piano version simultaneously in Britain and Germany in 1832 as op. 21, to be followed by a full score in 1835.[50]

A noteworthy and now almost entirely forgotten means by which Mendelssohn's music was widely disseminated were readings by professional elocutionists (often actors and actresses beyond their prime), with a musical accompaniment ranging from a keyboard instrument to a large orchestra plus chorus. The practice of reading the *Dream* in particular was first popularized by the renowned English actress and writer Fanny Kemble (1809–93), who had known Mendelssohn personally and who had discovered that this highly profitable means of performance allowed her to tour England and North America according to her own schedule, while keeping production costs to a minimum.[51] The other Berlin incidental works of Mendelssohn quickly followed as fodder for similar performances. Almost needless to say, this means of production died out along with the profession of the elocutionists themselves, leaving in the public memory only the gentle satire of the practice embodied in Shaw's *Pygmalion*.

The list of theater productions associated with Mendelssohn's *A Midsummer Night's Dream* music starts with an oddity: on two occasions, the overture was associated with a performance of the play long before the incidental music was composed (and before such performances ever even took place in Germany). The first was the 1833 revival of Frederic Reynolds's highly adapted, often criticized 1816 London production that—whatever its failings—had at least managed to give the play a stage life again.[52] Luckily, Mendelssohn's overture had appeared in print by the time of the second run, adding to the success of the production. Particularly groundbreaking in terms of approach was Madame Vestris's 1840 production in *Covent Garden,* which padded the play out greatly with musical sequences and ballet dances, turning it into a proto-Hollywood spectacular. Mendelssohn's overture was used as a prelude to the whole phantasmagoria, which was staged in a pseudo-ancient Athenian forest. As pioneered by this production, the magical aspects of the play were subsequently often emphasized in a "Gesamtkunstwerk," drawing upon every resource of the composer's, choreographer's, and scene-painter's art. Productions along those lines naturally did not shy away from cutting the text extensively to provide greater space for music and dance, but the virtual standardization of such an approach quickly declined into routine. It was, moreover, ruinously expensive (casts often numbered nearly one hundred). Something had to give, and by the end of the nineteenth century new production methods began to be sought that were both artistically more innovative and more solicitous of the sorely tried impresarios' profit margins.[53]

From 1850 onward, performances that did *not* use Mendelssohn's music (completely, in part, in pared-down arrangements, or with additions) became the exception rather than the rule, with the result that audiences began to expect to hear the music in conjunction with the play.[54] Directors such as Samuel Phelps (1853–61 and 1875), Charles Kean (1856–59), John Ryder (1870); and F. R. Benson (1889–1916), all employed it. One of the Mendelssohn-based productions that provides an especially interesting insight into performance-practice issues was the production of the Benson Company, for which two complete sets of performance-parts (from around 1911 and, with additions, 1919) survive in the *Shakespeare Centre* in Stratford. What we can learn from these is that the director required more than Mendelssohn's extensive incidental music (the published score of which provided the basis for the parts, with the extra pieces in manuscript merely glued in and some numbers cut), so further songs, such as "Over Hill, Over Dale," choral pieces, plus a glee for four voices with piano accompaniment by R. J. S. Stevens on "Ye Spotted Snakes" were added, in combination with alterations to Mendelssohn's score itself—in this instance including an annotation that reads: "It is a good effect if everyone on the stage hums the last four bars." Whether this advice was followed and if so, how successfully, is not known, but we do at least have a detailed review by George Bernard

Shaw of a Benson Company production from the late 1880s, which seems to have scarcely differed from the 1911 parts in its use of incidental music. Extra works by Mendelssohn were evidently included; favorites seemed to have been two of the best-known *Songs without Words,* the so-called "Bees' Wedding" and the "Spring Song." Clearly, it had become standard to use only the supposedly "essential" bits of Mendelssohn's incidental music, namely the overture at the beginning, the nocturne at some point, the indispensable wedding march, and also the rustics' music. Other ingredients from the original score were optional. The Benson Company, for example, used Mendelssohn's "Scherzo" in its 1911 production, but not in 1919.

The early-twentieth-century reaction against the mass-spectacle method of staging the play was particularly marked in progressive director Harley Granville-Barker's 1914 production. This was surely a "modern" way of producing the *Dream:* he replaced the unwieldy sets with a simple system of patterned curtains, and out with the lavish scenery went Mendelssohn's music, which had become inextricably linked to the "old" production style—to be replaced by English folk music. Productions following this trend included those of Patrick Kirwan (1914, with Elizabethan music), Bridges Adams (after several productions with Mendelssohn's music, it was replaced by Purcell in 1921 and Elizabethan music in 1932/1934), E. Martin Browne (1937, with Elizabethan music), and Andrew Leigh (1938, with newly composed music). After 1957, Mendelssohn's score finally ceased to be used as a default even in Britain—much later than in Germany, where it had of course been banned during the Nazi period (and had to await reappraisal there until the twenty-first century, when the critical edition of the score was published as part of the complete works).[55] Nevertheless, the performance history of Mendelssohn's *Dream* continued under a new guise: in 1964, Sir Frederick Ashton, on the four-hundredth anniversary of Shakespeare's birth, created a ballet using Mendelssohn's music, which drastically compressed the action into one act. More famous and long-lasting was George Balanchine's ballet (1962, with a filmed version published in 1967), which followed Shakespeare's plot more closely and incorporated music from five other compositions of Mendelssohn in addition to the original. This crossover of genres marked the beginning of a period of experimentation with Shakespeare's works, and the *Dream* in particular, where remnants of its old Victorian splendor were retained parallel with postmodern stagings. Mendelssohn's music made a reappearance in a few of those landmark English productions, at least as a point of departure, namely those of Peter Brook (1970–73) and John Caird (1989–90). It was still considered standard, even if now fit only for parody.

Peter Brook swept away every tradition associated with the play, staging it in a blank white box, in which masculine fairies engaged in circus tricks such as trapeze artistry. His production saw notable innovations in terms of instrumentation: composer Richard Peaslee introduced a guitar and a wide range of percussion instruments (such as a snap). The music consisted of "jazzed-up" Mendelssohn, including newly composed pieces such as a "Jazz Waltz," but also the "Wedding March" blaring from loudspeakers while the musicians and fairies looked down at the action below from a catwalk around the top of the set.[56] John Caird's production was set in an Edwardian court, the actors dressed accordingly.[57] The music, composed by Ilona Sekacz and partly based on Mendelssohn, introduced an interesting, Baroque-style innovation: two bands were used, a brass band associated with Oberon and a woodwind band associated with Titania. Both groups also included horns, percussion, and a synthesizer. Parts of Mendelssohn's overture appeared throughout, especially the four opening woodwind chords, although here in new orchestration that included brass. The beginning of the overture was played fairly straight, with open curtain, but soon became increasingly bizarre, first through the addition of a rhythm section, then through an orchestration for the full band. Toward the middle, the overture was radically altered in a crudely syncopated fashion, but the approximate original length and overall scope was retained. The close returned to Mendelssohn's original music, albeit in a different orchestration with a heavy emphasis on synthesized sounds, which gave a deliberate impression of "artificiality." This pattern was followed throughout: The music tended to start with Mendelssohn, then gradually distanced itself. Much newly composed music was added, including a deliberately awful song for the fairies, which they duly start rehearsing as diagetic music. The overture finally resurfaced as a postlude. It is interesting to observe that the director was quite happy to adapt or distort Mendelssohn's music and the original setting of the play, but not, of course, Shakespeare's words. The latter were certainly sacrosanct—they could be cut, but not distorted or modernized—something that resurfaced in twentieth-century film adaptations, which left a more permanent fingerprint on the reception history of the music.

In performances today, Mendelssohn's complete music is not performed regularly in conjunction with the play—not the least because it is expensive to produce owing to its hybrid nature. Although there are relatively few vocal passages, it still requires a female choir plus soloists, not to mention a full early Romantic orchestra. In recent years, however, it has become fashionable again (more so in England than in Germany) to offer historically informed, half-staged performances of the (heavily cut) play with Mendelssohn's music in the foreground. Such a performance, for example, was given by the Orchestra and (female half of the) Choir of the Age of the Enlightenment at the Royal Festival Hall in London in 2005. The latest Royal Shakespeare Company production in Stratford-upon-Avon (premiered in 2005) uses Mendelssohn's magical opening chords as a point of reference at the beginning and also at the very, very end, long after most of the audience have left the hall, as a piquant farewell gesture to those few members of the public still lingering by the exits.

Given the popularity of the *Dream*—it is arguably the best loved and most frequently performed of Shakespeare's comedies—it is not surprising that it was also reinvented more than a dozen times in the medium of moving pictures. Mendelssohn's music played an important role in this strand of performance practice, as is evidenced most strongly in the first noteworthy attempt to turn the *Dream* into a film. German theater director Max Reinhardt had already tried his hand at the piece on the Berlin stage thirteen times between 1905 and 1934, followed by a more spectacular American outdoor production at the Hollywood Bowl—a first step toward "Hollywoodizing" Shakespeare—before he, on the strength of the latter production, was contracted by Warner Brothers to direct a filmed version. As a musical partner, he chose the Viennese opera composer Erich Wolfgang Korngold, with whom he had already collaborated on a Berlin production of *Die Fledermaus* in 1929. Korngold ended up staying six months in America instead of the originally intended six to eight weeks—because the music for the film gradually became one of the main points of emphasis.

For the film score, Korngold followed the nineteenth-century tradition of employing not only Mendelssohn's original music, but also excerpts from the *Songs without Words* (including the old favorite, the "Spring Song," plus a "Venetian Gondola Song," albeit both with added words) and—which was more of a novelty—the "Scottish" Symphony in the form of a choral adaptation of its finale. Korngold, however, showed great respect for the integrity of Mendelssohn's music. Whenever possible, he left the orchestration untouched, although he felt compelled to transpose the "Nocturne" down a semitone. Occasionally he thickened Mendelssohn's textures, especially in the lower voices, to compensate for the limitations of the single-track sound recording, with which the altogether more delicate scoring of early nineteenth-century orchestration would have been lost. In the sections of additional music composed by Korngold himself, he felt free to use percussion instruments, harp, saxophone, piano, guitar, and most notably a vibraphone. Korngold's meticulous care and resourcefulness soon established his authority over the directors and actors in matters that might affect the music. Such a practice had never been encountered before, but Korngold, on this film, established procedures that would influence the medium right up to the present day. As a result, the film of *A Midsummer Night's Dream* has 114 minutes of music[58] and represents one of those rare instances where the action and choreography is actually built around the music and not vice versa.

Nevertheless, with typical modesty, Korngold chose not to be credited at all as composer in the film's titles. Of course, Korngold left his interpretative fingerprints on the original work, for example by using the music of the "Wedding March" as running commentary to the action. It first appears near the opening as a foreshadowing of the forthcoming wedding ceremony, then in the middle as an ironic comment on Titania's affair (and enacted fantasy wedding) with Bottom—an idea made famous by the Benson productions. Finally, it comes back near the end, in the place intended by Mendelssohn, but not unaltered: it is seamlessly joined onto a song of Bottom and subsequently also rendered in a version with words. The wedding march music appears one final time, as exit music, ending the movie in a very different and much more mundane spirit from Mendelssohn's version of the play. Overall, the music features so prominently that the whole movie can be called an homage to Mendelssohn in Hollywood during a time when his music had started to be excluded from the concert stages in Germany.

A discussion of the *Dream*'s performance practice would not be complete without mentioning the influence Korngold's film score exerted in the genre. Two productions deserve particular mention in this regard, Woody Allen's *A Midsummer Night's Sex Comedy* (1982) and *William Shakespeare's Midsummer Night's Dream* (1999). Woody Allen's movie has notably less to do with Shakespeare than it does with Mendelssohn—it uses his music exclusively, not only the *Dream,* but also excerpts from the "Scottish" Symphony, the Violin Concerto in E minor, and the Second Piano Concerto. The overall mood in this instance is set not by the Mendelssohn overture, but by the "Wedding March" used for the opening credits—a not too subtle hint that there is a wedding in store. It quickly becomes obvious that the film is about Allen's usual topics—desire and lust, dysfunctional relationships, maybe love, but in any case obsession. Mendelssohn's music is employed in a Leitmotiv manner—the "Scottish" Symphony for pastoral scenes, the Violin Concerto for outdoor activities, the slow movement of the Piano Concerto where love could come into play, and the *Dream* whenever infidelity becomes an issue. The overture appears at minute 37 when the three couples (Andrew and Adrian, Maxwell and Dulcy, Leopold and Ariel) start swapping partners for the first time; their second attempt at straying is underlined by the Allegro Intermezzo about an hour into the movie. The overture makes a repeat entrance fifteen minutes later, when Leopold is about to shoot his unfaithful fiancée and her lover with an arrow, inadvertently almost killing the wrong guy. The final use of the *Dream*'s music is the one notable exception to Allen's otherwise consistent use of themes: the film ends with the overture when Leopold, the repressed, controlling superego, has expired, causing a magic ball to start glowing and rattling over Mendelssohn's "magical" opening chords, while his ghost speaks on his way to joining the souls of all the others who have died during lovemaking. The "magic" in this movie is as present as in the play, though in a rather twisted, typically Allenesque, way.

Mendelssohn's *Dream* music made a reappearance in a 1999 Hollywood adaptation with an all-star cast including Kevin Kline, Michelle Pfeiffer, and Calista Flockhart under the direction of Michael Hoffman, with a musical score by Simon Boswell. Although the words were little altered, Mendelssohn's music is tweaked quite liberally and serves by no means as the main musical resource. Oddly set in late nineteenth-century Italy, the film relies heavily on tunes taken from Italian popular nineteenth-century operas, including surprisingly excessive excerpts from *La Traviata* and the intermezzo from Mascagni's *Cavalleria Rusticana,* but also Puccini's *La Boheme,* Bellini's *Norma,* and Donizetti's *L'Elisir d'Amore*—all in all a very impressive "best of Italian opera" selection. The film also contains newly composed ghostlike, Indian-style, and English pastoral sections. Nevertheless, it cannot do without Mendelssohn entirely. His music is granted a generously extended appearance right in the beginning, with twinkling fireflies that seem like a reference more to Woody Allen than to Shakespeare: the scene opens, in the general tradition of many theater performances, with the overture (with the credits running), which is at first faithfully rendered, then recomposed (after about 3 minutes), with parts of the incidental music interpolated; after another 90 seconds, Mendelssohn's music emerges again, this time as diagetic music, from a gramophone. Mendelssohn then disappears entirely until the "Nocturne" makes an entrance (in rearranged form with a counter-melody) after almost 1½ hours, when the mixed-up couples wake up reunited after a night of confusion and miracle, paradoxically turning it into a morning song. It is followed by the seemingly unavoidable "Wedding March" a few minutes later, but the epilogue here is spoken over music from Mascagni's "Intermezzo," which, as it happens, ends in a very similar manner to the close of Mendelssohn's overture.

When we look at this extensive, varied, multimedia performance history of Mendelssohn's *A Midsummer Night's Dream* music, it becomes clear that it must be robust to survive all this as it has. Some prefer more of it, along the lines of Basil Dean's production at Drury Lane in 1924 that included not only the full incidental music, but also excerpts from the *Italian* Symphony, two string quartets, and seven other items, resulting in 3¾ hours running time. Others would like less, such as Dean's critic Herbert Farjeon, who claimed that "it would take up too much time to give *all* Mendelssohn and *all* Shakespeare," and he would rather sit through Shakespeare's *Dream* than Mendelssohn's.[59] The good thing is that each can have their own, "As you like it," so to speak, for we can hardly claim that there is any one "authentic" tradition of performance to which productions should ideally conform to do justice to both Mendelssohn and Shakespeare, or indeed to either separately. This lack of an original, composer-approved production style not only is liberating to performers, but also facilitates the refashioning of Mendelssohn's music from age to age and ensures its continuing relevance. Whether the music is being regarded with reverence, affection, or irony, it nevertheless remains a part of present-day theater by being played, and played with a frequency that Mendelssohn's other stage works have never enjoyed, or, in all likelihood, will ever achieve.

NOTES

The last section of this chapter originated as a lecture for the Royal Shakespeare Company/ Shakespeare Institute, Stratford upon Avon (August 2005). I wish to thank the staff of the Shakespeare Centre for their assistance of my research in their library.

1. Manuscript copy of a letter of Lea Mendelssohn to Henriette von Pereira-Arnstein, May 1821; quoted in Thomas Krettenauer, *F. Mendelssohn Bartholdys Liederspiel "Heimkehr aus der Fremde"* (Augsburg: Bernd Wißner, 1994), 55: "Sehr munter, leicht und musikalisch." Unless otherwise noted, all translations of German quotations are by the author.

2. See Sebastian Hensel, *Die Familie Mendelssohn 1729–1847* (Frankfurt: Insel, 1995), 175: "Ich mache dich zum Gesellen im Namen Mozarts, im Namen Haydns und im Namen des alten Bach."

3. Letter of Mendelssohn to Voigts; quoted in Rudolf Elvers, *"Nichts ist so schwer gut zu componiren als Strophen": Zur Entstehungsgeschichte von Felix Mendelssohns Oper "Die Hochzeit des Camacho"* (Berlin und Basel: Mendelssohn-Gesellschaft, 1976), 8–9: "Machen Sie doch ja keinen zu kurzen Dialog zwischen den Musikstücken. Sänger, Orchester, und Zuhörer müssen sich verpusten können. Ich halte ein paar Worte zwischen den Gesangstücken für höchst nothwendig."

4. Ibid, 10: "Den *Priester* auftreten zu lassen, wäre freilich gut, doch wird es auf den wenigsten Bühnen Deutschlands geduldet. . . . Und wenn dies hier geschieht, wie wird es dann erst in Österreich sein?"

5. Eduard Devrient, *My Recollections of Felix Mendelssohn-Bartholdy and His Letters to Me,* trans. Natalia Macfarren (London: Richard Bentley, 1869), 25.

6. See Carl Klingemann [Jr.], *Felix Mendelssohns Briefwechsel mit Legationsrat Karl Klingemann in London* (Essen: Baedeker, 1909), 69.

7. See Klingemann, 72.

8. Letter of Mendelssohn to Friedrich Rosen, Berlin, 9 April 1830; quoted in Klingemann, 78: "Von dem Festspiel weißt Du schon durch Klingemann das Nähere, es ist eine unserer liebsten Erinnerungen geworden und ich denke, es ist meine beste Komposition."

9. Devrient, *Recollections,* 92–93.

10. Ibid., 95.

11. Devrient felt obliged to justify the posthumous publication of the work against the composer's explicit wishes with the words: "The editors of his Nachlass believe to be obliged to not withhold a work from the musical world that gives witness of the freshest blossoming of Mendelssohn's talent and dramatic strength." See his preface to Felix Mendelssohn, *Heimkehr aus der Fremde,* op. 89 (Leipzig: Breitkopf & Härtel, [1851]).

12. Loewenberg recorded performances in Berlin, 1851 and 1890; Vienna, 1853 and 1862; Lucerne, 1867; Stuttgart, 1879; Leipzig, 1883; Frankfurt, 1883; Breslau, 1900;

Bremen, 1909; London, 1851, 1861 and 1896; Paris, 1865; Stockholm, 1901; Budapest, 1909. For a list, cf. Loewenberg, *Annals of Opera,* 1597–1940 (Totowa, N.J.: Rowman and Littlefield, 1978), 803.

13. W. A. Lampadius, *Felix Mendelssohn Bartholdy* (Leipzig: Leuckart, 1886). "Ich selbst wohnte nach M.'s Tode einer Aufführung bei einem Privatcirkel bei M.'s bester Freundin in Leipzig bei, wobei ich den verbindenden Text las."

14. See Loewenberg, 803.

15. See letter of Mendelssohn to Emanuel Geibel, Interlaken, 27 August 1847, Library of Congress, Washington (US-Wc). It seems possible that some of this music has been lost.

16. See R. Larry Todd, "On Mendelssohn's Operatic Destiny: *Die Lorelei* Reconsidered," in *Felix Mendelssohn Bartholdy: Kongreß-Bericht Berlin 1994,* ed. Christian Martin Schmidt (Wiesbaden: Breitkopf & Härtel, 1997), 113–40, which discusses the drafts contained in vol. 44 of the Mendelssohn Nachlass (kept in the Biblioteka Jagiellońska, Krakow, PL-Kj).

17. Todd, 126.

18. Franz Liszt, "Religious Music of the Future," in *An Artists Journey: Lettres d'un bachelier ès musique 1835–1841,* trans. Charles Suttoni (Chicago: University of Chicago Press, 1989), 236: "That music . . . will sum up both the THEATER and the CHURCH on a colossal scale. It will be at once both dramatic and sacred, stately and simple, moving and solemn, fiery and unruly, tempestuous yet calm, serene and gentle."

19. Donald Mintz, "The Sketches and Drafts of Three of Mendelssohn's Major Works" (Ph.D. diss., Cornell University, 1960), 20.

20. See letter of Lea Mendelssohn Bartholdy to Carl Klingemann, 30 December 1829; quoted in Klingemann, 71.

21. See Felix Mendelssohn, *Soldatenliebschaft: Komisches Singspiel in einem Akt,* ed. Salome Reiser (Wiesbaden: Breitkopf & Härtel, 2006), 150. (*Leipziger Gesamtausgabe der Werke von Felix Mendelssohn Bartholdy,* Series V/2).

22. See Felix Mendelssohn, *Die Hochzeit des Camacho* (Berlin: Laue, [1828]).

23. For example, "Nuptial Chorus from *The Wedding of Camacho,* Adapted to English Verses by G. H. Esq., of Edinburgh, Ed. Samuel Leigh" (London: n.p., 1830) and "Now bring ye forth the tapers brightly burning," Chorus of the Bridesmaids and Choristers, from the Opera *The Wedding of Camacho,* The English Words by F. E. Cox, The Music By F. Mendelssohn Bartholdy" (London: Lamborn, Cock, [c. 1880]).

24. For example, "Fond Hours, a duet," trans. H. Hudson (Dublin: Robinson and Bussell, [1838–52]).

25. "I Am a Roamer by Mendelssohn, Arranged as a Part-song for T.T.B." Arranged as a part-song for T.T.B.B. [by] H. Noble. [Words by] H. F. Chorley (London: Oxford University Press, 1939). It had also been published as "F. Mendelssohn Bartholdy's operetta entitled Son and stranger. The text freely adapted from the German of C. Klingemann esqu. By H. F. Chorley esqu. [No.] 4, I am a roamer bold and gay" (London: Ewer, [c. 1855]).

26. Todd also mentions performances of *Die Entführung aus dem Serail, Die Zauberflöte, Der Freischütz,* and *Der Templer und die Jüdin.* See Larry Todd, *Mendelssohn: A Life in Music* (New York: Oxford University Press, 2003), 297.

27. Letter of Mendelssohn to Immermann, Berlin, 18 February 1833, D-DÜhh 51.4897: "Eine Ouvertüre machte ich am liebsten selbst dazu, denn jede fremde bleibt dem Stück fremd, doch fürchte ich daß es meine Zeit nicht erlaubt, so sehr ichs wünsche; dann würde ich Ihnen mit der Musik entweder die jenige schicken, die hier gegeben worden ist, oder wenn sie hier dazu etwa eine ganz lustige gespielt haben, wie sie das bei Trauerspielen gern thun, so würde ich Ihnen eine andre auszufinden suchen. Aber ich will das Selbst Componiren doch nicht verschwören. Die Aufgabe reizt mich gar zu sehr."

28. The manuscript is located in D-B MN 56/1.

29. Letter of Felix to Abraham Mendelssohn, 28 March 1834, in Paul and Dr. Carl

Mendelssohn Bartholdy, eds., *Letters of Felix Mendelssohn Bartholdy from 1833 to 1847*, trans. Lady Wallace (Boston: Oliver Ditson, 1863), 26.

30. See Peter Ranft, *Mendelssohn: Eine Lebenschronik* (Leipzig: VEB Deutscher Verlag für Musik), 100–101.

31. Ernst Wolff, *Felix Mendelssohn Bartholdy* (Berlin: Schlesische Verlagsanstalt, 1906), 152: "durch moderne Ausdrucksmittel in den Geist der Antike einzudringen."

32. Letter of Mendelssohn to Ferdinand David, in *Letters of Felix Mendelssohn Bartholdy from 1833 to 1847*, 248.

33. Diary entry of Devrient, in *Eduard Devrient aus seinen Tagebüchern*, ed. Rolf Kabel (Weimar: Hermann Böhlhaus Nachfolger, 1964), 1:122.

34. Ibid., 5 October 1841; 1:126.

35. Ibid., 25 October 1841; 1:129: "Aber daß Tiecks Gegenwart so viel Andacht, Genauigkeit, Interesse für die geringsten Details, Unterordnung unter die Idee des Stückes beim Personal erzeugte, das erquickte mich ordentlich. So sollte es immer sein, wie herrlich wäre es dann."

36. Ibid., 13 April 1842; 1:143: "Bei den Abgängen der Schauspieler versuchte man einige Male zu klatschen, aber bei keinem der Musikstücke; und am Schluß der Vorstellung regte sich kein Laut. Mag sein, daß die Leute die Vorstellung als eine Art von Oratorium angesehen haben, in dem nicht applaudiert wird; schon dies ist eine Dummheit; dann, warum haben sie es bei den Schauspielern versucht? Warum nicht bei der Musik!"

37. A[ugust] Böckh, "Über die Darstellung der Antigone," in *Über die Antigone des Sophokles und ihre Darstellung auf dem Königlichen Schloßtheater im neuen Palais bei Sanßouc: Drei Abhandlungen von A. [August] Böckh, E. H. Toelken, Fr. [Friedrich] Förster* (Berlin: Schroeder, 1842), 79: "Die scenische Einrichtung war im Verhältnis zu der beschränkten Räumlichkeit höchst zweckmäßig getroffen. Damit der Blick in die Orchestra frei bleibe, müssen die Sitze, wo möglich in einer Rundung, aufsteigen; diesen Vortheil bot das kleine Theater schon dar, in welchem die Aufführungen stattfanden. Die Bühne ist fünf Fuß über die Orchestra erhöht; diese Verhältnis ist sehr ansprechend, und die handelnden Personen, namentlich der König, werden dadurch gegen den Chor angemessen hervorgehoben."

38. Ibid., 92.

39. Friedrich Förster, preface, in ibid., xi.

40. Letter of Mendelssohn to Droysen, Berlin, 2 December 1841, in Carl Wehmer, ed., *Ein tief gegründetes Herz: Der Briefwechsel Felix Mendelssohn-Bartholdys mit Johann Gustav Droysen* (Heidelberg: Lambert Schneider, 1959) 71: "Privatspaß."

41. Letter of Robert Schumanns to Clara, 24 March 1842; quoted in Wolfgang Boetticher, *Robert Schumann: Einführung in Persönlichkeit und Werk* (Berlin: Hahnefeld, 1941), 259: "Viel zu viel Musik und doch nicht tief und bedeutend genug. . . . Das Ganze gibt aber wie gesagt keinen reinen Kunstgenuß, 's ist halb Oper, halb Tragödie."

42. Public poster announcing the nineteenth performance of the London *Antigone* production on 30 January 1830.

43. Letter of Mendelssohn to Macfarren, Frankfurt, 8 December 1844, in Karl Mendelssohn-Bartholdy, *Goethe and Mendelssohn*, trans. M. E. von Glehn (London: Macmillan, 1874), 167.

44. Felix Mendelssohn, "War March of the Priests" from *Athalie* arranged for 2 pianos and 8 hands by E. [Ernst] Pauer (London: Augener, [1892]).

45. Gustav Droysen, "Johann Gustav Droysen und Felix-Mendelssohn Bartholdy," *Deutsche Rundschau* 3 (April–June 1902): 118: "Im Winter 1827 und 1828 bildete Mendelssohn aus seinen und seiner Schwestern musikalischen Freunden und Freundinnen einen kleinen, zuverlässigen Chor, der nach dem Vorbild der Zelter'schen Freitage Sonnabend Abends zusammenzukommen pflegte, um unter seiner Leitung seltene Musik zu üben. Doch wurde dann, gleichsam zur Belohnung, wohl auch ein Stück einer beliebten Oper gesungen."

46. See Claudius Böhm and Sven-W. Straps, *Das Leipziger Stadt- und Gewandhausorchester: Dokumente einer 250jährigen Geschichte* (Leipzig: Verlag Kunst und Touristik, 1993), 96.

47. Gooch/Thatcher's overwhelmingly vast, but still not entirely complete (or accurate) *A Shakespeare Music Catalogue* lists a total of 850 incidental compositions, of which 241 are arrangements of Mendelssohn's music, plus 117 operas using the play, not to mention countless nontheatrical compositions on the subject. Cf. Bryan N. S. Gooch and David Thatcher, *A Shakespeare Music Catalogue in Five Volumes* (Oxford: Clarendon, 1991), 2:969–1077.

48. August Wilhelm von Schlegel, *Sommernachtstraum,* in *Shakespeare's dramatische Werke* (Berlin: G. Reimer, 1830), 3:259.

49. Letter of Fanny Hensel to Rebecka Dirichlet, Berlin, 18 October 1843; quoted in Hensel, *Die Familie Mendelssohn,* 712–14: "Der Sommernachtstraum ist im Neuen Palais geträumt. . . . Es war wunderschön, und besonders die Musik ist das Zauberhafteste, was man hören kann. . . . Alle Kinder Berlins werden noch ihre Lust an dem Stück haben."

50. Although originally intended to appear under single opus number in conjunction with *The Hebrides* and *Calm Sea and Prosperous Voyage*—a set of three concert overtures—the work was published simultaneously in Germany and Britain (for four-hand piano and in parts; by Breitkopf & Härtel/Cramer, Addison and Beale) as op. 21. The full score followed in 1835.

51. For further reading on this subject area, see Marian Wilson Kimber, "Mr. Riddle's Readings: Music and Elocution in Nineteenth-Century Concert Life," forthcoming in *Nineteenth Century Studies* 21, and her "Reading Shakespeare, Seeing Mendelssohn: Concert Readings of *A Midsummer Night's Dream,* ca. 1850–1920," in *The Musical Quarterly* 89 (Summer-Fall 2006): 199–236. I would like to thank Marian Wilson Kimber for giving me access to these essays prior to publication and for her helpful comments on the present chapter.

52. For details about this production, see Trevor R. Griffiths, ed., *A Midsummer Night's Dream* (Cambridge: Cambridge University Press, 1996), 17–21.

53. See ibid., 2 and 21–24.

54. For a list of British productions and performance venues, see ibid., xiii–xv.

55. Mendelssohn's *Sommernachtstraum,* op. 61 and the composer's piano arrangements have appeared in editions by Christian Martin Schmidt as Series V/8 and Series V/8A of the *Leipziger Ausgabe der Werke von Felix Mendelssohn Bartholdy* in 2000 and 2001, respectively.

56. The prompt books are available at the Shakespeare Centre, Stratford. Six vocal pieces from this production have appeared in print (Hackensack: Boonin, 1975).

57. The prompt books, musical parts, and a videotape of the 1989 Royal Shakespeare Company production in Stratford are available at the Shakespeare Centre, Stratford.

58. A recording of the film music is available from CPO (999 449-2).

59. Griffiths, 50.

8

Mendelssohn and the Performance of Handel's Vocal Works

RALF WEHNER

Although Mendelssohn also championed other composers of the eighteenth century as well as the so-called "Alte Musik," namely Italian church music, with occasional performances,[1] these areas are marginal in his career in view of the intensity and continuity of Mendelssohn's dedication to the music of Johann Sebastian Bach and George Frederic Handel.[2] This study will discuss some aspects of Mendelssohn's editions and performances of some of Handel's works,[3] with special focus on *Solomon* (HWV 67), *Israel in Egypt* (HWV 54), *Joshua* (HWV 64), and *Alexander's Feast* (HWV 75).

It so happens that Handel's Ode for Cecilia's Day, *Alexander's Feast,* marks Mendelssohn's first and last contact point with Handel's music. Between Mendelssohn's eleventh birthday on 3 February 1820, when he was given an edition of this ode, and his last performance of a work by Handel in June 1846, when Mendelssohn conducted the ode, lies a stretch of twenty-six years. During these years Mendelssohn regularly poured over Handel's music, which greatly influenced his compositional approach.[4] A wealth of documents reveals Mendelssohn's multifaceted and flexible approach to this one-hundred-year-old music.[5] The situation with Handel's music was different from Bach's.[6] Handel's major vocal works were popular in Germany and were to a limited extent part of the repertoire of Singvereine and music festivals.[7] Handel's music nevertheless raised some performance issues not present in Bach's music: (1) the problem of German/English texts (no translations or bad German translations); (2) the problem of instrumentation and authenticity; in the early nineteenth century Handel's

Translated by Siegwart Reichwald

oratorios were performed in arrangements by Wolfgang Amadeus Mozart, Ignaz Franz Edler von Mosel, and other composers;[8] and (3) the problem of missing (unnotated) organ parts.

Mendelssohn approached these challenges with meticulousness and much enthusiasm. There is hardly another composer of the past (maybe not even Bach) with whom Mendelssohn grappled more intensely than with Handel. Already in 1833 it was said that "he has complete knowledge of Handel's works and has captured their spirit."[9] Over the course of Mendelssohn's career he also had to address many practical performance issues. In 1828 he wrote arrangements similar to Mozart's for his teacher Carl Friedrich Zelter; Mendelssohn looked at original sources,[10] copied them whenever possible,[11] and then incorporated the knowledge he had into his performances whenever possible. Mendelssohn's library included a representative cross-section of Handel's oeuvre.[12] Mendelssohn's critical study of these editions led to his attempts to publish new ones, resulting in his edition of *Israel in Egypt,* which reflects his editing ideals. There is also a substantial list of works by Handel with Mendelssohn's markings or additions. We have Mendelssohn's organ parts for *Solomon* (HWV 67), *Israel in Egypt* (HWV 54), *Dettingen Te Deum* (HWV 283), *Messiah* (HWV 56), and *Joshua* (HWV 64).[13] Some extant sources are handwritten full scores with additions of wind parts or single parts for other instruments (*Acis and Galatea* (HWV 49[a]), *Dettingen Te Deum, Israel in Egypt, Messiah*); printed scores with Mendelssohn's additions (*Alexander's Feast, Dettingen Te Deum, Israel in Egypt, O Praise the Lord* (HWV 254), *Samson, Zadok the Priest* (HWV 258);[14] some of Mendelssohn's performance materials; and finally many letters by Mendelssohn, expressing views about Handel's music and how to perform it.

All these sources help us understand Mendelssohn's pragmatic approach to performing. When no organ was available, he added wind parts despite his general disapproval of these types of arrangements. If a recitative was missing, Mendelssohn spontaneously composed one in the style of Handel to save the performance.[15] If there was not enough time before the performance to create a new, better translation of a work's text, he retained the old version for the choruses and translated only the texts of the solo parts, since they could be adjusted more quickly. While Mendelssohn had very clear ideas—especially later in his career—about how to perform Handel's music, he did not insist on his approach but was willing to compromise when conditions required it. This explains why Mendelssohn performed Mozart's arrangements, even when he had written his own.

A list of performances of Handel's vocal works under Mendelssohn's direction[16] (see table 8.1) shows the highest level of activity in the 1830s, especially during his Düsseldorf years (1833–35), when he performed no

Table 8.1. Performances of Handel's Vocal Works by Mendelssohn

Date	Place	Composition	HWV	Comments
26 and *28 May 1833	Düsseldorf	Israel in Egypt	54	music festival
*22 October 1833	Düsseldorf	Israel in Egypt	54	with tableaux vivants
22 November 1833	Elberfeld	Alexander's Feast	75	Mozart's version, with new text
9 March 1834	Düsseldorf	Messiah	56	presumably Mozart's version
*3 May 1834	Düsseldorf	Israel in Egypt	54	
17 August 1834	Düsseldorf	Dettingen Te Deum	283	Mendelssohn's version
*23 October 1834	Düsseldorf	Samson	57	only part I
*18 December 1834	Düsseldorf	Judas Maccabaeus	63	only part I
12 March 1835	Düsseldorf	Messiah	56	presumably Mozart's version
7 June 1835	Cologne	Solomon	67	organ part by Mendelssohn
*2 July 1835	Düsseldorf	Dettingen Te Deum	283	Mendelssohn's version
1 January 1836	Leipzig	Zadok the Priest	258	Mendelssohn's version
*4 February 1836	Leipzig	Acis and Galatea	49a	Mozart's version, final scene
*17 March 1836	Leipzig	Messiah	56	"Hallelujah"
23 May 1836	Düsseldorf	O praise the Lord	254	music festival, Mendelssohn's version
7 and 17 November 1836	Leipzig	Israel in Egypt	54	organ part by Mendelssohn
2 February 1837	Leipzig	Zadok the Priest	258	presumably 1 January 1836 version
16 November 1837	Leipzig	Messiah	56	Mozart's version, organ part by Mendelssohn
*4 and 14 December 1837	Leipzig	Judas Maccabaeus	63	recitative "Oh let eternal honours" and air "From mighty Kings" (Clara Novello)
*8 January 1838	Leipzig	Jephta	70	accompagnato "Ye sacred priests" and air "Farewell" (Clara Novello)
15 February 1838	Leipzig	Zadok the Priest	258	"historical concert," presumably 1 January 1836 version
3 June 1838	Cologne	Joshua	64	music festival, organ part by Mendelssohn
*15 November 1838	Leipzig	Rodelinda	19	air "Holy, holy, Lord God almighty," adaptation of the air "Dove sei? amato bene" (Mary Shaw)

Table 8.1. (*continued*)

Date	Place	Composition	HWV	Comments
*13 December 1838	Leipzig	*Messiah*	56	air "He was despised" (Mary Shaw)
10 January 1839	Leipzig	*Zadok the Priest*	258	presumably 1 January 1836 version
*10 January 1839	Leipzig	*Samson*	57	recitative "Relieve, Thy Champion" and air "Return, oh God of hosts" (Mary Shaw), pianoforte: Mendelssohn
*24 January 1839	Leipzig	*Messiah*	56	air "He was despised" (Mary Shaw)
19 and *21 May 1839	Düsseldorf	*Messiah*	56	Mozart's version (*"Hallelujah")
*12 December 1839	Leipzig	*Judas Maccabaeus*	63	air (Sophie Schloss)
25 June 1840	Leipzig	*Dettingen Te Deum*	283	organ part by Mendelssohn
1 January 1841	Leipzig	*Zadok the Priest*	258	presumably 1 January 1836 version
*21 January 1841	Leipzig	*Israel in Egypt*	54	"historical concert"
*21 January 1841	Leipzig	*Messiah*	56	Mozart's version, in "historical concert"
25 April 1842	Berlin	*Zadok the Priest*	283	presumably 1 January 1836 version
15 and *17 May 1842	Düsseldorf	*Israel in Egypt*	54	additional wind instruments instead of organ
1 January 1843	Leipzig	*Zadok the Priest*	258	presumably 1 January 1836 version; conductor not named
*26 January 1843	Leipzig	*Israel in Egypt*	54	
*25 December 1843	Berlin	*Messiah*	56	chorus "For unto us a Child is born," organ part by Mendelssohn
*1 January 1844	Berlin	*Messiah*	56	"Hallelujah," organ part by Mendelssohn
*6 March 1844	Berlin	*Theodora*	68	air "Angels, ever bright and fair" (Charlotte Anne Birch), pianoforte: Mendelssohn
*11 March 1844	Berlin	*Rodelinda*	19	air "Holy, holy, Lord God almighty," adaptation of the air "Dove sei? amato bene" (Charlotte Anne Birch), pianoforte: Mendelssohn
31 March 1844	Berlin	*Israel in Egypt*	54	organ part by Mendelssohn
1 June 1846	Aachen	*Alexander's Feast*	75	Mozart's version

* partial performances

fewer than seven oratorios and other large-scale works in their entirety or in part; in contrast, during that time he performed only two Bach cantatas. Based on his extensive experience in Düsseldorf, Mendelssohn presented selected pieces in his later positions at Leipzig and Berlin. During the 1840s his interests shifted, and he performed mostly excerpts of works, accommodating the nineteenth-century programming conventions outside of music festivals. As was the case with Bach's repertoire, Mendelssohn found his favorite pieces among Handel's oratoric works, some of which he performed often (*Israel in Egypt, Messiah, Zadok the Priest*); a few sometimes (*Alexander's Feast, Dettingen Te Deum*); and several only once (*O Praise the Lord, Joshua, Solomon*) or partially (*Samson, Judas Maccabaeus, Acis and Galatea*).

EARLY ARRANGEMENTS—THE FIRST ORGAN PART

Mendelssohn was critical of the type of contemporaneous arrangements used at the Berlin Singakademie[17] under Carl Friedrich Zelter; in 1833 he wrote to William Horsley:

> We had last year Solomon and Joshua performed in public, and to-morrow there is Samson; but I do not know whether I shall go; fancy that they put wind-instruments to it, during or after the rehearsal, whenever the harmony appears to them not rich enough; a thing Mozart did with the utmost delicacy and carefulness after much study, is now done in a thoughtless hurry, Handel is improved by a set of tedious imitations and sentimental dissonances, there are flutes and clarinets which make me shudder. And yet the public cannot be alledged as the reason for it, for they like truly what they call old music, and the room is always crowded when there is something of Handel's to be heard.[18]

Mendelssohn knew these types of arrangements well; as a nineteen-year-old teenager he had written similar arrangements of *Dettingen Te Deum* (HWV 283) and *Acis and Galatea* (HWV 49ᵃ).[19] In 1834 when looking for a fitting work by Handel for Düsseldorf, Mendelssohn remembered the arrangements and wrote to his friend Devrient in Berlin: "Five or six years ago Zelter asked me to instrument the 'Dettingen Te Deum' and the 'Acis and Galatea' of Handel. I did so, gave him the scores, and have heard nothing more of them since; but I know that they are in the library of the Singakademie. Now I wish very much to have them."[20] In the meantime, however, Mendelssohn had become critical of them:

> In the score of "Acis" (which was performed with the announcement, "Newly instrumented by F. M. B.")[21] I have found, amongst many good things, several which I could not now endorse, and want to correct before it can pass into other hands, because I consider this matter of re-instrumenting as requiring the utmost conscientiousness. Now it happens that I recollect having done some

still more arbitrary things in the "Te Deum" than in "Acis," and I must expunge these faults (as I now regard them), as I cannot annul the score.[22]

The *Dettingen Te Deum* was performed in 1834 and 1835 only after extensive revisions. Luckily, almost all orchestral parts are extant.[23] Mendelssohn expanded the orchestra, adding flutes, clarinets, and horns—in some movements even contrabassoon and a third trumpet. The main goals were to vary colors through various timbral combinations and to deal with the exposed trumpet parts, which were extremely difficult for the nineteenth-century performer. Keeping the structure intact, Mendelssohn reorchestrated the high passages in the trumpets, having them mostly covered by the oboes. He thus catered to the taste of his audience for a fuller wind sound. For example, he rescored the bass aria, *Thou are the King of Glory* (originally scored for trumpet and basso continuo), for pairs of flutes, oboes, clarinets, bassoons, two horns, and three trumpets.[24] Also, the eight-measure-long intrada before the chorus "We therefore pray thee" for two trumpets was rewritten for fourteen wind instruments. In later performances Mendelssohn moved away from his earlier arrangements inspired by Mozart. These arrangements appeared in print only after Mendelssohn's death.[25]

During his stay in Rome in 1830 Mendelssohn was given a full score of Handel's *Solomon* (HWV 67) by Fortunato Santini.[26] Mendelssohn wrote to his family about his plan "of arranging Handel's Solomon for future performance, with proper curtailments, etc."[27] Although Mendelssohn commented eight weeks later that he had nearly completed his arrangement of *Solomon*,[28] it took another eighteen months before the project showed tangible results. While he was enthusiastic about the oratorio, Mendelssohn believed that it needed extensive cuts, rescoring, and a new text before it could be presented to the public. In August 1832 Mendelssohn told his friend Klingemann:

> I plan to perform a large work by Handel here this winter, the oratorio *Solomon;* the *Singakademie* must do it and they have already consented, and the music is some of the most beautiful the old man has come up with. As I looked through the score the other day and thought about the performance, I noticed the terrible translation written underneath. . . . [C]ould you translate the text to *Solomon* into German or rewrite it?[29]

The following paragraph from the same letter gives some ideas about Mendelssohn's envisioned changes:

> Numbers 1–6 remain; after number 6 (the chorus in F Major) follows the ensuing recitative; the aria in E [Major] by Solomon is cut, as well as the next aria in A [Major] by the queen. Zadok's recitative right after the duet in B Minor and the aria, also the next recitative and aria by Solomon are cut. In the second part, after the opening chorus, will be that recitative, which introduces the trio

with the two women; the preceding arias and recitatives are cut. Then everything stays in until after the chorus in A [Major]; Zadok's recitative and aria are cut as well as the final chorus of the second part, which will be replaced by the chorus in D [Major] from the third part ("Praise the Lord with Harp and Tongue").[30]

Mendelssohn changed the order of movements, reduced the number of choruses to twelve, and limited the recitatives and arias to only the most important ones. He also had specific ideas about the new text: "There are places where the words must not only be translated but rewritten, as some of them are stupid, including Solomon's and the queen's recitatives in the first part, which are too philistine for my stomach. . . . How am I going to make that work?"[31] Klingemann helped him, fulfilling the task to Mendelssohn's satisfaction, who found his translations to be excellent. In the end, however, Mendelssohn informed his friend that the Singakademie had decided on a different version altogether, rejecting Mendelssohn's ideas.[32]

It was not until 1835 that Mendelssohn came back to *Solomon,* when he directed the performance at the music festival in Cologne.[33] Ironically, Mendelssohn had to start with the 1832 Berlin Singakademie version, since he was using their parts. In a somewhat humorous letter Mendelssohn mocked this version and in doing so explained what seems inappropriate to him:

> [T]he changes are limited to the bass trombone, a few oboes, and horns which Rungenhagen added, and which we now have to "write off again." They want to change Handel, but they don't even know how to do that correctly. . . . To us, who know that a bass trombone and oboes are live animals, it is not fun to see such a crude person, who commits animal cruelty; there are oboes having to play in G sharp Minor in their low register—true horror to the oboe heart, and a terrible bass trombone part! It sounds like an old comb. They want to rescore G. F. Handel, but they would crawl under the table if the big guy was still alive.[34]

The main focus of Mendelssohn's preparations for the Cologne performance was the creation of an organ part, for which he received help in England from the knowledgeable George Smart, who had helped him with *Israel in Egypt* in 1833:

> Yet I must try to ask you a musical question, which nobody can answer as well as you and which is of much interest to me and to the amateurs of this country. You know, all the Oratorios of Handel have been performed without the organ in this country; the want of harmony was made up by wind instruments, additional accompaniments, etc., very badly sometimes. I have now succeeded for the next festival at Cologne, when *Solomon* is to be performed, to have an organ in the Orchestra and hope to see this custom adopted afterwards in all the other performances of Handel in this country. Now I should like to know

how the organist plays it in England, whether there exists a written part for him, or whether he plays only the chords of the thorough-bass, which are marked in the score; I know that the full organ comes in always towards the end of the Choruses which produces a very good effect, but I should like to know whether such places are marked or are entirely left to the choice of the organist, and whether there are any other rules followed by the organ players in the Oratorios. . . . I hope yet to receive some lines from you about this subject. And how do you perform the part of Solomon in your country? It is written for a C alto, but I cannot fancy king Solomon with an alto voice and should wonder if Handel really could.[35]

One of the results of this inquiry was that the part of Solomon was, in fact, sung by an alto. Mendelssohn also created organ part (D-B, Mus. ms. autogr. F. Mendelssohn Bartholdy 28, fols. 261–76). He had worked on it right up until the first performance, incorporating even his first impressions of some of the rehearsals:

> My idea with the organ turned out well, although we had to go *per aspera ad astra;* in the first rehearsal with choir, orchestra, and organ everything sounded terrible and also went very badly, that I assumed the whole festival to be a flop. A few passages had sounded quite good, I added stops there, rewrote half the organ part overnight, added in some more effects I had just learned, and during the next rehearsal things turned around. The whole thing began to sound good, and with a few additions of a 16' stop here and a 4' stop there such an effect was created that by the third rehearsal everybody was enchanted, and I have to say that it is only since then, that I know how to perform Handel's things. Especially the chorus "Draw the Tear" sounded beautiful with principal 8' and Bordun 16' in thick scoring.[36]

The experience gained here taught Mendelssohn to try to always include the organ in his performances. Since organ parts were mostly nonexistent, he either created them himself or had them written out based on his model. The main effect of the organ, which was positioned behind the orchestra for the *Solomon* performance, was created by not having it played continuously. Rather, it was used only at musically fitting passages (mostly when building toward a climax and at the end of movements, also for choruses and parts of arias, but not during recitatives). Mendelssohn based his organ parts somewhat on Handel's figured bass, but deviated when he felt it necessary. An excellent organist himself, Mendelssohn notated his organ parts the way he would have played them, as can be seen in his letters and the preface to *Israel in Egypt.* Because he assumed that improvisation played an important role in Handel's own performances, Mendelssohn generally followed Handel's indications but also felt free to go beyond them. He sometimes ignored and sometimes followed the *tasto solo* indications, had the organ double the bass sometimes but not always, supported the choral parts (especially in fugue expositions), or underscored or changed the character of a certain passage through long-held chords or newly composed counter-melodies. He showed himself always engaged as composer, never following any predictable patterns. Mendelssohn even changed his own organ parts for a different performance setting, when the acoustics of the hall or the sound of the orchestra called for it.[37] This explains why the *Dettingen Te Deum* and *Israel in Egypt* have several different organ parts; but it also makes it extremely difficult to capture Mendelssohn's complex approach to performing Handel. Mendelssohn's critical eye, seen in his constant revisions of his own compositions, can be found also in his arrangements of other composers' works.

We cannot draw generic conclusions about Mendelssohn's arrangements of the *Dettingen Te Deum* or *Israel in Egypt,* since every performance was different. We also must assume that works performed only once, such as *Solomon* or *Joshua,* would have differed in subsequent performances—not in basic approach but in the details. All that is left for posterity are snap-shots, seen in some surviving parts or a marked full score. These documents give us only limited information, leaving many questions about Mendelssohn's performances of Handel's choral works unanswered. Appraisals of Mendelssohn's organ parts have differed, depending on the perspective of the writer and the sources taken into consideration. Contemporaneous writers saw the use of the organ in Handel's oratorios as a positive development; Chrysander became the first critical voice.[38]

ISRAEL IN EGYPT (1833–45)—PERFORMANCES AND EDITION

No other work by Handel received more of Mendelssohn's attention than *Israel in Egypt* (HWV 54). He performed this oratorio the most, and it was the only work by Handel that Mendelssohn published an edition of. Benedict remembered that already in Naples in 1831 Mendelssohn could play choruses from *Israel in Egypt* from memory.[39] At the 1833 Lower Rhine Music Festival in Düsseldorf Mendelssohn performed the oratorio in its entirety in German translation by Carl Breidenstein;[40] Mendelssohn used the Arnold edition with changes based on English text booklets and the autograph score, which he consulted in London shortly before the performance. Six months later Mendelssohn directed from the piano (without orchestra) a partially staged performance with ninety singers, writing in great detail about it in a letter to his family.[41]

Israel in Egypt seems to have been especially fascinating, not only to the audience but also to Mendelssohn, who experimented heavily with it, as every performance showed a distinctly different approach. He wrote different organ parts for it and adapted an organ part for orchestra for the 1842 performance at the Lower Rhine Music Festival in Düsseldorf, when no organ was available.[42] Mendelssohn's edition of *Israel in Egypt* was eventually published in England.[43]

In June 1835 Mendelssohn wrote in his notebook about his plan to publish three oratorios with organ accompaniment.[44] When he negotiated publication details with Simrock a few years later, the composer turned editor fought rigorously—somewhat uncharacteristically—for preserving the original text of the work without cuts or changes in movement order or instrumentation. Essential changes for a modern performance were to be marked as such:

> I had thought, I would for this purpose write organ parts, which need to appear in smaller print or in a different color in the full score with the goal of 1) preserving Handel in its original if wanted, 2) providing my organ part if wanted and an organ is available, and 3) including in an appendix a modern arrangement of the organ part for clarinets, bassoons, and other wind instruments for the event that no organ is available. Such a score could be used for all performance settings of oratorios, and the authentic Handel would be brought to Germany.[45]

This project, however, as well as plans for an edition of *Samson* (HWV 57), *Judas Maccabaeus* (HWV 63), and *Messiah* (HWV 56) with Breitkopf and Härtel in 1839 failed. For his publication of *Samson* Mendelssohn looked at Arnold's edition and stated, "I find it so full of mistakes, so far from accurate in the details that it is impossible to give a new edition without the manuscripts . . . and the other editions of Handel which may exist."[46] He then turned to William Sterndale Bennett with detailed questions about figured bass, tempo indications, and the use of the organ; he also asked Bennett to compare specific passages in Arnold's edition with the original.[47] While *Samson* and the other editions never materialized, Mendelssohn nevertheless gained valuable insights for his 1844 edition of *Israel in Egypt*. The inherent problems in Arnold's edition were evident not only to Mendelssohn, but also to members of the Handel Society, founded in 1843, "for the production of a superior and standard edition of the works of Handel."[48] Despite similar goals, there were differences of opinion regarding the musical text of such an edition, expressed in the correspondence[49] between Mendelssohn and the society's council, represented by George Alexander Macfarren.[50] The Handel Society wanted a performance edition with tempo indications, dynamics, and, in specific cases, even the addition of trombones. Mendelssohn insisted on his ideal of authenticity with few, marked additions. This led to strong disagreements, seen in a letter to Moscheles, who was also involved with this edition, having already been the editor of *L'Allegro, il Pensieroso ed il Moderato* (HWV 55):

I regret the difficulty with the Handel Society, but I cannot alter my views on the subject. On less important points I am ready to give way; as, for instance, in reference to the accidentals,—although there, too, I prefer the old method, on account of the long bars. But I cannot possibly introduce my marks of expression into a score of Handel's, nor my tempi, nor anything else, unless it is to be made perfectly clear what is mine and what Handel's; and as he has put his pianos and fortes and his figured basses where he thought them necessary, I must either omit them or leave the public in doubt as to which is his marking and which mine.[51]

Mendelssohn's insistence paid off, as most of his ideas were realized. In 1845–46 Cramer, Addison and Co. published "THE | WORKS | OF | HANDEL. | LONDON, | Printed for the Members of | The Handel Society. [. . .], Vol. V: ISRAEL in EGYPT, | An Oratorio, | Composed in the Year 1738; | By | George Frederic Handel." The remarks to the user explain,

> The Editor Is alone responsible for the directions of Piano and Forte and other Marks of Expression; for all such Descriptions of the Movements as stand within brackets, (those which are not so placed being the only indications for which the Original Manuscripts furnish authority;) for the suggestion of the Times according to Maelzel's Metronome; and for the Figuring of the Organ Part.
> The Adaption of the Instrumental Parts for the Pianoforte, Intended as an Accompaniment to the Voices, in the absence of the orchestra, is by The Editor; For which also he is alone responsible.

Mendelssohn's organ part and a piano reduction appears underneath the full score,[52] which also includes dynamics and metronome marks. Mendelssohn also wrote a detailed preface,[53] which includes source descriptions, some critical remarks about problematic passages, and explanations about the organ part and the piano reduction:

> I have now only to add a few remarks concerning the Organ Part and Pianoforte Arrangement; for both of which I am responsible. As for the Organ Part, I have written it down in the manner in which I would play it, were I called upon to do so at a performance of this Oratorio. These works ought of course never to be performed without an Organ, as they are done in Germany, where additional wind instruments are introduced to make up for the defect. In England the Organist plays usually ad libitum from the Score, as it seems to have been the custom in Handel's time, whether he played himself, or merely conducted and had an Organist under his control. Now as the task of placing the chords in the fittest manner to bring out all the points to the greatest advantage, in fact of introducing, as it were, a new part to Compositions like Handel's, is of extreme difficulty, I have thought it useful to write down an Organ Part expressly for those who might not prefer to play one of their own. I must leave it to the Organist to choose the stops according to the strength and number of the Chorus Singers, to the nature of the instrument, andc.; but I have indicated six gradations of strength, PP, P, MF, F, FF, and FFF; meaning by

the last the whole power of the full Organ, and by the first one soft stop of eight feet alone. Whenever the word *Bassi* appears in the Organ Part, I want the Organ *not to play at all,* (the notes being written merely to enable the Organist to follow the performance); and where the word *Organo* comes after it, the Organist is to resume playing. There are also two Violoncello parts for the accompaniment of the Recitatives to be found in the Organ Part; I have written them likewise, in order to indicate to the performers (should they not choose to follow their own fancy) the manner in which I would place the chords. The descriptions of movements, metronomes, pianos and fortes, andc., which I would introduce had I to conduct the Oratorio, are to be found in the *Pianoforte Arrangement.* Whoever wishes to adopt them, can easily insert them in the Original Score, and he who prefers any other is not misled so as to mistake my directions for those which Handel wrote himself.

—Felix Mendelssohn-Bartholdy.

London, 4th July, 1844.

In her work for the modern Halle Handel Edition Annette Landgraf was able to discover further details about Mendelssohn's role in the history of performances and editions of Handel's works. For a performance in Düsseldorf in 1833, for example, Mendelssohn included additional movements from English sources, which led to the mingling of sources, since the added movements were recitatives from a pasticcio by Handel's assistant John Christopher Smith Jr., an aria from a later version of *Israel in Egypt* (1756), and a "Hallelujah" from the second version of *Esther* (HWV 50b).[54] Mendelssohn based his edition of *Israel in Egypt* on a printed score of Arnold's edition (ca. 1791), which was based on a London print by William Randall. Mendelssohn compared these printed editions with the autograph (GB-Lbl, R.M.20.h.3.), all of which included only parts 2 ("Exodus") and 3 ("Moses' Song"), but not part 1 ("The Lamentation of the Israelites for the Death of Joseph"). These sources also did not contain trombone parts found in Handel's 1739 performance score (D-Hs, M C/262); thus Mendelssohn did not know about them.[55] This two-part version was commonly used throughout the nineteenth and twentieth centuries. The work therefore began with the recitative from part 2, "Now there arose a new king over Egypt," under the caption "Part the first." Even from the perspective of modern Handel philology these "shortcomings" do not lessen the accomplishments of Mendelssohn, who set new editorial and artistic standards with *Israel in Egypt.*

For the performance at the Garnison Church in Berlin on Palm Sunday in 1844 Mendelssohn had risers installed for 400 performers. He used the performance material of the 1836 Leipzig performance; cellos and basses accompanied the recitatives, and the organ gave customary support in the arias and choruses.[56]

Joshua (1838)

For the Lower Rhine Music Festival in Cologne in 1838 Mendelssohn was able to program both a composition by J. S. Bach and Handel's oratorio *Joshua* (HWV 64).[57] On the title page of his copy of the Arnold edition, "JOSHUA, | A Sacred Oratorio, | In Score; | Composed in the Year 1747." (GB-Ob, Deneke 10/2), Mendelssohn wrote, "Zur Aufführung in Cöln beim | Nieder Rheinischen Musikfest eingerichtet | zu Pfingsten 1838 | FMB" ("adapted for the performance in Cologne at the Lower Rhine Music Festival at Pentecost 1838"). He then crossed out the word *eingerichtet* ("adapted") and wrote *bezeichnet* ("marked"). This correction is interesting and deserves mention, because it reflects a change in Mendelssohn's relationship to Handel's works. The word used earlier, *eingerichtet,* is close in meaning to *Bearbeitung* ("arrangement"), which seemed no longer appropriate to Mendelssohn for his specific role in preparation for performance. His markings are in pencil throughout. Movements were numbered or given titles for easier orientation.[58] The "Introduzione" was omitted and the work began with the first chorus, "Ye sons of Israel," which Mendelssohn titled as "No. 1" and "Anfang." The score contains indications about instrumentation, such as "Org" (organ) and "senza Organo"; on page 14 Mendelssohn added "senza" before the printed abbreviation "Org."

While the organ part is no longer extant, there is a loose folio with wind parts for some movements, which matches indications in the score. A closer look shows that these are not added wind parts—as was the case with the *Dettingen Te Deum.* Rather, they are simplifications of especially tricky passages. Mendelssohn tried these types of changes in Handel's *Zadok the Priest* in 1835 and again in 1838 in J. S. Bach's Orchestral Suite in D major (BWV 1068) for his first historical concert in Leipzig on 15 February, around the same time that Mendelssohn prepared *Joshua* for performance.

Changes were necessary whenever Handelian trumpets were called for. The first passage is found at the beginning of part 2 in the solemn March during the Circumvection of the Ark of the Covenant. Mendelssohn lowered the exposed trumpet 1 part, keeping the thematic material intact for the more flexible horns (see examples 8.1 and 8.2). In the ensuing chorus, "Glory to God," Mendelssohn gave the high passages in the trumpets to the oboes.

Mendelssohn also rescored the trumpet parts for the chorus "Almighty ruler of the skies!" and the final chorus of the second part, "Behold! the list'ning sun the voice obeys." Mendelssohn had specific reasons for these changes before this final chorus and after Joshua's recitative "Brethren, and friends, what joy this scene imparts." At the end of the recitative there is only one measure in the Arnold score of a fanfare with the indication,

EXAMPLE 8.1.   Handel, *Joshua,* "March during the Circumvection of the Arc of the Covenant."

"Flourish of Warlike Instruments andc."[59] Following the next brief recitative, "Thus far our cause is favour'd," was another indication for the repeat of the fanfare. Mendelssohn wrote two short fanfares, seen in examples 8.3 and 8.4. With the indication "attacca no. 45 Chor" Mendelssohn moved straight into the final chorus of part 2. The work was performed without extensive cuts (besides the "Introducione" two arias were omitted) and without the additional instruments to enrich the timbre—as was the case in the *Dettingen Te Deum.* More important than the fact that this was the first time *Joshua* was performed at the Lower Rhine Music Festival is Mendelssohn's growing concept of authenticity in performances of Handel oratorios.

EXAMPLE 8.2.   Mendelssohn's adaption.

EXAMPLE 8.3.   Mendelssohn's "Flourish of Warlike Instruments" A.

EXAMPLE 8.4.   Mendelssohn's "Flourish of Warlike Instruments" B.

ALEXANDER'S FEAST (1846)

Mendelssohn's last performance of a work by Handel took place on 1 June 1846 at the Lower Rhine Music Festival in Aachen. The star of the festival was the Swedish singer Jenny Lind.[60] Helpful information about Mendelssohn's performance approach is found in his letter to the committee, discussing possible repertoire:

> Of the two other oratorios I would prefer *Athalia* [HWV 52]; while *Esther* [HWV 50] contains much beautiful music, it is not as rich as the former. Both need to be diligently edited. I don't mean the instrumentation and type of arrangement customary for Handel's works here in Germany, but rather, first a

good translation, placing the movements strewn about in the appendix and bundled together in the full score in the correct order, and finally, the creation of an organ part. The last point leads to the question if you will be able to have an organ available? There is no need for a large organ, but it needs to be a good and pure one, to be clearly heard within thick musical textures. I have always refused the customary way of replacing the organ with clarinets, bassoons, and trombones in Handel's works, and I will not consent to it—and am even less willing to write them. But if you have a good translation and a satisfactory organ in the orchestra, and if you know a musician who can produce the organ part, I will correspond with him about the order of the pieces.[61]

After the decision had been made to actually perform *Alexander's Feast* (HWV 75), Mendelssohn wrote:

The movement order needs to follow exactly the order in the printed score; I would like no changes. When looking at the enclosed leaf of the text booklet, I noticed once again how terribly jerky and defaced the Ramler translation is in many places, and I remembered, that I asked to have a new translation done, which I had forgotten. I propose therefore to at least print and use the new translation of the recitatives where the Ramler translation has too many obvious problems; the choruses will have to retain the old text because of the high number of copies, and the arias might cause problems, which are not present in the recitatives, since you (if you agree with my plan) will only have to have single sheets written for the soloists and their recitatives.[62]

Mendelssohn mailed the translation and two (now lost) recitatives, which were to be accompanied by two cellos and a bass. About the setup of orchestra and chorus Mendelssohn told the committee to use the proven "wedge" stage setup. The large chorus was positioned on risers with steps on the left and the right; in the middle was a wedge like a triangle with the smaller end closest to the conductor.[63] A newspaper drawing about a comparable event illustrates this arrangement in detail (see figure 8.1).[64] Klaus Wolfgang Niemöller explains the history and reasons for this setup:

The sound ideal of performances of Handel oratorios presented to the audiences of the Lower Rhine Music Festivals of the nineteenth century, was not just achieved through additional instrumentation, but also depended on the ratio between chorus and orchestra—and beyond that the placement of the soloists. For the conductor the positioning of hundreds of performers was an important aspect of the performance. . . . At first it was customary since the music festival in Aachen in 1825, at which Ferdinand Ries performed the Mozart arrangement of *Alexander's Feast,* to place the orchestra in two parts with the best professional musicians as the smaller group and a larger "ripieno" group, which worked effectively within the framework of piano and forte, for the latter of which the back of the group entered. Related to this division of the orchestra was the "wedge" set up, in which the orchestra was pulled forward to the conductor like a wedge between the chorus, which guaranteed immediate contact to the soloists. This wedge-form orchestra set up, which was

FIGURE 8.1.   "Wedge" stage setup. "Das niederrheinische Musikfest in Aachen," *Illustrirte Zeitung* 7, no. 161.

also preferred by Friedrich Schneider as conductor of oratorios at music festivals, was established by Mendelssohn at the Lower Rhine Music Festival as the customary stage design for years to come.[65]

For the 1846 performance of *Alexander's Feast* Mendelssohn tried to bring together all elements of a good performance: an adequate translation, secco recitatives accompanied by low strings, and a stage design based on the acoustical needs. Mendelssohn was always willing to compromise when necessary; he was not able to have an organ for the performance and used Mozart's arrangement instead. In the end he was a practical-minded musician who was willing and able to react to specific circumstances of each performance.

NOTES

1. See also Ralf Wehner, "'. . . ich sehe sie nun zugleich alle durch und lerne sie kennen . . . ;' Felix Mendelssohn Bartholdy und die wirklich alte Musik," *Basler Jahrbuch für historische Musikpraxis* 21 (1997): 101–27.

2. The best overview of Mendelssohn's approach to earlier music is found in Susanna Großmann-Vendrey, *Felix Mendelssohn Bartholdy und die Musik der Vergangenheit,* Studien zur Musikgeschichte des 19. Jahrhunderts, no. 17 (Regensburg: Bosse, 1969).

3. Included in the Händel-Werkverzeichnis (HWV) is Bernd Baselt, *Verzeichnis der Werke Georg Friedrich Händels,* brief edition (Leipzig: Deutscher Verlag für Musik, 1984); for a detailed discussion of works mentioned in this chapter see Bernd Baselt, *Händel-Handbuch,* vol. 2, *Thematisch-systematisches Verzeichnis: Oratorische Werke, Vokale Kammermusik, Kirchenmusik* (Leipzig: Deutscher Verlag für Musik/Kassel: Bärenreiter, 1984).

4. Wilgard Lange, "Händel-Rezeption bei Felix Mendelssohn Bartholdy" (diss. University of Halle, 1980); Annette Landgraf, "Ein 'leibhaftiger Enkel Händelschen Stammes:' Felix Mendelssohn Bartholdys Musikschaffen unter dem Einfluß seiner Auseinandersetzung mit den oratorischen Werken Händels," *Händel-Jahrbuch* 44 (1998): 76–88.

5. Only a few, preliminary overviews have been written on this topic; see Wilhelm Altmann, "Mendelssohns Eintreten für Händel," *Die Musik* 12, no. 8 (1912–13): 79–85; Hellmuth Christian Wolff, "Mendelssohn and Handel," *Musical Quarterly* 45, no. 2 (April 1959): 175–90; Großmann-Vendrey, *Felix Mendelssohn Bartholdy und die Musik der Vergangenheit;* as well as Wilgard Lange, "Mendelssohns Händel-Bearbeitungen," in *Georg Friedrich Händel im Verständnis des 19. Jahrhunderts, Bericht über die wissenschaftliche Konferenz zu den 32. Händelfestspielen der DDR am 13. und 14. Juni 1983 in Halle (Saale),* ed. Walther Siegmund-Schultze, Wissenschaftliche Beiträge 1984, no. 38 (Halle, Saale: Martin-Luther-Universität Halle-Wittenberg, 1984), 70–77. While further research published on specific works exists, a more exhaustive study remains to be done.

6. See William Charles Smith, *Handel: A Descriptive Catalogue of the Early Editions* (London: Cassell, 1960; 2nd ed., Oxford: Blackwell, 1970); for Samuel Arnold's Complete Edition (1787–97), see Jacob Maurice Coopersmith, "The First Gesamtausgabe: Dr. Arnold's Editions of Handel's Works," *Notes* 4 (1947): 277–92, 439–49. As a thank-you gift for his directorship of the music festival in Cologne, Mendelssohn received this bound edition in 32 volumes in 1835, extant as GB-Ob, Deneke 1–32; for German edition see Bernd Baselt, "Early German Handel Editions during the Classical Period," in *Handel Collections and their History,* ed. Terence Best (Oxford: Clarendon Press, 1993), 238–48; relevant for Mendelssohn was the 1820s, four-volume edition of Handel's *Chandos-Anthems* by J. O. H. Schaum, see Siegfried Flesch, "Die Händel-Ausgabe von J. O. H. Schaum," *Händel-Jahrbuch* 39 (1993): 105–12.

7. The Lower Rhine Music Festival played a pivotal role; see Julius Alf, *Geschichte und Bedeutung der Niederrheinischen Musikfeste in der ersten Hälfte des neunzehnten Jahrhunderts,* eds. Gerd Högener and Fritz Kulins (Düsseldorf: Droste, 1987); and Klaus Wolfgang Niemöller, "Die Händel-Pflege auf den Niederrheinischen Musikfesten," *Händel-Jahrbuch* 44 (1998): 89–99.

8. A conference in 1992 in Halle (Saale) ("Händel-Bearbeitungen des 18. und 19. Jahrhunderts. Bearbeitungsprinzipien, aufführungspraktische Einrichtung, quellenmäßige Überlieferung") dealt with these issues; see *Händel-Jahrbuch* 39 (1993): 13–194.

9. Letter from 25 March 1833 by Carl Breidenstein to Otto von Woringen; quoted in Großmann-Vendrey, 70: "er hat eine vollständige Kenntnis von Händels Werken und ist mit dessen Geiste vertraut." For an overview see the chapter "Vokalwerke Händels, die Mendelssohn gekannt hat" in Felix Loy, *Die Bach-Rezeption in den Oratorien von Mendelssohn Bartholdy,* Tübinger Beiträge zur Musikwissenschaft (Tutzing: Schneider, 2003), 168–79.

10. During his visits to London in 1829, 1833, and 1844; some of the relevant documents—based on Großmann-Vendrey—are quoted in Rainer Heyink, "Original oder Bearbeitung? Felix Mendelssohn Bartholdy und seine Annäherung an die 'Werktreue' bei Händel," *Göttinger Händel-Beiträge* 6 (1996): 254–68, especially 257–59; see also Thomas Schmidt-Beste, " 'Alles von ihm gelernt?' Die Briefe von Carl Friedrich

Zelter an Felix Mendelssohn Bartholdy," *Mendelssohn-Studien* 10 (1997): 25–56, especially 46–53.

11. The best known example is *Dixit dominus* (HWV 232); Mendelssohn had copied the work in 1829 in London during his illness, at that time he labeled the work as "one of the most energetic and sublime of the great composer"; see letter of 7 November 1829 to George Frederick Anderson; quoted in Großmann-Vendrey, 39. In January 1837 Mendelssohn gave the autograph to the Viennese collector Aloys Fuchs (A-Wn, Mus. Hs. 16.536); Mendelssohn ordered a copyist to make a duplicate (GB-Ob, MS. M. Deneke Mendelssohn c. 75).

12. For these editions before 1833 see Peter Ward Jones and Rudolf Elvers, "Das Musikalienverzeichnis von Fanny und Felix Mendelssohn Bartholdy," *Mendelssohn-Studien* 8 (1993): 85–103; for the available sources eleven years later see Mendelssohn's own list, "Musikalien (1844)," GB-Ob, MS. M. Deneke Mendelssohn c. 49, fol. 29–30; see *Catalogue of the Mendelssohn Papers in the Bodleian Library, Oxford,* vol. 3, compiled by Peter Ward Jones, Musikbibliographische Arbeiten, vol. 9 (Tutzing: Schneider, 1989), 285–99; see also R. Larry Todd, "Mozart according to Mendelssohn: a Contribution to Rezeptionsgeschichte," in *Perspectives on Mozart Performance,* Cambridge Studies in Performance Practice, ed. R. Larry Todd and Peter Williams (Cambridge: Cambridge University Press, 1991), 158–203; facsimile of fol. 29r with the Handel entries on page 186.

13. The complete organ parts by Mendelssohn for *Messiah* and *Joshua* are considered lost. The periodic mention of an organ part for *Jephta* (for Cologne 1842 performance) is based on erroneous information in Glenn Stanley, "Mozarts 'Messias' und Mendelssohns 'Israel in Ägypten'—Zur Frühgeschichte der Aufführungspraxis historischer Musik," in *Kongreßbericht zum VII. Internationalen Gewandhaus-Symposium: Wolfgang Amadeus Mozart—Forschung und Praxis im Dienst von Leben, Werk, Interpretation und Rezeption anläßlich der Gewandhaus-Festtage in Leipzig vom 3. bis 6. Oktober 1991,* Dokumente zur Gewandhausgeschichte (Leipzig: Peters, 1993), 94–100.

14. The majority of these sources are located in GB-Ob, see *Catalogue of the Mendelssohn Papers in the Bodleian Library, Oxford,* vol. 2, compiled by Margaret Crum, Musikbibliographische Arbeiten, vol. 8 (Tutzing: Schneider, 1983), 41–43.

15. In connection with the performance of the final chorus from *Zadok the Priest* on the last day of the Birmingham Music Festival (28 August 1846) Mendelssohn composed a recitative in the style of Handel, sung by the tenor Charles Lockey; see Frederic George Edwards, *The History of Mendelssohn's Oratorio "Elijah"* (London: Novello, Ewer, 1896), 93–95; a facsimile of this recitative is reproduced as special supplement in *The Musical Times* 43, no. 707 (1 January 1902).

16. Instrumental works are not of importance in this context, as Mendelssohn only occasionally incorporated Handel's themes in his improvisations on the piano. An exception is the public performance of the "Variations on The Harmonious Blacksmith" from the Suite No. 5 in E major (HWV 430) within the context of the historical concert on 21 January 1841. Handel's operas can also be completely excluded from this study.

17. Werner Bollert, "Die Händelpflege der Berliner Sing-Akademie unter Zelter und Rungenhagen," in *Sing-Akademie zu Berlin. Festschrift zum 175jährigen Bestehen,* ed. W. Bollert (Berlin: Rembrandt, 1966), 69–79.

18. Letter from 16 January 1833 to William Horsley; Karl Mendelssohn-Bartholdy, *Goethe and Mendelssohn (1821–1831),* 2nd ed., trans. M. E. von Glehn (London: Macmillan, 1874), 102.

19. An early analysis of this work is found in Nicholas Kilburn, "Additional Accompaniments to Handel's 'Acis,'" *Sammelbände der Internationalen Musikgesellschaft* 3 (1901–1902; reprint, Hildesheim: Olms, 1970), 129–38 (page citations are to the reprint edition).

20. Letter from 30 September 1833; Eduard Devrient, *My Recollections of Felix Mendelssohn-Bartholdy and his Letters to Me,* trans. Natalia Macfarren (London: Bentley, 1869), 161.

21. The only documented performance of Mendelssohn's arrangement of the *Dettingen Te Deum* took place on 13 January 1831 in Berlin under Zelter; see Schmidt-Beste, 56; Mendelssohn was in Rome at that time.

22. Letter from 9 June 1834; Devrient, 163.

23. Klaus Wolfgang Niemöller, "Die Händelüberlieferung im historischen Notenarchiv des Musikvereins Düsseldorf. Zur Händelpflege des 19. Jahrhunderts im Umkreis von Mendelssohn und Schumann," in *Georg Friedrich Händel—Ein Lebensinhalt. Gedenkschrift für Bernd Baselt (1934–1993)*, ed. Klaus Hortschansky and Konstanze Musketa, Schriften des Händel-Hauses (Halle, Saale: Händelhaus, 1995), 207–25, especially 217–24; for a catalog, see Susanne Cramer, *Die Musikalien des Düsseldorfer Musikvereins 1801–1929: Katalog* (Stuttgart: Metzler, 1996), 142–67.

24. See musical examples in Hellmuth Christian Wolff, "Mendelssohn and Handel."

25. Georg Friedrich Händel, *Te Deum, zur Feier des Sieges bei Dettingen*, instrumentation by Felix Mendelssohn (Leipzig: Kistner, [1869]).

26. For Santini's interest in and collection of Handel's works, see Karl Gustav Fellerer, "Fortunato Santini als Sammler und Bearbeiter Händelscher Werke," *Händel-Jahrbuch* 2 (1929; reprint, New York: Johnson Reprint Corp., 1968), 25–40; and Rudolf Ewerhart, "Die Händel-Handschriften der Santini-Bibliothek in Münster," *Händel-Jahrbuch* 6 (1960): 111–50.

27. Felix Mendelssohn, *Letters from Italy and Switzerland*, ed. Paul Mendelssohn Bartholdy and Carl Mendelssohn Bartholdy, trans. Lady Wallace (Boston: O. Ditson, 1862; reprint, Freeport, N.Y.: Books for Libraries Press, 1970), 23 November 1830, 65 (page citations are to the reprint edition).

28. Ibid., 17 January 1831, 97.

29. Letter from 15 August 1832 to Carl Klingemann, *Felix Mendelssohn Bartholdys Briefwechsel mit Legationsrat Karl Klingemann in London*, ed. Carl Klingemann (Essen: Baedecker, 1909), 98–100: "Ich habe nämlich vor, gegen den Winter hin einen grossen Händel hier aufzuführen, das Oratorium Salomon; die Singakademie soll wieder dran und hat es schon zugesagt, und die Musik ist wohl eine der schönsten, die dem alten Herrn eingefallen sind. Als ich nun aber neulich mir die Partitur durchsah und mir alles zur Aufführung überlegte, fiel mir auf einmal die entsetzlich schlechte Manuskript-Übersetzung auf, die darunter stand. . . . willst Du mir den Text zum Salomon ins Deutsche übersetzen oder bearbeiten?" [all translations by Siegwart Reichwald].

30. Ibid.: "Die Nummern 1–6 bleiben alle; nach Nummer 6 (dem Chor aus f-dur) kommt das folgende Rezitativ; die Arie aus E von Salomon bleibt weg, ebenso die folgende Arie aus A b/d von der Königin. Zadoks Rezitativ nach dem Duett in h-moll samt seiner Arie, ebenso Rezitativ und Arie von Salomon, die darauf folgen, bleiben weg. Im zweiten Teil kommt gleich nach dem Anfangschor das Rezitativ, welches das Terzett mit den beiden Frauen einleitet, die vorhergehenden Arien und Rezitative bleiben weg. Dann bleibt alles bis nach dem Chor aus a; Zadoks Rezitativ und Arie bleibt weg und ebenso der Schlusschor des zweiten Teiles, an dessen Stelle ich den Chor aus d aus dem III. Teil (praise the lord with harp and tongue) setzen will."

31. Ibid.: "Noch müsste der Text an einigen Stellen nicht übersetzt, sondern geradezu geändert sein, weil er an manchen Stellen gar zu dumm ist; dahin gehören besonders die Rezitative Salomons und der Königin im ersten Teil, die zu philiströs für meinen Magen sind. . . . Da hilf Dir nun raus."

32. See letter from 5 December 1832 to Carl Klingemann, ibid., 102–103.

33. See Klaus Wolfgang Niemöller, "Felix Mendelssohn-Bartholdy und das Niederrheinische Musikfest 1835 in Köln," in *Studien zur Musikgeschichte des Rheinlandes*, Beiträge zur rheinischen Musikgeschichte (Cologne: Volk, 1965), 46–64.

34. Letter from 31 March 1835 to his family, Großmann-Vendrey, 77; Carl Friedrich Rungenhagen was Zelter's successor: "Die Veränderungen beschränken sich auf eine Baßposaune, ein paar Hoboen und Hörner die Rungenhagen dazu geschrieben hat,

und die wir nun wieder davon schreiben müssen. So haben sie wohl die Lust Händel abzuändern, aber nicht einmal das können sie ordentlich. . . . Aber für uns, die wir wissen, daß eine Baßposaune oder eine Hoboe lebendige Thiere sind, ist es gar keine Wonne, solch einen Rüpel zu sehen, der mit ihnen Thierquälerei treibt; es sind da Hoboen in Gis moll in der Tiefe zum Ausfüllen zugefügt, von denen jedes Hoboenherz schaudern muß und eine armselige Baßposaune! Die klingt wie ein alter Kamm; denn wollen sie G. F. Händel instrumentieren und würden vor Angst unter den Tisch kriechen wenn der dicke Herr noch lebte."

35. Letter from 27 March 1835 to George Smart, H. Bertram Cox, and C. L. E. Cox, *Leaves from the Journals of Sir George Smart* (London: Longmans, 1907; reprint, New York: Da Capo Press, 1971), 289–90 (page citations are from the reprint edition); the year of the letter is erroneously given as 1838.

36. Letter from 26 June 1835 to Carl Klingemann, *Felix Mendelssohn Bartholdys Briefwechsel mit Legationsrat Karl Klingemann in London,* 182–83: "Mein Einfall mit der Orgel war der allerglücklichste, obwohl wir erst per aspera ad astra mussten; denn in der ersten Probe mit Chor, Orchester und Orgel klang und ging alles so entsetzlich schlecht, dass ich die ganze Idee und somit das ganze Fest für verrechnet ansah. Ein paar Stellen hatten gut geklungen; auf die fusste ich noch, schrieb die halbe Orgelstimme in der Nacht danach um, brachte die Effekte hinein, die ich erst hatte kennen lernen, und bei der nächsten Probe bekam ich Oberwasser. Das Ding fing an zu klingen, mit ein paar Zusätzen von 16 Fuss hier, 4 Fuss dort bekam es auf einmal solche Wirkung, dass in der dritten Probe alles entzückt war, und ich muss sagen, dass ich seitdem erst weiss, wie man Haendelsche Sachen aufführen soll. Namentlich der Chor 'draw the tear' klang mit Prinzipal 8 F. und Bordun 16 F. in dicken Akkordlagen wunderschön."

37. About the organ part for *Israel in Egypt* Mendelssohn wrote: "You will notice the massive amount of changes everywhere, which were continuously added with each new performance; but that's how it has to be: regional, size of the choir, the orchestra, etc. make for constantly new constelations" ("Sie werden die Masse Veränderungen hin und her bemerken, die bei jeder neuen Aufführung hineingemacht wurden; aber so muß es auch sein: Local, Stärke des Chors, des Orchesters etc. bedingen immer wieder eine andre Anordnung"). Letter from 3 April 1844 to Jacob Bel; Reinhold Sietz, "Heinrich Dorn in Köln," *Jahrbuch des Kölnischen Geschichtsvereins* 29–30 (1954–55): 301.

38. For a detailed discussion with musical examples, see Friedrich Chrysander, "Mendelssohn's Orgelbegleitung zu Israel in Aegypten," in *Jahrbücher für Musikalische Wissenschaft,* vol. 2, ed. Friedrich Chrysander (Leipzig: Breitkopf and Härtel, 1867; reprint Hildesheim: Olms, 1966), 249–67 (page citations from reprint edition); Karl Gustav Fellerer, "Mendelssohns Orgelstimmen zu Händelschen Werken," *Händel-Jahrbuch* 4 (1931; reprint, New York: Johnson Reprint Corp., 1968), 79–97 (page citations from reprint editions); Hellmut Federhofer, "Zur Generalbaßpraxis im 19. Jahrhundert," *Musik und Kirche* 60, no. 1 (1990): 1–10, and "Zu Felix Mendelssohns Händel-Interpretation im Urteil der Mit- und Nachwelt," *Musicologica austriaca* 8 (1988): 27–39.

39. Jules Benedict, *Sketch of the Life and Works of the Late Felix Mendelssohn* (London: Murray, 1850), 18: "[H]e performed from memory some of the finest choruses of Handel's 'Israel in Egypt,' the 'Messiah,' and some of his 'suite de pièces' for the 'clavecin.'" The Berlin Singakademie had rehearsed *Israel in Egypt;* they also gave it its German premiere on 8 December 1831 (Mendelssohn was not present).

40. Breidenstein had not only translated the text; in 1826 Simrock published his piano vocal score and choir parts. Mendelssohn also used the parts in later performances.

41. Letter from 26 October 1833 to his sister Rebecka Dirichlet, *Letters of Felix Mendelssohn Bartholdy from 1833 to 1847,* 8–14.

42. Mendelssohn's score of single movements for flutes, clarinets, bassoon, horns, trombones, cello, and bass with the title "Orgelstimme zu Händel's Israel in Aegypen für

Instrumente, zum Düsseldorfer Musikfest 1842" is part of D-B, MA Ms. 8; see Hans-Günter Klein, *Felix Mendelssohn Bartholdy, Autographe und Abschriften: Katalog,* Staatsbibliothek zu Berlin—Preußischer Kulturbesitz, Kataloge der Musikabteilung, 1. Reihe, Bd. 5 (München: Henle, 2003), 121.

43. For more detailed information see Großmann-Vendrey, 192–96; and R. Sterndale Bennett, "Mendelssohn as Editor of Handel," *Monthly Musical Record* 86 (1956): 83–94.

44. GB-Ob, MS. M. Deneke Mendelssohn g. 6, entry from 5 June 1835 into diary; quoted in Großmann-Vendrey, 192.

45. Letter from 10 July 1838 to Simrock, *Felix Mendelssohn Bartholdy; Briefe an deutsche Verleger,* ed. Rudolf Elvers (Berlin: de Gruyter, 1968), 219: "Ich hatte mir gedacht, ich würde dann zu dem Zwecke die Orgelstimme machen die müßte aber mit kleinen Noten oder mit Noten von einer anderen Farbe in der Partitur stehen, sodaß man 1) den ganzen puren Händel hätte, wenn man wollte, 2) meine Orgelstimme dabei, wenn man wollte und eine Orgel hätte, und 3) in einem *Anhang* etwa die Orgelstimme für Clarinetten, Fagotten und andre Blasinstrumente des jetzigen Orchesters arrangirt, in Ermangelung der Orgel. Dann wäre eine solche Partitur bei allen Instituten für Oratorienmusik zu brauchen, und man hätte doch endlich den wahren Händel in Deutschland."

46. Letter from 3 April 1839 to W. Sterndale Bennett; Karl Mendelssohn-Bartholdy, 153.

47. See Bennett, 83–94.

48. Stated at the front of each volume; the society already ceased to exist in 1848 for lack of subscriptions, having published 16 volumes, the last of which would appear in 1858.

49. Seven Mendelssohn letters were printed in Karl Mendelssohn-Bartholdy, 169–85. Mention of the Macfarren's response letters in Großmann-Vendrey, 194–95.

50. Members of the council of this society were William Sterndale Bennett, William Crotch, Charles Lucas, Edward Francis Rimbault, Ignaz Moscheles, Thomas Molleson Mudie, Sir George Smart, and Henry Thomas Smart; they all, like Macfarren, produced their own editions as well.

51. Letter from 7 March 1845 to Ignaz Moscheles; *Letters of Felix Mendelssohn to Ignaz and Charlotte Moscheles,* trans. and ed. Felix Moscheles (London: Trübner, 1888), 251–52.

52. This piano vocal score is an adaption of the printed piano vocal score by Carl Breidenstein (see note 40), which was pointed out in Chrysander, 251. Mendelssohn had ordered Breidenstein's score on 27 May 1844 from Simrock, which was quickly sent to him in London.

53. The most important passages of this four-page-long preface are quoted in Clive Brown, *A Portrait of Mendelssohn* (New Haven: Yale University Press, 2003), 41–44.

54. See *Israel in Egypt: Oratorio in Three Parts,* HWV 54, Hallische Händel-Ausgabe, Serie I, Bd. 14, Teilband 1: Part I–III, ed. Annette Landgraf (Kassel: Bärenreiter, 1999), xxvi.

55. Mendelssohn did not want to follow the wishes of the council to write trombone parts: "I will not write Trombone parts," letter from 28 December 1845 to Macfarren; Karl Mendelssohn-Bartholdy, 182–85.

56. For letters and discussion, see Großmann-Vendrey, 176–78.

57. For more about the preparations, see Großmann-Vendrey, 89–100.

58. Mendelssohn followed the movement numbering of the piano vocal score by Johann Heinrich Clasing (Hamburg: A. Cranz, [1823(?)]).

59. Handel's note in the full score about the use of the "Warlike Symphonie," which is based on a movement from the first version of the opera *Riccardo I* (HWV 23), was part of all early editions of *Joshua* and caused problems in performances. Mendelssohn did not follow Clasing's four-measure-long version.

60. For the context of the music festival, see Reinhold Sietz, "Die Niederrheinischen Musikfeste in Aachen in der ersten Hälfte des 19. Jahrhunderts," *Zeitschrift des Aachener Geschichtsvereins* 72 (1960): 109–64.

61. Letter from 17 January 1846 to the committee; quoted in Großmann-Vendrey, 113–14: "Von den beiden anderen [Oratorien] würde ich Athalia vorziehen, obwohl Esther auch viele große Schönheiten enthält, doch scheint sie mir nicht so reich wie die erstere. Beide aber bedürfen erst einer sorgfältigen Bearbeitung. Ich verstehe hierunter nicht Instrumentierung und Arrangement, wie sie bei den meisten Händelschen Werken in Deutschland gebräuchlich sind, sondern zunächst eine gute Übersetzung, eine richtige Anordnung der einzelnen theils im Appendix zerstreuten, theils in der Partitur gehäuften und nicht nacheinander zu singenden Stücke, endlich Ausarbeitung der Orgelstimme. Dies letztere führt wieder auf die Frage, ob Sie eine Orgel in Ihrem Locale werden haben können? Es bedarf gar keiner sehr großen, indeß einer guten, reinen und durch die großen Musikfestmassen deutlich hörbaren. Gegen die gewöhnliche Art, dieselbe durch Clarinetten und Fagotten und Posaunen in den Händelschen Werken zu ersetzen, habe ich mich stets gewehrt und würde mich mit einer Bearbeitung in diesem Sinne nicht einverstanden erklären, viel weniger sie selbst übernehmen können. Haben Sie aber eine gute Übersetzung, können Sie eine genügende Orgel im Orchester haben und wissen Sie einen dortigen Musiker, der die Ausarbeitung der Orgelstimme übernähme, so würde ich mich mit ihm über die Anordnung der Stücke verständigen."

62. Letter from 3 April 1846 to the committee; quoted in Großmann-Vendrey, 116: "Die Anordnung der Stücke im Alexanderfeste bitte ich genau nach der Reihenfolge zu machen wie in der gedruckten Partitur, ich wünsche keine Änderung darin. Auf dem eingelegten Blatte des Textbuches ist mir aber wieder aufgefallen, wie entsetzlich holprig, ja entstellend die Ramlersche Übersetzung an vielen Stellen ist und ich erinnerte mich, daß ich vor einigen Jahren eine andere Übersetzung machen ließ, die ich seitdem wieder ganz vergessen hatte. Ich schlage Ihnen deshalb vor wenigstens die Recitative in denen bei Ramler zuweilen offenbare Widersinnlichkeiten stehen nach dieser neueren Übersetzung drucken und singen zu lassen; die Chöre müssen wohl der vielen Exemplare wegen den alten Text behalten und auch in den Arien möchten Schwierigkeiten dadurch entstehen, die in den Recitativen wegfielen, weil Sie (im Falle Sie meiner Meinung beitreten) nur einzelne Blätter für die Solosänger mit deren Rec. schreiben zu lassen brauchten.

63. A letter in connection with the performance of *Paulus* at the 1840 Schwerin music festival was published in Hans Erdmann and Hans Rentzow, "Mendelssohns Oratorien-Praxis: Ein bisher unbekannter Brief des Meisters vom Jahre 1840," in *Musica* 6 (1952), 352–55. This article also contains Mendelssohn's own drawings of the stage setup, which is similar to Aachen's.

64. Dr. Brühl, "Das niederrheinische Musikfest in Aachen" *Illustrirte Zeitung* 7, no. 161 (1 August 1846): 67–69.

65. Klaus Wolfgang Niemöller, "Die Händel-Pflege auf den Niederrheinischen Musikfesten," 97–98: "Die Klanggestalt, in der die Händel-Oratorien dem Publikum der Niederrheinischen Musikfestes des 19. Jahrhunderts dargeboten wurde, ist jedoch nicht nur durch die ergänzenden Instrumentierungen bestimmt, sondern in ihrer Wirkung auch abhängig vom Verhältnis zwischen Chor- und Orchesterklang, darüber hinaus durch die Position der Solisten. Die Aufstellung von Hunderten von Mitwirkenden war für alle Dirigenten ein wesentlicher Aspekt der Aufführung. . . . Zunächst hatte man daher seit dem Aachener Musikfest 1825, auf dem Ferdinand Ries das *Alexanderfest* in der Mozart-Instrumentierung aufführte, das Orchester zweigeteilt in ein kleineres mit den besten Berufsmusikern und ein größeres mit den "Ripienisten," was sich "in betreff ihrer Wirksamkeit, namentlich hinsichtlich des Piano und Forte, bei welchem letzteren nur die hintere Masse eingriff, sehr vorzüglich" zeigte. Verbunden

war diese Orchesteraufteilung mit einer keilförmigen Gesamtaufstellung, bei der die kleine Orchestergruppe keilförmig zwischen dem Chor bis nach vorn zu dem Dirigenten vorgezogen war und so den unmittelbaren Kontakt mit den dort aufgestellten Gesangssolisten hatte. Diese keilförmige Orchesteraufstellung, die auch Friedrich Schneider als Musikfestdirigent für Oratorienaufführungen bevorzugte, wurde auf den Niederrheinischen Musikfesten durch Mendelssohn für lange Zeit zur verbindlichen Form."

9

From Notation to Edition to Performance:
Issues in Interpretation

JOHN MICHAEL COOPER

This essay is addressed to two principal readerships: performers who work from printed editions of Mendelssohn's music and prospective editors of that music. It centers around two highly subjective aspects of musical interpretation: notation (manuscript and printed) and performance. It views musical notation as a flexible system of conventionalized symbols that, individually and collectively, are always subjective and usually context-sensitive within a given work. Proceeding from this view, it treats the basic acts of reading, studying, and learning notated music as acts of realizing the pitches, timbres, durations, and larger structures it symbolizes. Finally, it stipulates that conventions of notation and performance alike have historically differed from one place to another and that both have changed considerably over time: the greater the geographic or historical distance between a performer and the origination of the notation used as the basis of interpretation, the greater the challenges in realizing that notation so that the resulting sound resembles what the composer originally envisioned.

In brief, notation mediates between composers and performers, and performers use notation to mediate between composers and audiences. Because these interrelationships are both subjective and liable to change over time, any study concerning relationships between notation and performance is likewise inherently subjective. Empirically verifiable consistency has little place here; hard-and-fast proof, even less. For that reason, these remarks are best treated not as rules, guidelines, or principles, but as suggestions, reflections, or simply food for thought.

The crux of this intermedial complex—that is, of the intersection between notation and interpretation—is that musical notation (like virtually any written information) possesses great connotative as well as denotative power. Consequently, musical performance is an unquantifiable mixture of responses to notation's objective subjects (such as pitch and duration) and its less tangible, suggestive ones (phrasing, relative dynamics and tempos, and so on). A few basic assumptions about how performers and composers approach musical notation bear this out:[1]

1. Sensitive performers respond intuitively and substantively to subtleties of notation—aspects that almost inevitably invite interpretive license even though they do not explicitly affect the durational, timbral, or tonal essentials of the work. A performer will probably interpret the figures and differently, even when the part provides no objective criterion for pacing the crescendo and decrescendo and even less of one for determining the length of the dynamic peak (the space between the ends of the hairpins).

2. Sensitive performers responded intuitively to their instruments. Accordingly, in performance we are likely to change the technique we employ to realize a given passage as we execute it on different instruments; indeed, in all likelihood the differences in technique correlate neatly with the differences in the instrument. A pianist will probably adapt his or her technique to achieve a comparable interpretation on a Steinway, a Bösendorfer, or a Baldwin (to say nothing of a Stein, a Graf, or an Erard).

3. Composers, too, respond intuitively to the instruments that they have at their disposal.

   a. When these instruments are employed in composing a piece (as for example when a composer writes out a work at the piano), the music naturally reflects the qualities peculiar to that instrument, making the most of the instrument's strong points, shying away from its limitations, and (presumably) avoiding its impossibilities altogether.

   b. When the instruments at a composer's disposal are not directly employed in composing a piece (as in the case of stage works and orchestral or orchestral/choral compositions, which almost inevitably are either composed at the keyboard or notated as a kind of translation of the events and sounds in the composer's aural imagination), the notated music tends to reflect his/her assumptions about how performers will respond to the notation in reading it.

4. For composers, the primary realization of the aural imagination is notation. Accordingly, in advanced notational stages (fair copies, performance materials, and the like, rather than sketches and drafts)[2]

composers tend to notate the music with an eye to how they imagine others will interpret it. This notation naturally reflects not only "essential" musical components (pitch and basic durational parameters) but also nuances that will aid performers in realizing the work sensitively (i.e., in sensitively conveying it to listeners).

If this were all there were to it, the challenges of moving from notation to performance would be fairly straightforward. Sensitive performers and composers could converse musically and intelligibly because of their shared familiarity with conventions of notation and their awareness of the implications of the scriptorial nuances that enrich the basic durational, timbral, and tonal information conveyed by musical notation. But very few latter-day musicians actually work from manuscript notation in performing nineteenth-century repertoires. Instead, as a practical matter we work from printed editions of the music—and this is where the real complications arise. For even in the nineteenth century, when copyright law and publication conventions facilitated or encouraged flexible and context-sensitive renderings of musical texts,[3] the technical and technological obstacles entailed in printing music impeded conveyance of the intuitive and finely calibrated subtleties characteristic of manuscript notation. Consequently, dissemination in print inevitably obscured or (in some instances) obliterated the notational nuances that facilitated performers' sensitive renderings of the music. Technological progress has addressed many of these problems in the meantime, but other forces have conspired to renew the crux—for since the last third of the nineteenth century the scholarly and performing musical publics have increasingly approached musical compositions not as flexible and context-sensitive texts, but as stable works whose essentials and incidentals alike are largely impermeable to circumstantial change. Modern printed music, accordingly, aims to be standardized and universally comprehensible—"reader-friendly," in a word—so that notational idiosyncrasies facilitate comparable renderings of the same work even under radically different performance circumstances and in the hands of different interpreters.

In other words, the cultivation of notational nuance and individuated interpretation common until the nineteenth century—i.e., until it became expected and necessary for composers to disseminate their works in print—has become a thing of the past, supplanted by practices that favor notational and textual consistency. And the intimacy of communication between composers and interpreters that empowered performers in those earlier ages has given way to a culture that tends to curtail individual interpretive license, generally permitting substantive textual deviation only when obvious errors or inconsistencies are present in the essentials of the standardized musical text. Although the values of textual authority in latter-day print culture are not without merit, they contravene those of the cultures in which and for which composers disseminated their music in the eighteenth and nineteenth centuries.

One further observation needs to be added to the above generalizations: the fact that performers and scholars alike have historically been troubled by gaps between "scholarly" and "practical" editions. These gaps (evidenced by a given edition's approach to the music's textual sources and to the task of differentiating between editorial and authorial information) are as old as the idea of the critical edition itself,[4] but they are especially relevant to Mendelssohn scholars for two reasons. For one thing, most critical editions continue (for reasons that are generally valid, at least in principle) to aim for uniform, stable presentations of their musical texts despite the often-elaborate critical annotations that identify, describe, comment on, or reproduce textual variants and editorial judgment calls.[5] Anachronistically, a modern edition's authority resides in its claims to textual objectivity and stability, rather than its flexibility and encouragement of interpretive nuance. Second, and more importantly, the bulk of Mendelssohn's musical output continues to circulate predominantly in editions that are textually critical only in the crudest sense of the word, if at all: the editions released under the general editorship of the composer's lifelong friend Julius Rietz and published by Breitkopf and Härtel (Leipzig) as Mendelssohn's *Sämtliche Werke* (Collected Works; N.B. not Complete Works) between 1874 and 1877. There are better alternatives, of course; most significantly, the new and truly critical Leipzig *Gesamtausgabe*[6] as well as individual text-critical editions published by Bärenreiter, Carus-Verlag, and Henle-Verlag, among others.[7] Collectively, these latter publications have materially improved the prospects for interpreters who want a reliable edition as their starting point.

But old habits die hard: the Rietz editions and their spin-offs still dominate the market, and they probably will do so for some time. In any event, since even the authoritative versions now available continue to grapple with the notational issues discussed here, conscientious performers would do well to be aware of them and their implications for interpretation. The following remarks focus on three of these issues: repeated notes, undulating notes, and hairpin crescendo-decrescendo markings.

REPEATED NOTES

The editorial and performance issue of note-groupings centers around the tendency of modern notational and editorial practice to write out most or all notational abbreviations that group two or more repeated notes together, such as the figures ♪ ♪ and ♪˙ commonly encountered in nineteenth-century manuscript and printed notation, and to regularize beamings for notes that are not repeated. The assumptions behind the latter-day practice seem to be that the abbreviatory notations were simply conveniences designed to save valuable time, ink, and space in earlier practice and that they do not affect performers' realizations of the corresponding music. Both assumptions are true to some extent, but both also require qualification if one considers the notational and performance issues set out above. For while it is clearly more convenient to write one note, one stem, and one abbreviatory symbol than to write out all the notes and stems entailed in it, the abbreviation may also be more than "simply" a convenience, at least in some instances or some contexts. Similarly, regularized beamings for notes that are not repeated (for example, using 𝄞♪♪♪♪♪♪♪♪ instead of 𝄞♪♪♪♪♪♪♪♪ in a notational context where the former predominates, even when the copy-text gives the latter) assume that the deviation from the norm in a given musical text is a coincidence or accident, immaterial to the performer's or analyst's reading of the affected passage. In both cases, the assumptions are problematic, because they fail to acknowledge notation's suggestive power and performers' capacity to respond to that power. For repeated and changing notes alike, this power resides not least of all in the relationship of any given passage to its context. A few examples may serve to illustrate this point.

In the instance of repeated notes, one main problem is that the written-out equivalent of an abbreviation subverts potentially useful hierarchies among the notes affected. Implicitly, all notes are phraseologically equal, whereas abbreviations implicitly privilege the first note of each group and any notes that fall outside the abbreviations. One clear example of this problem occurs in the little-known concert aria *Infelice! / Ah, ritorna, età dell'oro* (1834), based on texts Mendelssohn compiled from several opera seria libretti by Pietro Metastasio (1698–1782).[8] In the cabaletta of this aria (Allegro vivace, 𝄴) the harmonic rhythm as well as the notation indicate a pulse of ♪ ♪. But in Mendelssohn's setting of lines 22–25 of Metastasio's poem (mm. 157–66) this pattern is broken—explicitly at first, then implicitly (see example 9.1). The interpretive import of the accompaniment notation in mm. 158–60 (beat 2) is quite clear: the last eighth note in each group of four should be separated slightly from the first three, and perhaps also from the next group of three. The irregular phrasing evidently has to do neither with text declamation (since the notes in question consistently fall on un-

EXAMPLE 9.1.   Mendelssohn, *Infelice! / Ah, ritorna, età dell'oro* (1834), mm. 158–66 (condensed score). Copy-text: autograph full score, Staatsbibliothek zu Berlin—Preußischer Kulturbesitz, Mus. ms. autogr. F. Mendelssohn Bartholdy 28.

accented words or syllables) nor with the relationship between the soprano solo and the string accompaniment (since the notes in question fall on rests as well as sung portions of the beats); instead, it seems to have been provided in order to add interest to an otherwise routine accompaniment. But how is the parallel material in mm. 162–66 to be treated?

This passage illustrates both the suggestion potential of notated note-groupings and the importance of context—for here the interpreter has to deal with at least two contexts: the predominant metrical and rhythmic notation of the cabaletta and, in mm. 162–66, the sub-context provided by the preceding measures. In all likelihood, any reading that responds to the idiosyncratic beaming in mm. 158–60 will interpret the transposed parallel passage in mm. 162–64 in light of that sub-context (i.e., will apply the same approach in the second group). This interpretive parallel, however, contravenes the notation in the second group of measures—indeed, a (perhaps unrealistically) positivist or literalist approach to the notation ("if Mendelssohn had wanted mm. 162–64 to be interpreted as parallel to mm. 158–60, he probably would have written them so") would insist that the two groups be differenti-

ated. In view of this contradiction, it seems clear that the edition should reproduce the notation of these measures as it stands: printing this passage as a

whole in regularized form (i.e., ♫♫♫♫ ♫♫♫♫ throughout) would misrepresent

the source and the potentially meaningful difference between the two groups
of measures. By contrast, reproducing the Notenbild of the original empow-
ers the interpreters to make sense of the contradictory suggestions of the notation according to their context and their own artistic judgment, and enables
them to establish their own interpretation of the patterns, repetitions, and exceptions within the composer's notation.[9]

This passage from the 1834 *Infelice* aria is both exceptional and exceptionally useful in that the aria exists only in manuscript and was therefore
never submitted to the generally normative (and hence potentially corrup-
tive) notational practices of print dissemination. As a "pure" instance, it suggests that as a rule notes that are grouped together (in this instance under a
single beam) should be treated as a group, and that notes individually recognized in the notation should be somehow distinguished from the
grouped notes in performance. Moreover, this passage's evident creation of
a new sub-context that subverts the performance implications of the notation suggests that interpreters' decisions as to the relative autonomy given
to individual notes and the implications of any notated note-groupings may
be contextually "nested" (i.e., may depend on the relationship of the immediate context to broader contexts in the work at hand).

The latter generalization bears significantly on performance when we
consider the balance of abbreviated to written-out repeated notes in
nineteenth-century editions of Mendelssohn's music: most editions of the
day (including those carefully proofed by the composer) set out to establish
the interpretive implications of a given notational pattern, but very few, if
any, adhere to that notational pattern so consistently that it seems to be
purely routine and thus devoid of suggestive differentiation. In the purely
instrumental music, examples of these repeated notes abound; in fact,
Mendelssohn poked fun at himself for his fondness for employing rapid
repeated-note accompaniments in his woodwind writing.[10] In those instances the composer's envisioned interpretation seems clear: all notes
should be equal; if any notes are privileged, they should be the first of the
group in any given abbreviation.

Several examples of this notational issue are found in the autograph full
score for the Violin Concerto in E minor, op. 64, held in the Biblioteka
Jagiellońska, Krakow. One occurs in the winds in the coda of the first
movement (più presto, mm. 473–80; see example 9.2). In modern editions
this passage is consistently reproduced in groups of four eighth notes

𝅘𝅥𝅮𝅘𝅥𝅮𝅘𝅥𝅮𝅘𝅥𝅮 𝅘𝅥𝅮𝅘𝅥𝅮𝅘𝅥𝅮𝅘𝅥𝅮 , an editorial decision that seems unobjectionable. But the autograph offers a different record of Mendelssohn's thinking here: in mm. 473 and 475 the clarinets, bassoons, and horns have a whole note comprised of repeated eighth notes; the same is true of both clarinets, both horns, and the second bassoon in m. 474, and of the first bassoon in m. 478. On the other hand, in mm. 477 and 480 the first bassoon, along with the clarinets and the second bassoon, has the same nominal figure (eight repeated eighth-notes) notated in two groups of four, all on the same pitch.

This passage raises several questions: (1) whether the notational disparity (eighth notes in groups of four or eight repeated notes) has any potential interpretive significance; (2) if so, how this should be reflected in a modern edition; and (3) whether the difference has any hope of being discernible in actual performance.

In answer to the first question I would propose that the notational differentiation at the very least records Mendelssohn's understanding of subtly differentiated phrasings in the winds: the re-articulation of the B in the first bassoon in m. 477 makes sense, because the second half of the measure marks the beginning of a new phrase rather than a continuation of the material of the previous measures. Similarly, the reiterated half note in m. 480 makes sense because of the cadential gesture (which also results in an octave leap in the cellos and basses). Moreover, if we apply the reasoning offered above concerning the relative autonomy or subsidiarity of notes within groups, the notation implies that the rule in the first three and a half bars of this passage is for a seamless stream of eighth notes, whereas the following measures should convey a slight half-note pulse—more pronounced than what would be achieved simply by changing notes—by means of subtle accents on each change.

The second question may be answered only by observing that editors (who are of course to a greater or lesser extent bound by the publisher's house style) should explain their procedure for presenting and differentiating these notational idiosyncrasies in the front matter or critical report, as appropriate. In principle, all notes grouped together by shorthand in the original notation should also be grouped in the modern typeface. My own preference is to reproduce the musical shorthand literally,[11] since interpreters who are bothered by figures such as 𝆑 are probably not sufficiently literate to produce a sensitive reading anyway. Alternatively, that figure may reasonably be written out as 𝅘𝅥𝅮𝅘𝅥𝅮𝅘𝅥𝅮𝅘𝅥𝅮 𝅘𝅥𝅮𝅘𝅥𝅮𝅘𝅥𝅮𝅘𝅥𝅮 and its interpretive implications commented on in the editor's notes. By extension, more esoteric shorthand may be indicated by a ligature sign (a horizontal square

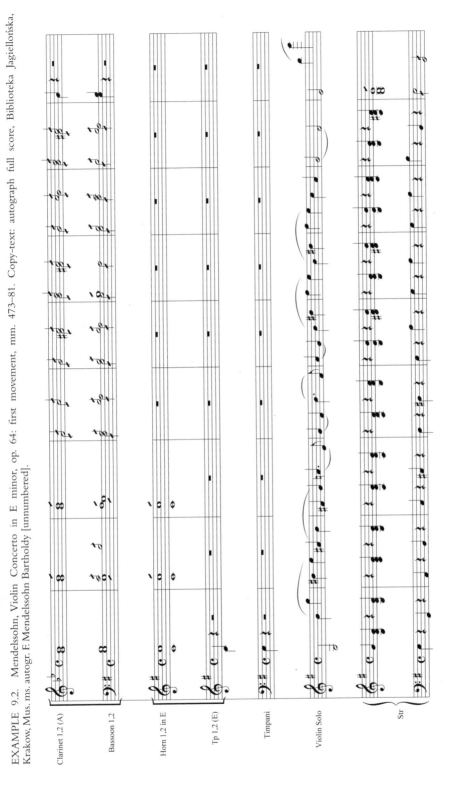

EXAMPLE 9.2. Mendelssohn, Violin Concerto in E minor, op. 64: first movement, mm. 473–81. Copy-text: autograph full score, Biblioteka Jagiellońska, Krakow, Mus. ms. autogr. F. Mendelssohn Bartholdy [unnumbered].

bracket placed above or below the entailed notes, e.g., ⌐♪♪♪♪♪♪♪⌐ for

♪)—again, with appropriate editorial clarification.

The last question is both the easiest and most difficult: is there any realistic hope of such subtle differentiations coming across in performance? Certainly not, I think, unless the editor respects it and performers are aware of it. But once performers become aware of the issue, they can of course respond to it with the same sensitivity they generally employ to bring out other, more conventionally recognized, subtle interpretive differences without necessarily emphasizing them. In such a reading audiences may perceive Mendelssohn's writing as many of his contemporaries did: extraordinarily nuanced and rarely (if ever) routine.

UNDULATING NOTES

The same reasoning also has implications for the abbreviation denoting a measured oscillation between two notes—most commonly, ♩__♩ or

♩__♩ . Similar to the devices sometimes referred to in violin technique as the *ondeggiando* or *ondulé* or the so-called "fingered tremolo," this figure is ubiquitous in mid-nineteenth-century music. Like the abbreviations discussed above, it appears in manuscripts and contemporary editions frequently, but not so uniformly as to suggest that it is completely interchangeable with its written-out equivalents. Again, at issue is not so much a "correct" or "incorrect" print presentation of the manuscript notation, but the retention or suppression of the notation's connotative power: if notes subsumed into an abbreviation are subtly less present than those explicitly written out and these notational hierarchies reflect the composer's thinking and offer cues to interpreters, then the ondulé abbreviation suggests a textural transparency that is (a) differentiated from the transparency of literally comparable passages that are fully written out and (b) not necessarily an obvious feature of the moment at hand.

Among the works in which the interpretive potential of this figure is evident, one of the best-known is *Die Hebriden,* op. 26, a concert overture whose orchestration has been celebrated from the start.[12] Among this overture's picturesque orchestrational effects are its delicate transferences of layers of thematic and motivic material in the upper, middle, and lower orchestral registers, a feature that (in the words of R. Larry Todd) "obscures the barrier between musical and visual imagery and evokes the synaesthetic, romantic qualities of the overture."[13] The effect of a transparent accompanimental undulation emerges early on in the overture, passing from the middle strings (mm. 13–20) to the upper strings (mm. 21–22) and back to the middle strings (mm. 23–25). In this passage, the undulation is sometimes written out, sometimes abbreviated (see examples 9.3a–b). By contrast, at the outset of the development section the strings' undulation is consistently notated in shorthand (see example 9.3c).[14]

Initially, these notational particulars might seem arbitrary or capricious, but I believe they are telling indicators of substantive differences in the relationship between the overture's thematic and motivic material—and the fact that the engravers of the first edition of the score and parts closely followed the abbreviations and writings-out of the autograph suggests that the differences between the two were not entirely incidental. In the first two instances (as in the presentation of the second subject in mm. 47ff, where the notation is likewise mixed), the smooth rippling of the accompaniment is integrally entwined with the concurrent thematic material, sharing the same registers and essentially enveloping it. The context for example 9.3c is quite different. Conspicuously static rather than flowing, the accompanimental gesture now stands in opposition to the registers and timbres of the thematic material rather than complementing it—a visual conveyance of the notation that seems to call for an undulation that is no longer simply smooth, but shimmering.

To be sure, these subjective observations resist objective verification. On the other hand, this is also the nature of notation as well as interpretation: both, as discussed at the outset of this essay, are notoriously fickle and liable to individualized interpretation. What is more, there is a certain logic to Mendelssohn's notation, whatever its intuitive dimensions. In the first two passages the undulation is an accompaniment to regular, flowing, clearly directional thematic material, and there the image of the notation reflects change, direction, and fluidity. In the third passage, at a point where the overture seems to struggle to regain momentum, the undulation visually suggests stasis, calm, pellucidity. The busy visual effect of modern editorial realizations of this notation contravenes the music's context and import.

The best way to avoid this implicit stylistic conflict, I believe, is to retain the composer's original notation. If, however, one is working with a publisher whose house style precludes this, the editor may at least provide the performer with the relevant information by employing the techniques described above: provide a ligature bracket and comment accordingly in the editorial notes.

EXAMPLES 9.3A–B.   Mendelssohn, *Die Hebriden,* op. 26, abbreviations in string parts: (a) mm. 13–16; (b) mm. 19–26. Copy-text: autograph full score, Bodleian Library, Oxford, MS M. Deneke Mendelssohn d. 71. Used by permission. (Perforated slurs and editorial indications in Roman font reflect reading given in first edition of orchestral score and parts.)

EXAMPLE 9.3C.   Mendelssohn, *Die Hebriden,* op. 26, abbreviations in string parts at beginning of development section. Copy-text: autograph full score, Bodleian Library, Oxford, MS M. Deneke Mendelssohn d. 71. Used by permission. (Perforated slurs reflect reading given in first edition of orchestral score and parts.)

OPEN AND CLOSED (DIAMOND-SHAPED) HAIRPIN DYNAMICS

The ubiquity of so-called hairpin crescendo-decrescendo markings — ⩤ ⩥ — in nineteenth-century music is well known; less well known, however, is that these paired, open-ended markings occur far less frequently in the manuscripts of Mendelssohn and some of his contemporaries than do the diamond- or lozenge-shaped figures known in German as *Schwellzeichen* ("swell signs"; i.e., ◁▷. Most modern editions treat the two as interchangeable, replacing the closed hairpins with open ones.[15]

Like the other notational variants discussed above, these two markings differ little in their absolute import: both clearly apply to dynamic strength, and both clearly denote a gradual increase followed by a gradual decrease. They differ, however, in their implications concerning the peak of this swell: ⩤ ⩥ suggests a dynamic peak of some length, while ◁▷ suggests an immediate decay. When the editor substitutes the latter for the former, the substitution almost inevitably requires an editorial judgment call concerning the space between the two open ends (i.e., the relative length or duration of the dynamic peak)—a judgment call that is seldom if ever identified in critical notes, despite its subjective nature and interpretive import. Perhaps most importantly, Mendelssohn himself used both symbols frequently but evidently *not* interchangeably—suggesting, again, that the notation's connotative value is lost when performers proceed from modern editions without consulting an earlier one (or any surviving autograph sources).

The interpretive significance of these different notated signs is underscored by the fact that for composers and copyists they were related but different characters from calligraphic, orthographic, and graphological perspectives, much as "a" and "ä," "r" and "ř," or "ss" and "ß" are. Because nineteenth-century ink pens had to be pulled (never pushed) across the writing surface, Mendelssohn's and other composers' diamond shapes were produced in the sequence $\underset{2a\ \ 2b}{\overset{1a\ \ 1b}{\diamond}}$, whereas hairpin dynamics were produced as $\underset{2}{\overset{1}{<}}\ \underset{4}{\overset{3}{>}}$. The former seems to have posed problems for nineteenth-century music engravers and lithographers, who in many instances clearly tried to reproduce it but produced awkward alignments and very slight gaps between the two open ends. Still, Mendelssohn's copyists and engravers—especially those with more reputable firms such as Breitkopf and Härtel (Leipzig), J. Ewer and Co. (London), N. Simrock (Bonn), and Pietro Mechetti (Vienna)—clearly treated the two symbols as different scribal challenges. Autograph hairpin dynamics are generally accurately (often elegantly) reproduced in contemporary editions, whereas autograph diamond-shaped hairpins are executed comparatively clumsily: despite obvious efforts to the contrary, a tiny space usually separates the wide ends of the hairpins, and there are often slight discrepancies in alignment.

The autograph for the Violin Concerto is one of dozens that tend to corroborate the notion that Mendelssohn recognized a distinction between open and closed hairpins. The two occur in the same context but with different musical functions at the presentation of the second subject in the exposition and recapitulation of the first movement. As shown in example 9.4 (the presentation from the exposition), in mm. 135–38 the solo violin clearly has a closed hairpin, suggesting a sharply contoured peak to its crescendo, whereas the statement of the second subject in the winds offers greater length to the peak of the crescendo (the entire first half of m. 137). By contrast, the preparation in mm. 144–47 for the violin's extension of the theme is clearly given in closed hairpins for the winds and the soloist alike.

One further note should be made about closed or diamond-shaped hairpins, at least as far as their interpretive possibilities for players of stringed instruments are concerned. As Clive Brown has pointed out,[16] a number of eighteenth- and nineteenth-century treatises suggest that diamond-shaped hairpins over individual notes may have implied the application of vibrato—which until the early twentieth century was consistently discussed as an ornament rather than a staple of the tone.

This suggestion is reinforced by a passage in Ferdinand David's edition of the celebrated Ciaconna from J. S. Bach's Partita No. 2 in D minor for Violin Solo, BWV 1004. David (1810–73; concert master of the Leipzig Gewand-

EXAMPLE 9.4.   Mendelssohn, Violin Concerto in E minor, op. 64: first movement, mm. 131–40.

haus Orchestra from 1836 to the end of his life, a close friend of Mendelssohn, and the soloist who gave the public premiere of the Ciaconna as well as Mendelssohn's Violin Concerto) published his edition in 1843 with Breitkopf and Härtel. Providing a diplomatic transcription of the sonatas' and partitas' musical texts as they appear in an eighteenth-century manuscript then considered to be Bach's autograph,[17] as well as David's own detailed realization of the solo part (including bowings, articulations, fingerings, and other elaborations), the edition is a treasure trove of information concerning mid-nineteenth-century violin performance practices. It also realizes David's recommended realization of the arpeggiated passages from the Ciaconna (mm. 89–120 and 201–208), which are simply labeled "arpeggio" by Bach. And here, in the middle of David's thirty-second-note realizations of one of the arpeggiated passages, the edition provides the engraved version of closed hairpins beneath the main notes of the theme (see example 9.5). In this instance, the rhythmic context and texture preclude any realistic application of a "real" crescendo-decrescendo (i.e., one interpreted with "open" hairpin

EXAMPLE 9.5.   J. S. Bach, "Ciaconna" from Partita No. 2 in D minor, BWV 1004, mm. 93–96, as edited by Ferdinand David (1843) and notated in eighteenth-century manuscript.

dynamics)—but it is quite realistic to conjecture that David used the symbol to indicate that those notes be emphasized by a selective application of the ornament of vibrato. Such an application would bring out the "subject" of Bach's complicated variations for mid-nineteenth-century listeners and performers, for whom the Ciaconna as a genre was at best obscure.[18]

If one accepts that the closed hairpins also functioned as an indicator that vibrato was to be used when they occur—and instances of this abound in Mendelssohn's vocal music as well as his orchestral works; certainly the passage from the Violin Concerto given in example 9.4 is a viable candidate—then there is all the more reason for modern editors and performers not to equate them with their open counterparts, for the apparently stable performance implications of the latter do not, as far as I can discern, embrace the further dimension of added vibrato. By reproducing the closed hairpins faithfully, editors will empower performers to elect whether or not this connotation works in any given context. And by treating open and closed hairpins as similar but not absolutely interchangeable, performers can open up a new range of historically and musically sensitive expressive possibilities as they interpret Mendelssohn's music.

CONCLUSION

On the face of it, much of the material in this essay may seem directed more at editors than at performers. It is not. On the contrary, I hope these observations will encourage performers to treat the relative paucity of obviously detailed performance cues in the musical notation of Mendelssohn and his contemporaries not as evidence of those composers' adherence to some universalized, objective, and normative lexicon of comparatively bland performance practices, but as evidence of the obligation to approach mid-nineteenth-century notation as something that invites or compels pronounced individualized subjectivity in performance. From such a perspective, the tendency of later composers and editors to provide more detailed notational information reflects a view of notation as something that prescribes (or even proscribes) rather than describes. Mendelssohn's notation reflects profoundly his keen belief in the value of interpretive subjectivity and nuance, as well as the flexible rather than reified status of musical artworks. If editors respect that notation and reproduce it faithfully, they will empower performers of Mendelssohn's music to retain a degree of choice and artistic discretion that is not only historically appropriate, but also greater than that generally permitted by modern editorial philosophies.

NOTES

1. See also chapter 1 ("Introduction: The Task of the Editor") in James Grier, *The Critical Editing of Music: History, Method, and Practice* (Cambridge: Cambridge University Press, 1996), 1–37, esp. 19–37.

2. On the issues of the aesthetics of the textual status of sketches and other "preliminary" compositional materials, see especially Bernhard R. Appel, "Zum Textstatus von Kompositions-Skizzen und -Entwürfen," *Jahrbuch des Staatlichen Instituts für Musikforschung Preussischer Kulturbesitz* 32 (1999): 177–210; further, Jeffrey Kallberg, "Chopin and the Aesthetic of the Sketch: A New Prelude in E-flat Minor?" *Early Music* 29 (2001): 408–22.

3. The best discussion of this issue remains Jeffrey Kallberg's "Chopin in the Marketplace," in *Chopin at the Boundaries: Sex, History, and Musical Genre* (Cambridge, Mass.: Harvard University Press, 1996), 161–214.

4. For an eloquent exploration of how this dichotomy came into being and its ramifications for modern scholars and performers, see Ludwig Finscher, "Gesamtausgabe—Urtext—Musikalische Praxis: Zum Verhältnis von Musikwissenschaft und Musikleben," in *Musik—Edition—Interpretation: Gedenkschrift Günter Henle,* ed. Martin Bente (Munich: G. Henle, 1980), 193–98.

5. Far from being confined to the disciplines of musical practice and musical scholarship, this issue figures prominently also in literary scholarship, where variorum editions and online variorum editions are well-established tools for those who wish to interpret (for example) works of Cervantes, Dickinson, Donne, or Shakespeare with a realistic scholarly awareness of textual pluralism in those works. To my knowledge the only comparable effort in music is the pilot project for the Online Chopin Variorum Edition, headed by Professor John Rink (see http://www.ocve.org.uk/ accessed 8 January 2008).

6. Officially, now the Leipziger Ausgabe der Werke von Felix Mendelssohn Bartholdy (formerly ". . . der Werke Felix Mendelssohn Bartholdys"). Originally established in 1959 by the Internationale Felix-Mendelssohn-Gesellschaft (Basel) in collaboration with the Deutsche Staatsbibliothek (East Berlin) and the Deutscher Verlag für Musik (Leipzig), the Leipziger Ausgabe was resurrected by Breitkopf and Härtel in 1992,

after a publication hiatus of some twenty years. Under the general editorship of Christian Martin Schmidt and with institutional support from the Sächsische Akademie der Wissenschaften zu Leipzig, the Ausgabe has been making up for lost time in recent years: as of April 2008, it had released an impressive total of nineteen volumes since 1997.

7. Particularly important among these are Christopher Hogwood's editions of the major concert overtures, published by Bärenreiter-Urtext beginning in 2003; the Carus critical editions of most of the sacred works (Stuttgart, 1967–97); and Henle-Verlag's Urtext editions of a number of the keyboard and chamber compositions.

8. Traditionally, the 1834 aria has been misconstrued as an early version of the aria posthumously published as Mendelssohn's op. 94, but that composition uses different texts from different arias and was composed for a different voice-part; despite some thematic and stylistic affinities, there is no evidence that Mendelssohn or his contemporaries consider the two arias as anything but autonomous. See my "Mendelssohn's Two *Infelice* Arias: Problems of Sources and Musical Identity," in *The Mendelssohns: Their Music in History*, ed. John Michael Cooper and Julie D. Prandi (Oxford: Oxford University Press, 2002), 43–97.

9. This approach differs from that employed by some leading music publishers, whose editorial guidelines specify that as a rule repeated notes with a value of one-sixteenth and smaller may be abbreviated, but eighth notes are to be written out. See, for example, Georg von Dadelson, *Editionsrichtlinien musikalischer Denkmäler und Gesamtausgaben* (Kassel: Bärenreiter, 1967); further, Bernhard R. Appel, Joachim Veit, and Annette Landgraf, *Editionsrichtlinien Musik* (Kassel: Bärenreiter, 2000), passim.

10. See his letter of 7 April 1834 to Fanny Hensel, ed. and trans. in my "Mendelssohn's Two *Infelice* Arias," 48.

11. "Musical shorthand" to refer to figures of the sort discussed above rather than indications for *colla parte* doubling and so on.

12. See especially R. Larry Todd, *Mendelssohn: The Hebrides and Other Overtures* (Cambridge: Cambridge University Press, 1992), esp. 84–88; further, Thomas S. Grey, "*Fingal's Cave* and Ossian's Dream," in *The Arts Entwined: Music and Painting in the Nineteenth Century*, ed. Marsha L. Morton and Peter L. Schmunk (New York: Garland, 2000), 63–99.

13. Todd, 88.

14. Although example 9.3c gives only mm. 96–102, the autograph, orchestral parts, and score edition retain the undulating abbreviation in the strings through m. 120. The only exception, as reflected in the example, occurs in m. 98—and here the autograph full score reveals that the composer wrote out the sixteenth notes because the measure was originally to cut off on the downbeat. This quarter note (with its black note head) was then extended to include four written-out sixteenth notes that extended to an eighth note and eighth rest on beat two, and was then further extended to beat three.

15. The qualifier "most" is necessary because some editors have begun restoring the lozenge-shaped symbols in recent years. The most notable advocate of the sign is Christopher Hogwood, whose editions of Mendelssohn's major concert overtures (opp. 21, 24, 26, 27, and 32, as well as the posthumously published *Ruy Blas* and "Trumpet" overtures), published by Bärenreiter Urtext, are exemplary as models of source-critical editorial method and performance-minded practicalities. I wish to thank Professor Hogwood for sharing his thoughts on the hairpin vs. lozenge issue with me in personal communications.

16. See Clive Brown, "Bowing Styles, Vibrato and Portamento in Nineteenth-Century Violin Playing," *Journal of the Royal Musical Association* 113 (1988): 111–19, esp. 118–19.

17. See Klaus Rönnau, "Bemerkungen zum 'Urtext' der Violinsoli J. S. Bachs," in Bente, 417–22.

18. On David's and Mendelssohn's efforts to address this generic obscurity by promoting the sonatas and partitas as works that resonated with predominant themes in the mid-century Bach revival, see my "Felix Mendelssohn Bartholdy, Ferdiand David und Johann Sebastian Bach: Mendelssohns Bach-Auffassung im Spiegel der Wiederentdeckung der 'Chaconne,' " *Mendelssohn-Studien* 10 (1997): 157–79.

10

Mendelssohn's Tempo Indications

SIEGWART REICHWALD

Much has been written and debated about the tempi of music by Bach, Mozart, Beethoven, Brahms, Mahler, and even Stravinsky. The generation of Mendelssohn, Schumann, Berlioz, and Chopin, however, seems to have been skipped in this discussion. This is surprising, since in many ways these composers hold the key to understanding and decoding tempo conventions of the late eighteenth to mid-nineteenth centuries, for they had to come to terms with the changes in tempo indications away from traditional tempo terms toward the "technological" and seemingly more accurate metronome marks. While Mendelssohn played a highly influential role both as composer and as performer, this chapter will focus mainly on Mendelssohn's approach to tempo as composer.

MENDELSSOHN AND THE METRONOME

For his twenty-sixth birthday on 3 February 1835 Mendelssohn was given a metronome by Karl Gottlieb Kyllmann (1803–78) with the complaint that the composer never included metronome marks in his printed music.[1] A look at Mendelssohn's published works before February 1835 confirms that the composer preferred not to publish metronome marks. His arrangement for four hands of his overture to *A Midsummer Night's Dream* is the only printed work with metronome marks prior to 1837. While it is not known whether Mendelssohn had owned a metronome before 1835, there are a few metronome marks in some autographs of his early works (see table 10.1). Surprisingly, these works are the only compositions with metronome marks in all his autographs. Mendelssohn clearly did not use

Table 10.1. Metronome Marks in Mendelssohn's Autographs

Works	Source of metronome markings	Modern edition with metronome markings
Six Little Pieces Date: 1820	D-B MN 1	
Sinfonia No. 8 in D major (string version) Date: 6–27 November 1822	D-B MN 2	LMA I/2
Symphony No. 1 in C minor, op. 11 Date: 1824, revised 1829	RPS MS 109	LMA I/4, p. 172

the metronome as part of his compositional routine, when dealing with the tempo terms for his works. The metronome marks in the autograph score of the Symphony No. 1 in C minor, op. 11, for example, are made in pencil, indicating that Mendelssohn added these marks for a particular performance.[2] He chose not to include them in the published version (Berlin: Schlesinger, 1834; London: Cramer, Addison, and Beale, 1839).

The next mention of the metronome in Mendelssohn's correspondence came under very unusual circumstances. After having been informed of the death of his father, Mendelssohn quickly had to make arrangements for the upcoming concerts in Leipzig before leaving for Berlin. His instructions to Heinrich Conrad Schleinitz (1802–81), written on 20 November 1835, include metronome marks for the performance of his *The Fair Melusine* overture.[3] Since Mendelssohn had been unable to find another conductor, he asked the timpanist Friedrich August Grenser (1799–1861) to rehearse the overture. While the inclusion of the metronome mark ($\downarrow$ = 96) might indicate Mendelssohn's lack of confidence in the timpanist's musical abilities, it also reflects the composer's growing uneasiness over the potential for wrong tempo choices by the conductor. Several months earlier Carl Klingemann wrote about the performance of the overture by their good friend and highly regarded musician Ignaz Moscheles:

> At the last Philharmonic-concert your Melusine was launched,—it's actually better not to say anything, as much as it irks me, the success was only one-tenth of what I had expected. . . . By the way, I was convinced that the tempo of the overture was too slow, and I diligently shared my concern after the rehearsal; M[oscheles] appeared to listen and promised to take a quicker tempo in the performance. But I did not notice that, it was and stayed too slow, which made the cheery section lose its impact.[4]

Another interesting mention of the metronome is in a letter from Fanny seven months later, in which she asks for metronome markings for two movements of the unpublished *Paulus;* Fanny and brother Paul had been arguing over the correct tempi.[5] Maybe it is not quite as surprising then that Mendelssohn included metronome marks in his published score of *Paulus* (a composition he viewed as his first mature major work) in 1837, despite the fact that it was not until 1839 that Mendelssohn mentioned the metronome again. In a letter to Breitkopf & Härtel Mendelssohn was distressed over performances with the wrong tempi: "Does the full score of my Psalm 42 include metronome marks? I have heard the choruses since my departure in tempi that were horrifying to me."[6] Six months later Mendelssohn followed up on this issue:

> A while back there was some discussion about the addition of tempi to my Psalm 42 according to Mälzl's metronome. I had forgotten to bring it up again, but I was approached about them again from somebody outside this area, and since I have heard wrong tempi so many times, I would like it, if the right tempi would be made known. They are as follows: no. 1 Chor ♩=92, no. 2 ♪=88, no. 3 Allo assai ♩=112, no. 4 Allo maest.ass. ♩ 116, più Anim. 𝅗𝅥=92, no. 5 Andante ♪=132, no. 6 ♩=152, no. 7 Maest.ass. ♩=116, Molto Allo vivace 𝅗𝅥=100, poco più Anim. 𝅗𝅥=108. I am asking you kindly, to send somebody over for a quarter of an hour with one of your metronomes to ensure that mine works correctly, and is not phlegmatic or sanguine. Maybe you can include these marks in your current or future copies.[7]

Despite Mendelssohn's earlier inclusion of metronome marks in *Paulus,* he was skeptical of the tool, and he obviously did not use it on a regular basis. Again, the metronome is a rarely used performance tool, only preventing wrong tempi. Mendelssohn did not customarily refer to the numbers of the metronome scale when determining tempo terms. (As a side note, a comparison of the suggested metronome marks with the Breitkopf & Härtel 1839 edition of Psalm 42 reveals discrepancies. Did Mendelssohn revise his marks when given a metronome by Breitkopf & Härtel? Since some terms remain unchanged, Mendelssohn obviously did not discover his metronome to be faulty. Based on the letter, it seems safe to assume, however, that the score contains Mendelssohn's revised metronome marks.)

After his use of metronome marks in *Paulus* and his frustrations with bad performances of Psalm 42, Mendelssohn included metronome marks for many major works. Table 10.2 is a list of most scores with metronome marks published during Mendelssohn's lifetime. This is not a comprehensive list, as it is based for the most part only on the holdings of the Bodleian Library. As mentioned above, Mendelssohn did not include metronome marks in most of his autographs. Neither did he write metronome marks in printed scores of his own compositions or of other composers for performances. Except for the *Six Little Pieces* (1820) Mendelssohn never wrote down any metronome marks for his solo piano works or Lieder.

Table 10.2. Mendelssohn's Works with Published Metronome Marks

Work	Contemporaneous publication	Modern edition with metronome markings
	BODLEIAN LIBRARY	
Incidental Music to Sophocles's *Antigone*, op. 55 Date: 4 February 1842–[1843]	London: Ewer [1843]; Leipzig; Kistner [1843]	
Overture to *A Midsummer Night's Dream*, op. 21 Date: 6 August 1826–10 July [1832]	PS 4 hands by FMB; Leipzig: Breitkopf & Härtel [1832]	
Serenade and Allegro giojoso, op. 43 Date: 1 April 1838	piano part; Bonn, Simrock, [1839]	LMA II/10
Symphony no. 3 in A minor, op. 56 ("Scottish") Date: 30 July 1829–20 January 1842	PS 4 hands by FMB; London: Ewer [1842]	LMA I/5
St. Paul [*Paulus*], op. 36 Date 1833–36	Bonn: Simrock [1837]	Carus
Wie der Hirsch Schreit (Psalm 42), op. 42 Date: 22 December 1837	Leipzig: Breitkopf [1839]	Carus
Da Israel aus Aegypten zog (Psalm 114), op. 51 Date: 9 August 1829–September 1840	PS by FMB; Leipzig: Breitkopf & Härtel [1840/41]	Carus
Lobgesang. Eine Symphonie-Cantate nach Worten der heiligen Schrift, op. 52 [*Hymn of Praise*] Date: July–27 November 1840	Leipzig: Breitkopf & Härtel [1841]	Carus

Work	Publication	
Die erste Walpurgisnacht, op. 60 Date: 16 July 1831–15 July 1843	VS; London: Ewer [1844]	
Elijah [*Elias*], op. 70 Date: 15 August 1844–47	Bonn: Simrock [1847]	Carus
Three String Quartets op. 44 Cello Sonata no. 1 in B-flat major, op. 45 Piano Trio no. 1 in D minor, op. 49 Date: 18 July 1839–?23 September 1839	Leipzig: Breitkopf Härtel [1840] Leipzig: Kistner [1839] London: Ewer [1840]	
Piano Trio no. 2 in C minor, op. 66 Date: 30 April 1845	London: Ewer [1846]	
6 sonatas, [organ], op. 65 Date: 14 July 1839–1845	Leipzig: Breitkopf & Härtel [1845]	LMA IV/6

RICHARD MACNUTT'S PRIVATE COLLECTION

Work	Publication	
Psalm 95, op. 46 Date: 6 April 1838	Leipzig: Kistner	Carus
Overture in C major for Wind Instruments, op. 24 Date: 27 June 1826	PS 4 hands by C. Czerny; Bonn: Simrock [1839]	

In 1842 Mendelssohn again mentioned his birthday present in a letter to Breitkopf & Härtel:

> Included here is the full score of my symphony [op. 56], which Henschke brought to me yesterday, and which I perused hastily and corrected. The metronome marks are according to *my* [emphasis in original] metronome (it really is truly mine, Herr Kyllmann from Wald near Solingen gave it to me as a present), but I would like to make sure, that they are correct. I ask you therefore, before the numbers are engraved, to have them checked with one of your metronomes by C. M. David, who knows the exact tempi; and if he finds them to be correct, you can confidently proceed with the engraving. If he finds them to be wrong, please let me know.[8]

Mendelssohn trusted the judgment of a competent musician over his metronome. He still could not relate to metronome numbers. This letter also suggests that Mendelssohn might have used the publisher's metronome in the past to determine the marks in his printed scores. His metronome marks were not for him or his own performances. They were only guidelines to prevent completely wrong tempi chosen by, in Mendelssohn's mind, incompetent performers. At the same time, Mendelssohn approached the addition of metronome marks with the usual care.

As it became routine to include metronome marks for major works, Mendelssohn seems to have become somewhat more confident in his own use of the metronome. Yet it was still not, and never would be, a regular enough tool to take with him on his trips, as this letter from Interlaken, written on 26 August 1847, shows:

> Since I don't have access to a metronome here, I have not looked at the marks. I would like to check them, however, before they are printed, and I am requesting that you include the metronome marks for part one [of *Elijah*] with the rest of your mailing.[9]

The follow-up letter, written a month later on 21 September 1847, shows again Mendelssohn's diligence in dealing with metronome marks:

> There are no mistakes in the metronome marks of part one. In part two, however, they are not yet engraved for many of the movements (only toward the end were they there), and on the list you sent me yesterday two tempi are missing, the Allegro of no. 26 (which should presumably be ♩=92, since it reappears in no. 30, where it is marked that tempo) and the Allegro moderato, ♩=100, in no. 30 on page 312. Maybe you can send me these two tempi (unless I forgot to write in the second one) with the rest of part two. I also had to change (correct) metronome marks in part two; I had written ♩=60 in no. 32, it should be ♩=66.[10]

While Mendelssohn used the metronome more routinely for the publication of his own works later in his career, there is not much evidence that he warmed up to the metronome as a rehearsal tool. The following excerpt from a letter to Mr. Bartholomew from Leipzig on 28 July 1846 is the exception:

> Dear sir: Here are the metronome marks which I beg you will give the director of the choruses; but tell them that I cannot promise they will be exactly the same, but nearly so I think.[11]

MENDELSSOHN AND TEMPO

In March 1831 the young Mendelssohn spent some time with Berlioz in Rome. Berlioz, in his memoirs, recounted an interesting conversation about tempo:

> One day, when I spoke of the metronome and its usefulness, Mendelssohn said sharply, "What on earth is the point of a metronome? It's a futile device. Any musician who cannot guess the tempo of a piece just by looking at it is a duffer."
>
> I could have replied that in that case there were a good many duffers, but I held my peace.
>
> At that time I had hardly published anything. Mendelssohn only knew my *Irish Melodies,* with piano accompaniment. One day he asked to see the score of the *King Lear* overture, which I had just composed in Nice. He read it through slowly and carefully, and was about to begin playing it on the piano (which he did, with incomparable skill) when he stopped and said, "Give me the right tempo."
>
> "What on earth for? I thought you said that any musician who couldn't guess the tempo was a duffer?"
>
> He would not admit it, but these ripostes, or rather unexpected thrusts, annoyed him intensely.[12]

This passage has frequently been quoted to contrast Mendelssohn's and Berlioz's personalities, characterizing Mendelssohn as rigid, opinionated, and somewhat snobbish. A closer look at this conversation, however, helps us understand Mendelssohn's conceptual approach to tempo. He initially stated that the composition itself contains all the information necessary to determine the correct tempo. Mendelssohn believed musical works to be inherently logical, which meant that careful study of a musical work would lead a competent musician, who understands the complicated but precise musical language, to that tempo. Mendelssohn's clear idea of tempo was based on two important aesthetic principles. First, music is precise communication based on logic. Second, the composer imbues a composition with its meaning; the performer decodes its content and communicates it to the audience. The following excerpt from a letter by the philosopher Georg Wilhelm Friedrich Hegel (1770–1831) shows that Mendelssohn was concerned about the aesthetic underpinnings of his craft, and it might indicate Hegel's influence on Mendelssohn's thinking:

The emotions evoked by music in the listener's mind belong to the realm of idealized pseudo feelings [*ideale Scheingefühle*] or imagined affects. Hence real logic in music is at least not provable. That this is so can easily be demonstrated by causing an able composer to continue another musician's composition. Most probably he will continue in a way different from the original author's procedure. However, if he masters his craft [*wofern er sein Handwerk versteht*], he will manage to do so in a way that . . . need not be less plausible. . . . Hence, logic in music is a logic of appearance [*des Scheins*] and form, which cannot be tested by comparisons with genuine conclusions pertaining to reality.[13]

Just three months after his conversation with Berlioz Mendelssohn wrote about the precision of expression of music to Zelter:

I require no under-current of thought when I hear music, which is not to me "a mere medium to elevate the mind to piety," as they say here, but a distinct language speaking plainly to me; for though the sense is expressed by words, it is equally contained in the music. This is the case with the "Passion" of Sebastian Bach.[14]

The rest of the conversation with Berlioz now makes more sense. The seeming contradiction of Mendelssohn's request for the right tempo is resolved, as he presumably just wanted a "shortcut" from the composer. In order to arrive at the right tempo himself, Mendelssohn would have had to study Berlioz's composition in more detail.

Some of Robert Schumann's notes about Mendelssohn help us to further our grasp of his ideas about tempo. In one of his entries Schumann wrote, "His judgment of musical matters, for example on compositions— the most penetrating thing imaginable, going right to the heart of the matter. He spotted the mistake and the cause and effect immediately and without fail."[15] Clearly Mendelssohn was consistent in his view, finding the answers in the score. Another anecdote from Schumann's notes raises some interesting issues of tempo and interpretation of a musical work:

On 14 March 1837. To him early, at 9:30. The day before, Beethoven's Ninth Symphony. Mendelssohn took the first movement unbelievably fast; it was so distressing for me that I walked out on the spot. I told him so, expressing myself bluntly and to the point. He was astonished, "he would never have imagined the movement otherwise." Then "the first three movements were *excessively* beautiful." Earlier he had felt that "the momentum of the first movement did not have its equal in music, that perhaps the end of the first movement of the Bach D minor Concerto was some long way behind it." "He would have liked perhaps a few touches of instrumentation to be otherwise, in the Scherzo (I know the spot), and one in the Adagio (where the violins answer the strong idea in the middle section [?bars 65–82]): in the first, the theme was inaudible and in the second the violins were too weak." "As for the last movement he didn't *understand* it." Meaning "it was the one he liked least."[16]

Obviously, Mendelssohn based his choices of tempi on *his* understanding of the work. The fact that he had definite ideas about passages that did not work well shows that he engaged himself artistically with the original text; however, he did not make any changes. Even his likes or dislikes were, according to Schumann, based on careful study. While Mendelssohn must have realized that choosing a tempo was somewhat a matter of interpretation, he tried to base his decision on the inner logic of the composition. Interestingly enough, neither Mendelssohn nor Schumann ever seemed to think that Beethoven's own metronome marks should be taken into consideration.

MENDELSSOHN'S TEMPO TERMS

In Mendelssohn's mind tempo terms were much more important than metronome marks. In the above-quoted letter to Zelter, Mendelssohn also notated several musical examples of medieval chant and Renaissance pieces he had heard during Holy Week in Naples. He not only notated chant rhythmically, he also used the terms "allegro" and "adagio" to give Zelter an idea of the tempi.[17] Italian tempo terms seem to have been an integral part of Mendelssohn's musical language—as had been the case for the generation before him. The arrival of the metronome in the second decade of the nineteenth century did not immediately change a composer's approach to tempo indications. The above-mentioned conversation between Berlioz and Mendelssohn shows that there was disagreement over the usefulness of this new tool. Thus Mendelssohn's generation was "caught" in the transition toward the consistent use of metronome marks. While Mendelssohn was trained to work with the old tempo conventions, he eventually warmed up to the metronome and made fairly consistent use of metronome marks at the end of his career. Relating Mendelssohn's metronome marks to his tempo terms therefore will give us some insights into the composer's terminology.

Clive Brown, in his book *Classical and Romantic Performance Practice 1750–1900,* has done a masterful job of untangling the conventions behind the Italian tempo terms. Brown has also shown the complexity and limitations of attempts to translate these conventions into metronome mark ranges. One of the complicating factors, according to Brown, is the other variants that determine tempo: meter, note values, percentage of fast note values, and types of rhythmic figurations.[18] Three of the most common examples of this relationship are the following: (1) smaller note values, notated in meters with higher denominators, are automatically considered faster and lighter (the same music notated in 2/2 and 2/4 would be performed faster and lighter in 2/4; (2) music in triple meter is considered to naturally have a faster pulse than music with the same tempo term in duple meter; (3) the choice of the tempo term is related to the fastest note values of the composition (the composer will chose a faster tempo term for a movement with sixteenth notes, even though the pulse for a movement with only eighth notes might be faster). The following observations apply Brown's approach to relating metronome marks to other tempo indications in the music of Felix Mendelssohn.

While fewer than 25 of Mendelssohn's more than 700 works contain metronome marks, we actually have over 270 tempo terms with metronome marks—mostly because of the large-scale choral orchestral works. Since *Paulus* was Mendelssohn's first published composition with metronome marks, it seems a good place to begin. Mendelssohn's careful revision process of the work is well documented and leads us to believe that he also made sure that his metronome marks would be accurate. In a letter to the composer Jacob Rosenhain, written on 13 January 1842, Mendelssohn affirms this by stating that "the metronome marks of my *St. Paul* are found in the full score, published by Simrock in Bonn, and which are indispensable for a performance."[19]

Table 10.3 organizes the metronome marks found in the 1837 edition of *Paulus* according to tempo terms first and to metronome marks within each basic tempo term second. Mendelssohn's choice of tempo terms is simple, consistent, and straightforward. He used mostly only the three basic tempo terms "adagio," "andante," and "allegro" with different qualifiers. The metronome marks show a clear delineation between these three tempo terms. While the range of metronome marks for each term seems rather broad at first, a closer look shows Mendelssohn's keen understanding of tempo conventions based on the above-mentioned relationships between tempo term, meter, and note values. The seemingly wide range of metronome marks from 54 to 88 for the adagio movements becomes narrower when considered within this relationship. If we take no. 14, ♩=60, as the central mark, the adjusted marks for the other movements seem logical. The subdivided movements have a faster pulse, which is adjusted according to the fastest note values. No. 7, ♩=54, has a slower pulse because of the eighth-note triplets.

The andante movements are all faster than the adagio movements in their overall speed. The andantino movement is the slowest at ♩=66, making the term "andantino" a bridge to the adagio. The central mark for andante movements seems to be ♩=72 for no. 19. The movements marked *andante con moto* are just a little faster. While the andante sostenuto movement no. 43 is marked the same as the andante no. 4 at ♩=112, the andante sostenuto

Table 10.3. Tempo Indications for *St. Paul*

Movement	Tempo term	MM	Meter	Fastest notes
	ADAGIO			
7. Aria	Adagio	♩=54	3/4	♪♪♪
14. Recitativo con Coro	Adagio	♩=60	c	♪ (triplet)
29b. Coro, m. 76	Adagio	♪=72	c	♪
18a. Aria	Adagio	♪=88	c	♪
40. Cavatina	Adagio	♪=88	c	♪
	ANDANTE			
35. Coro	Andante	♩=66	3/4	♪
13. Recitativo ed Arioso	Andantino	♩=66	c	♪
19. Recitativo	Andante	♩=72	c	♪
11. Coro	Andante con moto	♩=80	c	♪
1a. Ouverture	Andante	♩=84	c	♩
25. Duetto	Andante	♪=108	c	♪
4. Recitativo	Andante	♪=112	c	♪
43. Coro	Andante sostenuto	♪=112	c	♪
26. Coro	Andante con moto	♪=132	6/8	♪
	ALLEGRO			
20. Aria e Coro	Allegretto	♩.=56	6/8	♪
36b. Recitativo, Aria e Coro	Allegro assai moderato	♩=60	c	♪
31. Duetto	Allegro	♩=69	¢	♪
29a. Coro e Choral	Allegro molto	♩.=84	6/8	♪
15. Coro	Molto allegro con fuoco	♩=88	¢	♪, ♪♫
45b. Coro	Allegro vivace	♩=88	¢	few ♪
36a. Recitativo, Aria e Coro	Allegro molto	♩=92	¢	♪
22a. Coro	Allegro moderato	♩=92	c	♪
22b. Coro, m. 93		♩=138	c	♪
38. Coro	Allegro non troppo	♩=92	c	♪
21. Recitativo	Allegro di molto	♩=96	¢	♪
45a. Coro	Allegro maestoso	♩=96	c	♪, few ♪
18b. Aria	Allegro maestoso	♩=100	c	♫
42. Coro e Recitativo	Allegro moderato	♩=100	c	few ♪
8. Recitativo e Coro	Allegro moderato	♩=104	c	♪
6. Recitativo e Coro	Allegro molto	♩=108	¢	♪
12. Recitativo ed Aria	Allegro molto	♩=108	¢	♪
1c. Ouverture	Allegro	♩=112	3/4	♪
5. Coro	Allegro	♩=112	c	♪
28. Recitativo col Coro	Allegro	♩=120	c	♫
2. Coro	Allegro maestoso	♩=120	c	♫, ♪♪♪ (triplet)
23b. Coro	Allegro vivace	♩=132	c	♪
	OTHER			
33. Coro	Presto	♩=88	c	♪
36c. Recitativo, Aria e Coro	Con molto di volta	♩=112	3/2	♩
16. Choral	Con moto	♩=69	c	♪
1b. Ouverture	Con moto	♩=92	3/4	♪
27. Recitativo ed Arioso	Con moto	♪=92	3/8	♪
23a. Coro	Grave	♩=66	c	♪
3. Choral		♪=80	c	♪
9. Recitativo e Choral		♪=80	c	♪

movement will seem slower, as it has only eighth notes as the fastest note value versus the sixteenth notes of no. 4.

The jump from andante to allegro is much greater, if we take ♩=112 of the overture and no. 5 as the central marks. The reason for this is the much wider range of allegro tempi, which can be seen in the many qualifiers. "Allegretto" is the bridge term here; it is only a little faster than the central andante, given the time signature (6/8). The qualifiers can be placed in the following order, slowest to fastest: "allegretto," "moderato," "non troppo," "maestoso," "allegro," "vivace," "molto." The presto movement seems slower than the allegro molto movements, but it has continuous sixteenth-note motion almost throughout.

Comparing the "tempo mark scale" of *Paulus,* Mendelssohn's first inclusion of metronome marks, with that of *Elijah,* one of his last major works to be published, will help solidify our understanding of Mendelssohn's tempo conventions (see table 10.4). The central adagio mark is easily established at ♩=63. The andante movements have a wider range than those of *Paulus,* with several faster andantes, such as nos. 41 and 42, marked *andante con moto,* ♩=88, and *andante maestoso,* ♩=96. It seems that the tempo term "allegro maestoso," ♩=96 and 100, of *Paulus* has moved into the "andante" range of *Elijah,* slowed slightly to ♩=88. However, Mendelssohn did use maestoso in the allegro range twice, calling for a tempo far too quick to be included in the andante range (no. 21 b *allegro maestoso* and no. 22a *maestoso ma moderato*). The central andante mark is the same as in *Paulus* with ♩=72, prescribed for three movements (nos. 21, 31, and 33). The slower andante movements show the qualifier "sostenuto." A very interesting tempo mark is *andante grave e maestoso* for no. 11, ♩=84. One would expect any "grave" qualifier to slow the tempo down rather than speeding it up. A closer look shows that to be true here as well. "Maestoso," in this tempo scale, is a faster andante. The "grave" is balanced out by the "maestoso," calling in Mendelssohn's mind for a tempo between andante and maestoso. Why did Mendelssohn use these contrasting modifiers? May he have chosen the tempo term in this case (and in probably many other cases) not just to qualify the speed but also the mood of the movement, in this case expressing the tension and plodding solemnity of "Baal, we cry to thee?"

With the wider range of the andante tempo marks moving well into the allegro range of the *Paulus* tempo terms, the allegro markings in *Elijah* are generally faster, with a central allegro mark at ♩=144! It is probably actually the faster allegro terms that swayed Mendelssohn to expand the andante range and include the "maestoso" qualifier. While the metronome marks for

Table 10.4. Tempo Indications for *Elijah*

Movement	Tempo term	MM	Meter	Fastest notes
	ADAGIO			
36. Chor Recit.	a tempo: Adagio non troppo	♩=63	c	♪
14. Aria	Adagio	♩=63	c	♪
25c. Recit. c	Adagio	♩=66	3/4	♪
35. Recit.	Adagio non troppo	♩=72	c	♩ few ♪
21a. Aria	Adagio	♪=80	3/8	♬
	ANDANTE			
8b.	Andante sostenuto	♩=58	c	♪
8c.	Andante con moto	♩=63	6/8	♬
8a.	Andante agitato	♩=66	6/8	♬
25a. Recit.	Andante sostenuto	♩=66	3/4	♪
19a. Recit. und Chor	Andante sostenuto	♩=66	c	♪
32. Chor	Andante sostenuto	♩=66	c	♩
40.	Andante sostenuto	♩=69	c	♪
4. Aria	Andante con moto	♩=72	3/4	♪
23a. Recit. und Chor	Andante	♩=72	c	♪
33a. Recit.	Andante	♩=72	c	♪
31a Aria	Andantino	♩=72	c	♪
1. Chor	Andante lento	♩=76	c	♬
8d.	a tempo: Andante	♩=76	c	♪
41b. Chor	Andante sostenuto	♩=76	c	♪
39. Aria	Andante	♩=80	c	♬
11a. Chor	Andante grave e maestoso	♩=84	c	♪
41a. Chor	Andante con moto	♩=88	c	♬
42a. Chor	Andante maestoso	♩=96	c	♬
28. Terzetto	Andante con moto	♪=100	2/4	♪
37. Arioso	Andante sostenuto	♩=100	6/4	♩
	ALLEGRO			
33b. Recit.	Allegro	𝅗𝅥=92	c	♩
17. Aria	Allegro con fuoco e marcato	𝅗𝅥=92	¢	♬
25b. Recit.	Molto Allegro vivace	𝅗𝅥=92	c	♪
10d. Recit.	Allegro vivace	𝅗𝅥=92	c	♬
30a. Recit.	Allegro vivace	𝅗𝅥=92	c	♪
42b. Chor	Allegro doppio movimento	𝅗𝅥=96	c	♩ few ♪
5a. Chor	Allegro vivace	𝅗𝅥=96	c	some ♬
9. Chor	Allegro moderato	♩=96	c	♬
34. Chor	Allegro molto	𝅗𝅥=100	c	♬
24. Chor	Allegro moderato	♩=100	c	♬
30b. Recit.	Allegro moderato	♩=100	c	♬
23b. Recit. und Chor	Allo moderato	♩=100	c	♬
22a. Chor	Allegro maestoso ma moderato	♩=112	c	few ♬

(*continued*)

Table 10.4. (*continued*)

Movement	Tempo term	MM	Meter	Fastest notes
20. Chor	Allegro moderato ma con fuoco	♩=126	3/4	♪
7. Doppel-Quartet	Allegro ma non troppo	♩=126	¢	♪
29. Chor	Allegro moderato	♩=126	¢	♫♫ (3)
21b. Aria	Allegro maestoso	♩=132	3/4	♫
19c. Recit. und Chor	a tempo: Allegro	♩=144	¢	♫♫ (3)
10b. Recit.	Allegro vivace	♩=144	¢	♫
16. Recit. und Chor	Allegro con fuoco	♩=152	¢	♪
11b. Chor	Allegro non troppo	♩=160	3/4	♪
12. Recit. und Chor	Allegro	♩=160	¢	♪
	OTHER			
13. Recit. und Chor	Presto	♩=126	6/8	♪
5b. Chor	Grave	♩=58	¢	♪
Einleitung	Grave	♩=60	¢	♪
10a. Recit.	Grave	♩=60	¢	♪
18. Arioso	lento	♪=96	2/4	♪
10c. Recit.	Maestoso	♩=80	¢	♪
Overture	Moderato	♩=92	¢	♪
38.	Moderato maestoso	♩=76	¢	♫♫ (3)
15.	Piu adagio	♩=52	¢	few ♪
19b. Recit. und Chor	Piu animato	♩=80	¢	♪
22b. Chor	Piu animato	♩=138	¢	♫
36b. Chor Recit.	Piu mosso	♩=84	¢	♪
2. Duett	Sostenuto ma non troppo	♪=100	2/4	♪

the allegro movements for *Elijah* are generally faster than those of *Paulus*, the order of qualifiers stays the same.

The many different tempo indications found in *Elijah* show how intricate and complex Mendelssohn's tempo conventions were. Mendelssohn's "translation" into much more "flat" tempo indications through metronome marks makes it possible for us to begin to understand the subtleties of the old system. It also shows that while metronome marks themselves are precise in communicating a desired speed, they lack much in the expression of mood and character.

A third tempo scale of interest might be one based on compositions that also follow another set of conventions—sonata plan (see table 10.5). The tempo scale is more polarized. The adagio movements have a slow pulse, the andante marks are all slow, and the allegros are fast—some extremely fast. This is not a surprise, since sonata plan prescribes contrast between movements. Most striking are the consistently fast allegro marks. None have a quarter-note pulse, yet almost all have sixteenth notes.

Table 10.5. Tempo Indications for Works Based on Sonata Plan

Movement	Tempo term	MM	Meter	Fastest notes
	ADAGIO			
String quartet op. 44/3; III	Adagio non troppo	♩=54	3/4	♪
Symphony no. 3 op. 56; III	Adagio	♪=76	2/4	♬
	ANDANTE			
Trio, piano and strings op. 66; II	Andante espressivo	♩.=54	9/8	♪
String quartet op. 44/2; III	Andante	♩=60	¢	♪
Symphony no. 3 op. 56; Ic	Andante come 1mo	♩=72	3/4	♪
Symphony no. 3 op. 56; Ia	Andante con moto	♩=72	3/4	♪
Trio, piano and strings op. 49; II	Andante con moto tranquillo	♩=72	¢	♪
Sonata, violoncello and piano, no. 1, op. 45; II	Andante	♪=104	3/8	♬
String quartet op. 44/1 LMA; III	Andante espressivo ma con moto	♪=120	2/4	♪
String quartet op. 44/1; III	Andante espressivo ma con moto	♪=126	2/4	♪
	ALLEGRO			
String quartet op. 44/2; II: Scherzo	Allegro di molto	♩.=72	3/4	♪
Trio, piano and strings op. 49; I	Molto Allegro agitato	♩.=80	3/4	few ♪
Trio, piano and strings op. 66; III: Scherzo	Molto Allegro quasi presto	♩=88	2/4	♪
String quartet op. 44/1; I	Molto Allegro vivace	♩=88	¢	♪
String quartet op. 44/2; I	Allegro assai appassionata	♩=88	¢	♪
String quartet op. 44/3; I	Allegro vivace	♩=92	¢	♪
Sonata, violoncello and piano, no. 1, op. 45; III	Allegro assai	♩=92	¢	♪
Trio, piano and strings op. 66; I	Allegro energico e con fuoco	♩=92	¢	♪
String quartet op. 44/3; IV	Molto Allegro con fuoco	♩=96	¢	♪
Symphony no. 3 op. 56; Ib	Allegro un poco agitato	♩.=100	6/8	♪
Trio, piano and strings op. 49; IV	Allegro assai appassionata	♩=100	¢	♪
Sonata, violoncello and piano, no. 1, op. 45; I	Allegro vivace	♩=100	¢	♪
Symphony no. 3 op. 56; IV b	Allegro maestoso assai	♩.=104	6/8	♪
Trio, piano and strings op. 66; IV: Finale	Allegro appassionata	♩.=112	6/8	♪
Symphony no. 3 op. 56; IV a	Allegro vivacissimo	♩=126	2/4	♫, ♬ (3)
	OTHER			
String quartet op. 44/1; IV	Presto con brio	♩.=104	12/8	♪
String quartet op. 44/3; II: Scherzo	Assai leggiero vivace	♩.=152	6/8	♪
Trio, piano and strings op. 49; III: Scherzo	Leggiero e vivace	♩.=120	6/8	♪

CONCLUSION

While the results of this study show the complexity of Mendelssohn's tempo conventions, the process runs counter to Mendelssohn's intuitive approach to determining tempo based to a large extent on the content of the work—a completely different factor left out here for obvious reasons. Another factor left out is the larger context of a tempo term for a movement with multiple tempo markings, as well as the tempo relationship between movements (almost all of Mendelssohn's compositions with his tempo marks are multi-movement works). In the case of his choral-orchestral works, there is a very strong and extremely important tempo relationship between movements. Even in Mendelssohn's "Scottish" symphony the tempo relationship is arguably more important than in most symphonies of the Classic period, since Mendelssohn prescribes a performance with no breaks between movements. The best way then to gain an understanding of Mendelssohn's tempi is to perform and study his pieces with metronome marks with the ultimate goal of learning his musical language. The isolation of various tempo factors is, after all, of only limited use in attaining this goal, as it merely gives us the kind of shortcut Mendelssohn requested from Berlioz.

NOTES

1. *"Die Musik will gar nicht rutschen ohne Dich" Fanny und Felix Mendelssohn, Briefwechsel 1821 bis 1846,* ed. Eva Weissweiler (Berlin: Propyläen, 1997), 184.

2. Ralf Wehner, *Leipziger Ausgabe der Werke Felix Mendelssohn Bartholdys,* I/4, Symphony No. 1 in C Minor, Op. 11 (Leipzig: Internationale Felix-Mendelssohn-Gesellschaft, 2000), 172.

3. Felix Mendelssohn, letter to Heinrich Conrad Schleinitz, 20 November, 1835; Hellmut Meyer and Ernst Lagerkatalog 52, Nr. 441.

4. Letter from 22 April 1834, Carl Klingemann [Jr.], ed. *Felix Mendelssohn-Bartholdys Briefwechsel mit Legationsrat Karl Kligemann in London* (Essen, G. D. Baedecker, 1909), 126–27: "Im letzten Phiharmonie-Konzert ist Deine Melusine vom Stapel gelassen,—besser nichts sagen, so sehr mich's auch jammert, nicht viel, ein Zehnteil von dem Erfolg, den ich sicher erwartete. . . . Ich wahr übrigens durch und durch überzeugt, dass das Tempo der Ouvertüre zu langsam war, und habe mein Bedenken nach der Probe gewissenhaft vorgetragen,—M. schien drauf einzugehen und versprach es in der Aufführung etwas rascher zu nehmen; ich hab's aber nicht gemerkt, es war und blieb zu langsam, wodurch die frohe Partie sehr verlor."

5. Letter from 28 June 1836, Fanny Mendelssohn Hensel, *The Letters of Fanny Hensel to Felix Mendelssohn,* ed. and trans. Marcia J. Citron (Stuyvesant, N.Y.: Pendragon, 1987), 205–206.

6. Letter from 30 May 1839, Felix Mendelssohn, *Briefe and deutsche Verleger,* ed. Rudolf Elvers (Berlin: Walter de Gruyter, 1968), 95: "Stehn über der Partitur meines 42sten Psalms Metronombezeichnungen? Ich habe die Chöre einigemal seit meiner Abreise in einem Tempo gehört, daß es ein Graus war."

7. Letter from 29 November 1839, Felix Mendelssohn, *Briefe an deutsche Verleger,* 98: "Vor einiger Zeit war zwischen uns die Rede von Hinzufügung der Tempi nach Mälzls Metronom zu meinem 42sten Psalm. Ich vergaß nachher wieder davon anzufangen, doch bin ich in neuerer Zeit abermals von auswärts darum angegangen worden, und da ich grade diese Tempi leider sehr oft vergreifen gehört habe, so wäre mirs doch lieb, wenn die richtigen bekannt würden. Es sind folgende: No. 1 Chor ♩=92, No. 2 ♪=88, No. 3 Allo assai ♩=112, no. 4 Allo maest.ass. ♩ 116, più Anim. 𝅗𝅥=92, No. 5 Andante ♪=132, no. 6 ♩=152, no. 7 Maest.ass. ♩=116, Molto Allo vivace 𝅗𝅥=100, poco più Anim. 𝅗𝅥=108. Doch würde ich Sie bitten, mir durch Ueberbringer auf eine Viertelstunde einen Ihrer Metronome zuzuschicken, damit ich auch gewiß bin, daß meiner richtig geht, und nicht etwa phlegmatisch oder sanguinisch. Vielleicht können Sie die Bezeichnungen dann auf irgend eine Art in den jetzigen, oder etwaigen spätern Exemplaren eintragen lassen."

8. Letter from 18 October 1842, Felix Mendelssohn, *Briefe an deutsche Verleger,* 127–28: "Beifolgend die Partitur meiner Symphonie [op. 56], welche mir Henschke gestern brachte, und die ich in aller Eile durchgesehen und berichtigt habe. Die Metronombezeichnungen sind nach *meinem* Metronom (er gehört wahrhaftig mir erb und eigenthümlich; Herr Kyllmann aus Wald bei Solingen, hat ihn mir geschickt) aber ich wüßte nur gern, ob sie auch nach andern richtig sind. Deshalb bitte ich Sie, ehe die Zahlen gestochen werden, sie nach einem von Ihren Metronomen durch C.M. David, der die Tempi so genau kennt, vergleichen zu lassen, und findet er sie richtig, so können sie getrost gestochen werden. Findet er sie falsch, so bitte ich um Nachricht."

9. Letter from 26 August 1847, Felix Mendelssohn, *Briefe an deutsche Verleger,* 273: "Da ich jetzt keinen Metronom hier bekommen kann, so habe ich die Bezeichnungen nicht wieder durchgesehen. Doch möchte ich es gern ehe sie in der Partitur erscheinen, und bitte Sie daher mir bei der Zusendung des Restes der Correctur auch die *Metronome* für den 1sten Theil wieder mitzuschicken."

10. Letter from 21 September 1847, Felix Mendelssohn, *Briefe an deutsche Verleger,* 275: "Auch in den Metronombezeichnungen des ersten Theils ist kein Fehler. Dagegen stehen sie im 2ten Theile bei vielen Stücken noch gar nicht gestochen (nur gegen das Ende stehen sie wieder) und in der Liste die Sie mir in Ihrem Briefe gestern schickten, sind 2 Tempi nicht angegeben, nämlich das Allegro von no. 26 (welches indeß vermuthlich half=92 ist, da es in no. 30 wiederkommt und da richtig bezeichnet steht) und das Allegro moderato quarter=100 in no. 30 pag. 312. Vielleicht geben Sie mir diese beiden Tempi (wenn nicht etwa das letztere gar von mir vergessen ist) an, wenn Sie mir den Rest des 2ten Theiles senden. Auch habe ich Metron. Bezeichnungen des 2ten Theils ändern (berichtigen) müssen; ich hatte no. 32 ♩=60 angegeben; es muß aber ♩=66 sein."

11. Elise Polko, *Reminiscences of Felix Mendelssohn-Bartholdy,* trans. Lady Wallace (London: Longman, 1869), 304; quoted in José Antonio Bowen, "The Conductor and the Score: A History of the Relationship between Interpreter and Text in the Generation of Mendelssohn, Berlioz and Wagner" (Ph.D. diss., Stanford University, 1994), 219.

12. Hector Berlioz, *The Memoirs of Hector Berlioz,* ed. and trans. David Cairns (New York: W. W. Norton, 1975), 292.

13. Unpublished letter from Hegel to Mendelssohn, dated 30 June 1829; quoted in Bowen, 81.

14. Letter from 16 June 1831, Felix Mendelssohn, *Letters from Italy and Switzerland,* trans. Lady Wallace (Boston: O. Ditson, 1862; reprint, Freeport, N.Y.: Books for Libraries Press, 1970), 186.

15. Robert Schumann, *Erinnerungen and Felix Mendelssohn Bartholdy; nachgelassene Aufzeichnungen von Robert Schumann,* ed. G. Eismann (Zwickau: Predella, 1948); quoted in Roger Nichols, *Mendelssohn Remembered* (London: Faber and Faber, 1997), 159.

16. Ibid., 162.

17. Letter from 16 June 1831, Felix Mendelssohn, *Letters from Italy and Switzerland*, 186.

18. Clive Brown, *Classical and Romantic Performance Practice 1750–1900* (Oxford: Oxford University Press, 1999), 290.

19. "Ein ungedruckter Brief von Felix Mendelssohn-Bartholdy," *Signale für die Musikalische Welt* 36, no. 12 (1878): 177: "Es war mir eine große Freude mal wieder directe Nachrichten von Ihnen zu erhalten. . . . Die Metronombezeichnungen meines Paulus stehen in der Partitur welche bei Simrock in Bonn gedruckt u. zu einer Aufführung wohl unentbehrlich ist."

11

"For You See I Am the Eternal Objector": On Performing Mendelssohn's Music in Translation

JOHN MICHAEL COOPER

Few nineteenth-century composers were more linguistically proficient than Mendelssohn. Together with his younger sister, Rebecka, he studied classical Greek from the age of nine. At eleven he was studying Latin six hours a week, and some time late in 1820 or 1821 he was sufficiently versed in Ovid's dactylic hexameter that he penned *Paphlëis,* an extended mock-epic poem in German (modeled in part on Goethe's *Achillëis* and *Hermann und Dorothea*) running to more than 460 lines in that meter.[1] In 1825, at the age of sixteen, he prepared translations of Terence's first comedy, *Andria* (again in German but in the meter of the Latin original), and Horace's celebrated *Ars poetica.* Throughout his life he conversed and corresponded fluently in English, French, and Italian, as well as his native German. Privately, he was remarkably gifted at translating poetry and prose into German.[2]

Given the lifelong breadth and depth of this linguistic, cultural, and intellectual background, the issues of performing Mendelssohn's vocal works in languages other than German are naturally more plentiful and complex than is the case with the music of most of his contemporaries. Latter-day performers and scholars alike generally take it for granted that the translated versions were commercially necessary evils, unauthorized degradations of the poetry and the text/music relationships as the composer conceived them. This rule rests on two assumptions: (1) that the composer possessed only basic proficiency in the target language, and (2) that the composer was consequently on an unequal footing with the translator, who conversely was not sufficiently musical to interpret the musical language fully in words. The peculiarities of Mendelssohn's case make clear that these assumptions should not be applied unquestioningly to his output; indeed, they necessarily raise other, more complicated questions whose answers effectively negate the modern rule of thumb regarding translated versions of his music: What were the composer's thoughts on the communicative tensions that inevitably seem to arise between linguistic and sonorous modes of communication—most notably, when verbal and musical accentuations, phrases, and structures come into conflict? What factors determined whether a given composition was suitable or unsuitable for translation in his view? What role did genre play in his thinking on these issues, specifically as regards solo, chamber, and large-ensemble works? Most pressingly, what are the criteria by which latter-day performers and other interpreters can reliably differentiate between translations of his music that are artistically viable and those that are not?

Since the heart of the matter is the relationship between textual and musical meaning in Mendelssohn's vocal works, I begin this essay by reviewing some of his salient views on this issue. I then address the first three of the questions proposed above by examining Mendelssohn's interactions with English translators in some detail, followed by some more general remarks on the issues involved in French and Italian translations of his music. A third section deals with works that were conceived and composed in other languages (and in some instances translated back into German). The evidence offered in those three discussions then suggests some viable—if also inevitably conjectural—responses to the question of the authority and artistic viability of various translations of his music.

RED ROOFS: WORDS AND MUSIC IN SOLO WORKS AND ENSEMBLE WORKS

Latter-day assumptions about the relationships between words and music tend to differ from Mendelssohn's views. Many, perhaps even most, contemporary musicians tend to consider words (and language generally) as reasonably precise conveyors of meaning, and consequently to assume that the proper domain of music in texted compositions is to depict "the meaning" of the text in tones. In this view, the ideas behind well-chosen words can be understood objectively, and well-written music interprets the composer's understanding subjectively. But Mendelssohn held that language is inherently incapable of objectively conveying ideas, while music could convey ideas to every individual precisely. Music, in his view, is the language of the ideal, a language that each individual can understand in terms of his or her individual experience. And since the number of individuals' experiences through which a given musical expression of an idea will inevitably be filtered is potentially as great as the number of auditors, no two individuals are likely to use the same words to describe the same ideas conveyed by any given musical composition. Music is a universally comprehensible mode of communication, objective within the realm of subjective experience, while words are a notoriously unreliable means for effective communication.

Perhaps unwittingly, Mendelssohn himself generated a need to explain these views. The explanations were occasioned by works that at first blush might seem irrelevant to his vocal music: the *Songs without Words (Lieder ohne Worte)* for piano solo or instrumental chamber ensemble.[3] In the late 1820s, the composer began heading these piano miniatures "Lied," thus invoking, paradoxically, a genre that was by definition a musical setting of a German text.[4] Throughout his life Mendelssohn occasionally composed or wrote out these textless "Lieder" as album-leaves for friends and acquaintances. After they began to be published as *Lieder ohne Worte,* as *Songs without Words,* and as *Romances sans paroles* in the 1830s,[5] attempts to formulate in words the supposedly hidden or suppressed meanings or texts behind the piano compositions became common, especially in Germany. Already in 1830, after leaving such a Lied with Josephine von Müller, Mendelssohn had to explain that "precisely . . . the main thing about such a *Lied ohne Worte*" was "that everyone later thinks up its words and its meaning, and sets this out in his own way. . . . [I]t really depends only on one's disposition." He then instructed Fräulein Müller to "just invent the verses for [her]self."[6]

More famously, in 1841 Marc-André Souchay Jr. wrote to Mendelssohn proposing a series of detailed titles that he believed expressed the poems that he believed had to underlay the individual *Songs without Words* from the first four volumes—titles such as "resignation," "melancholy," "scene of a *par force* Hunt," "praise for the goodness of God" (for op. 19[b] nos. 1–4) or, more amusingly, "Boundless but unrequited love, which therefore often turns into longing, pain, rage, and despair, but always becomes peaceful once again" (op. 38 no. 1).[7] Mendelssohn tactfully but firmly drew on Souchay's proposed titles in affirming once again that words could express meaning only subjectively, whereas good music was universally comprehensible:

> There is so much spoken about music, and yet so little is said. I believe that words are entirely insufficient for that, and if I should find that they were sufficient, then I would write no more music. People usually complain that music is so ambiguous; that what they should think when they hear it is so unclear, whereas everyone understands words. But for me it is just the opposite, and not just with entire discourses, but also with individual words—these, too, seem to me so ambiguous, so unclear, so misleading in comparison to good music, which fills one's soul with a thousand things better than words.—What the music I love expresses to me is thoughts not too *unclear* for words, but rather too *clear*. I therefore find in all attempts to put these thoughts into words

something correct, but also always something insufficient [and] not universal; and this is also how I feel about your [suggestions]. But this is not your fault, but rather the fault of the words, which simply cannot do any better. If you ask me what I was thinking of in them [the *Lieder ohne Worte*], then I will say: just the song as it stands there. And if I had even one certain word or certain words in mind for one or another of these songs, I could not divulge them to anyone, because the same word never means the same things to different people, for only the song can mean the same thing, say the same thing, arouse the same feelings in one person as in another—a feeling which is not, however, expressed by the same words.—Resignation, melancholy, praise of God, a *par force* hunt: one person does not think of these in the same way as someone else. Resignation is for one person what melancholy is for another; a third person can't get a clear sense of either. Indeed, if one were by nature an enthusiastic hunter, for him the *par force* hunt and the praise of God could be pretty much the same thing, and for him the sound of horns would truly be the proper way to praise God. *We* [on the other hand] would hear nothing but the *par force* hunt, and however much we were to debate with him about it we would get absolutely nowhere. The words remain ambiguous, but we all understand the music.[8]

Whether we agree with Mendelssohn's views or not, their implications for the relationship between language and music are profound. Since music expressed ideas universally but words could only respond to ideas—and could do so only on an individualized basis—there was no call for the sort of detailed text-painting and musical imagery that one associates with the songs of (for example) Schubert and Schumann. Already in 1831 Mendelssohn had characterized such descriptive settings of texts as juvenile: "To me such things always seem like a game, rather like the paintings in children's primers in which the roofs are painted bright red so that the children will notice that they're supposed to be roofs."[9]

More generally, it follows that the main criterion for couplings of words with music is that they mutually respond to the same idea or ideas (or rather, that they do so at least in the composer's eyes). In Mendelssohn's view, when he set a text to music his task was to realize in tones the ideas he perceived to underlay the text, and to do so in such a fashion that the music would mediate between his and other auditors' understanding of the words. The same should be true when texts are invented or found to fit with music. Since both music and words were expressions of ideas, neither came first, neither should be privileged over the other, and neither should be protected from the other. They collaborate as equals in conveying ideas. As he put it to his close friend Carl Klingemann, who wrote the texts for eight of Mendelssohn's songs and the duet "Herbstlied" (op. 63 no. 4): "With your words, I have the singular feeling that I don't need to create any music: it is as if I read it between the lines, as though it already stood before me."[10]

Finally, it should be noted that the above remarks concern repertoires that center on explicitly individualized interpretation and performance—solo songs and works for piano solo. They do not necessarily apply to collective or staged repertoires (genres that in performance tend to assume more than one performer with text, such as part-songs, concerted or ecclesiastical choral music, operas and oratorios, etc.). Since Mendelssohn's contributions to those collective and staged genres tend to feature more obvious text-painting—more "red roofs," as he might put it—than his solo songs do, we may provisionally surmise that he considered those genres to require more conspicuous musical effort in conveying the ideas of the text.

English Translations

The complex legalities of early- and mid-nineteenth-century copyright law made it a practical necessity for composers to publish their compositions simultaneously or very nearly so in at least two countries; absent such publication, works would be effectively unprotected and thus vulnerable to piracy.[11] Theoretically, such unethical publications could take the form of plagiarized editions that credited one composer for another one's work; more commonly, they resulted in publishers' producing and selling compositions without remunerating the composer or his/her authorized publisher(s)—and, of course, without offering the composer opportunities for proofing and correcting their editions. This situation could easily raise artistic difficulties in the vocal music of composers less linguistically proficient than Mendelssohn, since they would be less able to evaluate issues of translation and text/music relationships in non-native editions of their music. Moreover, for practical reasons the need for carefully coordinated multinational releases increased with the composer's reputation. During the years of Mendelssohn's ascent to fame he could risk some flexibility in these simultaneous multinational publications. By the 1840s, however, his renown was such that he could allow exceptions only when there was little chance of a practical market for the work in broader markets. Finally, it should be remembered that under early- and mid-nineteenth-century copyright practice the rights to a work belonged to the primary publisher(s) once they were purchased from the composer. After music was published composers had no legal authority to control, review, or prohibit spin-off editions.[12]

These factors are readily evident in the publication histories of Mendelssohn's authorized publications of music in English translation (see table 11.1). Because the German Lied seems to have aroused little attention in England until the mid-1840s, none of his works in that genre were released in the 1830s. What is more, since even his greatest success in the domain of sacred music during those years, *St. Paul,* was (in the words of Peter Ward Jones) "at best a steady seller,"[13] English publications of his sacred music were likewise rather peripheral. His first major orchestral psalm setting (Psalm 115, op. 31) remained unpublished in England until it was picked up retroactively in 1845.[14] The orchestral psalm-settings opp. 42, 46, and 51 did appear in England and with English texts contemporaneously with their German counterparts, but these translations were uncredited—a subtle but clear suggestion of a perfunctory status for the English versions. And *St. Paul* was published with a credited English translation by William Ball, but Mendelssohn's first real opportunity to review and revise this text came only late in the publication process, as he was working through the proof-sheets for the first German edition (which included the English text beneath the German one).[15]

The situation changes in the 1840s. The first trigger for the change seems to have been a decidedly minor work: Mendelssohn's setting of Thomas Moore's poem "The Garland." In 1841 the composer offered the English version of this setting to Edward Buxton, a wool broker who had taken over the London music firm of J. J. Ewer and Co. out of love for music and would eventually become one of Mendelssohn's close friends; Buxton quickly accepted, and the song was released later that year—the first appearance of a solo song by Mendelssohn in England. In 1842, then, the composer's friend J. W. Davison, a prominent music critic, inquired on behalf of the London firm of Wessel and Stapleton as to whether Mendelssohn had works to sell them. By December the composer had offered them his op. 57 songs, which appeared in the summer of 1843 with Davison's "adapted" English translations of the texts (as well as the German ones). In the meantime, Ewer and Co. under Buxton's leadership undertook several major publications of the vocal music. The first English editions of the symphony-cantata *Lobgesang* (*Hymn of Praise*), op. 52, and the incidental music to Sophocles's *Antigone,* op. 55, coincided with a series of translated publications of Mendelssohn's songs beginning in 1843. First out were the six part-songs for male voices op. 50,[16] the part-songs for mixed vocal quartet op. 59, and then in 1844 the mini-cycle of part-songs "The First Day of Spring" from Mendelssohn's op. 48.[17] These were followed by a retrospective English translation of his op. 41 part-songs, which had been published with considerable success in Germany already in 1838, and then in 1845 and 1846 by English editions of his five previous volumes of solo songs (opp. 8, 9, 19[a], 34, and 47). Finally, having caught up with Mendelssohn's contributions to vocal chamber music and helped to launch the relatively new English interest in German song, Ewer and Co. also published the English editions of his opp. 63 and 71 collections (as well as numerous posthumous ones). Like Novello, Wessel and Stapleton seems to have gotten itself left out in the cold.[18]

Table 11.1. English Translations of Mendelssohn's Music Published during His Lifetime

Year of first English ed. / (Year first published)	Brief Title	Text source(s) / Translator	Publisher of English ed. (all in London)	Remarks
1836	St. Paul / Paulus, op. 36	Bible, A. B. Marx, A. Baur, J. Schubring, J. Fürst, Mendelssohn / Wm. Ball	Novello	
1838	As pants the heart. The 42nd Psalm / Der XVII. Psalm, op. 42	[Psalm 42] / [uncredited]	Novello	
1839	Da Pacem Domine: motett. Grant us thy peace: prayer. / Verleih uns Frieden. (Da nobis pacem, Domine. Gebet nach Lutherschen Worten mit lateinischer Uebersetzung)	Bible / [uncredited]	Novello	In English ed. words in English and German; in German ed. words in German and Latin.
1840/41 (1841)	When Israel out of Egypt came. The 114th Psalm / Der 114te Psalm, op. 51	[Psalm 42] / [uncredited]	Novello	
1841	Hymn of Praise / Lobgesang, op. 52.	Bible / [uncredited]	Novello	
1842	Come let us sing. 95. Psalm / Der LXXXXVste Psalm, op. 46	[Psalm 95] / [uncredited]	Novello	
1843	6 Songs / 6 Lieder, op. 57	Various / J. W. Davison	Wessel & Stapleton	
1843	Incidental Music to Sophocles's Antigone, op. 55	Sophocles / J. J. C. Donner / W. Bartholomew	Ewer	
1843	6 vocal quartets for two trebles, tenor, and bass . . . / Sechs vierstimmigen Lieder . . . im Freien zu Singen, vol. 3, op. 59 (SATB)	Various / W. Bartholomew		

(continued)

Table 11.1. (continued)

Year of first English ed. / (Year first published)	Brief Title	Text source(s) / Translator	Publisher of English ed. (all in London)	Remarks
1844 (1838)	6 Songs for Four-Part Mixed Chorus, to Be Sung Outdoors [], [vol. 1], op. 41 (SATB) / 6 vierstimmige Lieder [. . .] im Freien zu Singen	Various / W. Bartholomew	Ewer	English ed. includes pf reduction
1844 (1840)	The first fay of Spring. A ciclus of three vocal quarets / (from 6 vierstimmige Lieder . . . im Freien zu Singen, Vol. 2, op. 48) (SATB)	Various / W. Bartholomew	Ewer	Nos. 1–3 only.
1844 (1840)	6 vocal quartets for four male voices / 6 Lieder für vierstimmigen Männerchor, op. 50	Various / W. Bartholomew	Ewer	
1844	Die erste Walpurgisnacht / The First Walpurgis-Night, op. 60	Goethe / W. Bartholomew	Ewer	
1844	Incidental Music to Shakespeare's A Midsummer Night's Dream, op. 61	(Shakespeare) / Schlegel / Tieck / (E. Buxton)	Ewer	
1844	6 two-part songs / 6 zweistimmige Lieder, op. 63	Various / [uncredited]	Ewer	
1845 (1827)	11 Songs / 12 Gesänge . . ., op. 8	Various / W. Bartholomew	Ewer	Omits No. 12 (by Fanny Hensel) of original German ed. Nos. 10 and 11 by Hensel.
1845 (1830)	12 Songs / 12 Gesänge, op. 9	Various / W. Bartholomew	Ewer	Nos. 7, 10, and 12 by Hensel.

1845 (1833)	6 Songs / 6 Gesänge, op. 19[a]	Various / W. Bartholomew	Ewer	
1845/1846 (1837)	6 Songs / 6 Gesänge, op. 34	Various / W. Bartholomew	Ewer	
1844 (1840)	Fest Gesang, Hymns of praise / Festgesang	A. E. Prölss / W. Bartholomew	Ewer	German version for male chorus; English version for mixed chorus
?1845 (1835)	Not unto us, Lord / Non nobis Domine / Nicht unserm Namen, Herr, op. 31	Psalm 115 (Vulgate) / Luther / [uncredited]	Novello	First composed in Latin
1846 (1839)	6 Songs / 6 Gesänge, op. 47	Various / W. Bartholomew	Ewer	
1846	An die Künstler (Festgesang) / Cantata from Schiller's poem To the Sons of Art, op. 68	Schiller / W. Bartholomew	Ewer	
1847	Elijah / Elias, op. 70	Schubring, Mendelssohn, et al./ W. Bartholomew	Ewer	
1847	6 Songs, op. 71	Various / W. Bartholomew	Ewer	

Note: Includes only works originally written in languages other than English

These interactions naturally produced extensive correspondence between Mendelssohn and his English translators. By far the most important of
these was William Bartholomew (1793–1867), the in-house translator for
Ewer and Co. Mendelssohn wrote to Bartholomew in detail about questions, reservations, and problems he had with his translations. Sometimes
these reservations were of a general nature; sometimes they were quite specific. For purposes of this short text three examples must suffice to illustrate
the compositional care and artistic integrity of this translational discourse.
The first of these concerns the difficulties of formulating an appropriate English text for the chorus widely known in the English-speaking world as the
Christmas carol "Hark! The Herald Angels Sing"; the second, Bartholomew's
translations for the first English edition of the op. 59 choral songs; the third,
the Finale of Mendelssohn's incidental music for Shakespeare's *A Midsummer
Night's Dream*.[19]

"Hark! The Herald Angels Sing" is a posthumous contrafactum of the
chorus "Vaterland, in deinen Gauen" from the so-called Gutenberg cantata,
which Mendelssohn composed in 1840 for the Leipzig celebrations of the
quatercentenary of the invention of printing by movable type.[20] In its original version (appendix 11A, column 1) Bartholomew's text fit the rhythm
of the notes but departed from Mendelssohn's original in its theme and its
overall character; he also switched the positions of this movement and the
full chorus "Der Herr, der sprach, es werde Licht!" To both of these licenses
Mendelssohn objected vigorously:

> My thanks also for your translation of the Festgesang, the copy of which I have
> not yet received. I like your words very much; but there is one thing which
> strikes me: the words of the Lied no. 2 (which is No. 3 with you) seems [*sic*] to
> me much too pathetic, and indeed I think the whole loses its intended charac-
> ter if this Lied is not a patriotic (rather jolly and cheerful) affair. The creation of
> man I would never have composed in such a gay and soldierlike strain. This
> Lied was, as I wrote already to you, the chief feature of the whole thing and
> just its coming in immediately after the Chorale enhanced its effect. I should
> not like its coming after the great Chorus, as well for its sake as for the Lied's.
> But above all I should like to have the English words more congenial to the
> solemnly-gay Character of the German. It has been sung (I mean the Lied
> only) here and there in this country at solemn Occasions, and they have of
> course written different words to it, but they always kept the Character of pa-
> triotism and liberty, which I also wish to see preserved in the English version.
> Why could it not be a song to Guttenberg [*sic*] as well as in German? Or to any
> other great man more familiar to English ears?[21]

Bartholomew initially responded defensively, expressing a view of music
and words decidedly contrary to Mendelssohn's ideas discussed earlier in
these pages.[22] But he wrote again on 11 May with a more moderate position,

including with his letter a new text that adopted some of Mendelssohn's suggestions (see appendix 11A, column 2) and stating that if Mendelssohn still
disliked the verses he should let him know: "I will yet try again to please *you,*
for you deserve it for the sake of the beautiful music you give the world."[23]
Mendelssohn thanked Bartholomew for his effort but remained dissatisfied
with the text for the Festgesang:

> I cannot as yet agree to the version of the "Lied" in the "Festgesang." Pray do
> not be very angry with me! I even liked your first version better than the one
> you last sent. This last is a mixture of both, which I do not think effective, and
> indeed your introduction of Guttenberg [*sic*], and of the art of printing in En-
> glish verse, makes me aware that the difficulty is greater than I thought at first.
> I am almost sure now that Guttemberg [*sic*] and the graphic pen and all that is
> not the thing, and that nothing of the kind should be mentioned in the
> poëm.—But what then? you will say. I answer with the the [*sic*] French
> proverb, criticizing is easy, but the art is difficult. I do not know; but I neither
> wish the creation of man, nor the creation of typography, and yet I wish for
> something national, popular, and lofty at the same time. I am sure you would
> wish I was in the Pepper-Country (as we say in Germany.)[24]

Bartholomew sent another revision of the words on 26 June,[25] now
casting the hymn as a Jubilate calling on mortals to praise God (see appendix 11A, column 3). This attempt, too, failed to please the composer, who
now offered more specific suggestions for the translation:

> Many thanks for your kindness[,] for your last letter, for the new translation,
> for everything! Of course I like your Verses very much, but you must not be
> angry, if I still am as stubborn as an old post: the idea of a Jubilate, of a praise
> the Lord andc. to that song of mine has some thing [*sic*] in itself which hurts
> me. This is not the strain in which I would sing a Jubilate, a "Praise the Lord."
> While I read it just now again and again, an idea struck me: could you not ad-
> here to the first word of the German verses, and make this eternal no. 2 in-
> stead of a Jubilate, a song in honour to *your* country, to your "Vaterland"? *That*
> is the sense of my music, if it is "praise the land" instead of the "Lord" then my
> music is right; or perhaps "happy land" or "happy thou" or andc. Really the
> more I think of it, the more I think it could and should be done so! The first
> two stanza's [*sic*] in praise of your English "Vaterland" and the third where the
> G minor commences, speaking of darkness, of bad times which may surround
> that countries [*sic*] horizon for a little while, but which must soon vanish be-
> fore the sun, and ending with that same "happy land" or "happy anything" as
> the others. This national feeling is at heart the only thing which to my idea
> the music can truly express; sacred it will never be, and the more sacred the
> words are, the less my notes will seem so. If you approve of this idea, it would
> involve indeed a general alteration, and the whole would become much more
> of a hymn to God, the creator of England, than to Him the Creator of the
> world—but so much the better. Mr. Buxton who visits Germany in August as
> I understand, shall bring you the brass-Score as a small atonement for this
> endless trouble.[26]

Work on formulating an appropriate English version dragged on for some time yet, but Mendelssohn ultimately prevailed in prodding his translator to an English version whose words corresponded to the music of this *Festgesang*. Ultimately, the effort seems to have paid off. As shown in appendix 11A, column 4, and appendix 11B, Bartholomew finally decided to make the English version of the "Lied" a hymn to learning—the abstraction of Gutenberg's contribution as represented in the German text. The composer even managed to retain something of Bartholomew's idea of a Jubilate. Mendelssohn shifted the return to the textual refrain ("Learning dawn'd" / "Gutenberg") back by one phrase, closing the hymn with the line "Till the earth with one accord, / Shall adore and praise the Lord." The translated text capitalizes on the original's imagery of darkness and light (mm. 41 and 53) and uses this dichotomy to invoke metaphorically the work's larger dichotomies of ignorance and knowledge, danger and salvation. That result was achieved by Mendelssohn's collaborating with his translator by discussing the subject of the music, its position and role in the larger work, and its musical/textual sense. (The irony, of course, is that Mendelssohn's music is now known as a Christmas carol despite his efforts to ensure that it be known as expressing "national feeling," and especially despite his statement that "the more sacred the words are, the less [his] notes [would] seem so.")

Mendelssohn was equally meticulous in gestural as well as substantive matters in reviewing translations of his music. Bartholomew and Buxton sent him Bartholomew's translations of the texts for the op. 59 choral songs on 18 July 1843,[27] and Mendelssohn responded with another detailed set of questions, suggestions, and concerns on the 31st. Here, too, we find the composer fully conversant in the general and particular issues of the English translation as well as in the vocal declamation:

> Many thanks for yesterday's letter with the translation of the 6 songs. I like it very much and have only a few trifling objections to make, none to any of them as a whole, but only to some details[.] Your despair about Eichendorff['s] poetry has made me laugh very much; it is a very odd thing, and meant to be so, and would sound still more wild if translated litterally [*sic*]; I think your reason a very good one, and as a whole it corresponds with the German meaning perfectly, although I miss some details "O Lieb O Liebe" andc. (which by the bye is not adressed to a lady)[28] for which I am not sorry at all, as it sings the better, and is much easier understood, and is indeed much more the thing than a more litteral [*sic*] translation would be. My objections (for you see I am the eternal objector) are:
>
> 1) In no. 2, the last two stanza's [*sic*] and more particularly the last, and more particularly the last two lines, and most particularly the Corydon in them.[29]—Pray don't let us have Corydon, or any such name in it. I could never reconcile it to my feelings, if Corydon, or Phyllis, or Damon came in at the end. I would even wish that neither "he" nor "she" was mentioned, and that it

was something of love which the Tenor and Bass could say as well, as the Soprano and Alto. So it is in the German although it does not seem so, and although it is a rather difficult passage, of which a litteral [*sic*] translation would
not do at all. There are some more objections I have in that song. . . . Then I
would wish in the beginning of the last but one [i.e., penultimate] Stanza [m.
74] to have the German expression "zum Busen kehrt er zurück" [([it returns
to the bosom)]—at least the *returning,* because it is this word that gave me the
idea of coming back to the first subject and it does therefore well with the
music. And then it is so fine in the poetry to follow the Zephyr (or what wind
it may be) on its way: beginning first "more powerfully,"[30] "vanishing" then in
the bushes, and returning at last to the bosom or the feeling of the poet! But
before all, pray kill Corydon, because I detest him amazingly.

Now pray forgive me [*sic*] fastidiousness, and have my best thanks for the
difficult task you have again so masterly done. The altered notes, as you propose
them, will suit me completely.[31]

Like the previously quoted letter concerning the Festgesang, this letter
demonstrates Mendelssohn's appreciation of the technical, poetic, and stylistic issues involved in producing translations of musical settings. He carefully considers the essential idea ("the sense," as he put it in his letter of 16
July 1843) that underlay his music and tries to optimize the consistency between the "translated" words and that idea. He weighs options for adapting
the specific language in order to convey that idea to auditors in the target
language, at the same time guarding against unwarranted literary or topical
cross-references. He verifies that significant instances of text-painting come
across in the translated text. And, writing in English with wit and diplo-
macy, he firmly negotiates revisions so that the final translated text is consistent with his intentions.

As a final instance of Mendelssohn's collaboration in these brief remarks, the matter of the incidental music to *A Midsummer Night's Dream*
must be cited. This "translation" is especially complicated because of the
circumstances of the music's commission and the issues entailed in producing a poetically and musically sensitive and practical retroactive fitting of
modernized Shakespearean English to the German words Mendelssohn set
to music—that is, Ludwig Tieck's adaptation of Friedrich Schlegel's rather
free translation of the original play.[32] Buxton himself fitted the English texts
to Mendelssohn's music in this instance, but the end of the music's Finale
(Act 5, sc. 1, in the play) gave him problems. On 18 March 1844, with the
simultaneous English and German publication date of 1 May bearing down
hard on him, he wrote of the quandary to the composer:

For the M[id] S[ummer] N[ight's] D[ream] music we cannot fix an earlier
day than the 1st [of] May as I do not see a possibility of getting it ready earlier.
I have written in the words for all except one piece, viz[.] the first part of the
Finale, where the words are

Bei des Feuers mattem Flim*mern*	Through this house give glimmering light,
Geister, Elfen, stellt euch ein!	By the dead and drowsy fire:
Tanzet in den bunten Zim*mern*	Ev[']ry Elf & fairy sprite
Manchen leichten Ringelreihn!	Hop as light as bird from brier [*sic*]
Singt nach seiner Lieder Weise,	And this ditty after me
Singet, hüpfet, lose, leise!	Sing and dance it trippingly.

If you will be kind enough to compare these words with the music you will find either the one or the other must be altered, and more practically at the end of the movement rather than the beginning—there is nothing in the english [*sic*] that will fit the words *lose, leise,* andc.. . . . I beg you will put the thing in ship shape as soon as possible in order that the work will be got ready by the time you come. If we alter the text I'm afraid our orthodox people will carp at it, but I would rather have that done, than that any effect of the music should be lost. I think however it will be easier for you to alter the music, than for us to alter the words.[33]

Mendelssohn's response, written ten days later, produced the final version (different from the definitive one only in the absence of any long note values):[34]

As for the words of the Finale, <u>of course</u> the music must be altered[.] I propose thus [see example 11.1].

EXAMPLE 11.1.   Mendelssohn's suggestion for musical alterations to Accommodate Text in Finale of *Midsummer Night's Dream* Incidental Music, in letter to Edward Buxton of 28 March 1844 (GB-Ob, MS M. Deneke Mendelssohn c. 42, no. 39).

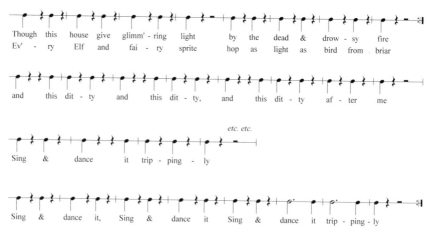

There is one further complication attendant to Mendelssohn's *Midsummer Night's Dream* music: the only musical primary sources that contain the "translated" text—that is, in this instance, the original Shakespearean English—are the English arrangements for voices with piano duet or piano solo; no orchestral materials prepared or published with Mendelssohn's supervision include English texts. Although this might suggest that Mendelssohn intended the English text to be heard with only the keyboard arrangement of his music, not the orchestral version, that impression is misleading. Mendelssohn himself conducted selections from op. 61 with voices and orchestra in concert on several occasions,[35] and a review of contemporary periodicals reveals that English audiences were no strangers to the work in its orchestral guise under other conductors. It does, however, indicate that the authority of the English and German versions should be linguistically differentiated.

French Translations

The steady spread of Mendelssohn's international fame during his last twenty-five years also made it lucrative for publishers in France and Italy to market his works. Once again, however, the exigencies of nineteenth-century publishing practice complicate the task of reconstructing his interactions with those venues. Aside from the comparatively undeveloped state of general research into Mendelssohn's reception in those countries, the biggest obstacle is that firms outside the countries of the primary publishers could, by arrangement with those publishers, act as distributors of his works without actually engraving them themselves. To distribute an already engraved edition was financially advantageous except when the work's genre or already-achieved renown ensured a high volume of sales. This situation easily permitted what modern readers might call "end-users" (i.e., individuals and groups who purchased the distributed products) to privately fit texts in their own language(s) to the music, without this being reflected in the official bibliographic record. As a corollary, much of Mendelssohn's music circulated in manuscript copies based on the printed sources, and when the music in question was vocal it naturally could have new texts in the target language fitted to it. Such official publication agreements as did exist did not require the composer's permission (again, because the copyright resided with the firm that had purchased the work).

Despite these difficulties, the surviving editions and correspondence permit a few observations about the French and Italian translations of his music up to about 1850.[36] In the early years of Mendelssohn's publishing activity, France might have seemed more likely than England as a potential market for his works. Felix's father, Abraham, was a pronounced Francophile, and the Paris-based house of Maurice Schlesinger collaborated with that of his father, Adolph Martin, Schlesinger in Berlin in producing Mendelssohn's first few published opera. As in England, however, no French or Italian publisher made a fortune from Mendelssohn's music until after his death and the commencement of the era of offset printing (the 1860s). Moreover, French and Italian firms typically undertook publication of Mendelssohn's instrumental works. *St. Paul* seems to have succeeded reasonably well in both France and Italy after it was finally published there in the early 1840s, but *Die erste Walpurgisnacht,* the *Lobgesang,* and *Elijah* were successful only in France. His French editions were typically arranged for or mediated by his German publishers; his Italian editions, by his French publishers. The correspondence with his French translators was more limited than that with Bartholomew, while the correspondence with his Italian translators was limited or nonexistent.

Does this rule out the relatively few editions of Mendelssohn's vocal music that appeared in Italy and France during his lifetime? To some extent, yes. But it is still helpful to be aware of the French and Italian editions that did appear with his cognizance—that is, to recognize those that have at least some historical authority—and to differentiate between these and later translations. Armed with this sort of awareness, we can study and evaluate the historically proximate French and Italian translations using the criteria Mendelssohn demonstrably employed in his English translations.

Mendelssohn's publication activities brought him into collaboration with five French publishers. Of these, Charles Simon Richault (normally styled Simon Richault) dealt exclusively in Mendelssohn's instrumental works during his lifetime. At the mediation of Mendelssohn's parents and the Berlin publisher Adolph Martin Schlesinger, the Parisian firm of Maurice Schlesinger participated in the publication of the prodigy Mendelssohn's op. 1 in 1823;[37] and although a falling-out interrupted the collaboration in the late 1830s,[38] matters had been repaired by the early 1840s. The Parisian Schlesinger released the first French editions of Mendelssohn's op. 34 songs and *St. Paul* as well as numerous instrumental works. The distinction of the first French edition of *Elijah* resides with Brandus and Co., established in 1846 when Louis Brandus (1816–87) purchased the firm of Maurice Schlesinger; that edition, however, was released only posthumously, in 1851. The Parisian firm of Alexandre Grus in 1843 published a French translation of Mendelssohn's op. 57 songs in collaboration with Benacci and Peschier (which at the time was based in Lyons), and Benacci and Peschier also published Book 5 of the *Lieder ohne Worte* and the French editions of *Die erste Walpurgisnacht* and the op. 63 songs, as well as the

A-minor Symphony (op. 56), the Second Cello Sonata (op. 58), and a piano-solo arrangement of three instrumental movements from the *Midsummer Night's Dream* incidental music. On the whole, Mendelssohn seems to have trusted Benacci more than his other French publishers. The surviving correspondence describes an unusually substantive relationship and demonstrates Benacci's conscientiousness in representing Mendelssohn faithfully in France (rather than simply exploiting his renown).

Insights into the French translations that resulted from these complicated interactions are offered by the translators' professional profiles and the few known letters surrounding the relevant publications. Certainly the most reputable of the named translators was the composer, critic, and poet Maurice Bourges (1812–81). House translator first for Maurice Schlesinger and then for Brandus, Bourges created the "paroles françaises" for Maurice Schlesinger's edition of *St. Paul* (1843) and Brandus's edition of *Elijah* (1851). He also served as translator for French editions of Bach's *St. Matthew Passion,* Weber's *Euryanthe* and *Oberon,* numerous Schubert songs, and Bellini's *La Sonnambula,* as well as authoring the libretto of Jean-Georges Kastner's "biblical opera" *Le dernier roi de Juda* (1844). His numerous contributions to the *Revue et gazette musicale de Paris* add to his credibility as a translator of Mendelssohn's works. There is no surviving documentation of any interaction between Mendelssohn and Bourges, either directly or through Schlesinger. But the composer's renewed association with Maurice Schlesinger in the 1840s suggests that he was not dissatisfied with the firm's representation of his *St. Paul* in Bourges's French translation.

Another named translator of Mendelssohn's works into French was Edouard Bélanger. Bélanger was associated primarily with the firm of Richault. Like Bourges, he established himself as a reputable translator of songs by Schubert and Beethoven. He also authored the French translation of Mendelssohn's posthumously published oratorio fragment generally known as *Christus* and a posthumously issued competitor to Bourges's French translation of *St. Paul.* But Bélanger priced himself out of the running for the role of Mendelssohn's preferred French translator in the late 1840s: according to Benacci and Peschier (to whom Mendelssohn offered his op. 71 songs in 1846), after the success of his Schubert translations Bélanger became "unapproachable" and demanded "exhorbitant" [*sic*] fees for each individual song.[39]

In at least one important instance, however, Bélanger's translation raised questions—for reasons that are understandable but also instructive in a broader sense. The work in question is *Die erste Walpurgisnacht* (op. 60), Mendelssohn's setting of Goethe's ballad centering on the eighth-century conflict between the pagan Saxon tribes of the Harz mountains and their Christian adversaries. Bélanger's translation reinterprets Goethe's historical protagonists in a sense that is both historical and disconcertingly contemporary: the poem's pagans are Gypsies, while the Christians are archers engaging in the "sport" of Roma/Gypsy-hunting, long officially sanctioned as legitimate recreation and evidently practiced clandestinely well into the twentieth century. The Parisian critic Léon Kreutzer praised Mendelssohn's music while issuing a withering critique of Bélanger's translation.[40] Certainly this "translation" goes some distance toward trivializing the "elevated symbolism" of ineluctable historical processes that were born of conflicts between that which is "old, established, proven, [and] reassuring" and "emergent renewals," as well as the poem's foregrounding of the midpoint in those processes by ending with the pagans' (temporary) victory.[41] On the other hand, by distancing the work from its literal historical subject and abstracting the cultural/ideological conflict as one that applied equally to contemporary contexts, Bélanger did precisely what the poet and composer themselves had done. Goethe first explained the poem to Carl Friedrich Zelter (whom he had invited to set the poem to music) strictly in terms of its literal historical subject and construed it in terms of its "elevated symbolism" only years later, when he learned that Mendelssohn had completed a setting and intended to have it performed publicly.[42] And at the first public performances Mendelssohn himself explained the cantata in terms of its historical subject;[43] only when he prepared the score for publication did he elect to preface it with the poet's symbolic explanation. By contemporizing the text for a French and predominantly Catholic audience (whose empathy for the poem's pagan Saxons would have been limited), Bélanger may have achieved the sort of consistency between idea and music that Mendelssohn had pleaded for in his letters to Bartholomew concerning the Lied from the Gutenberg cantata. And Kreutzer's insistence on a more literal interpretation might have been viewed by the composer as the sort of naiveté that had occasioned his responses to Müller and Souchay. (Unfortunately, whether Mendelssohn approved of or even saw Bélanger's free interpretation of the text of the *Walpurgisnacht* remains unclear.)

More direct surviving evidence concerns Louis Delâtre, who translated Mendelssohn's op. 57 songs for publication by Benacci and Peschier in 1843. On 13 August 1843 Delâtre sent his translations of the songs to Benacci, who immediately forwarded them to Mendelssohn for his approval and/or revisions with the assurance that the translator had done his best to convey the sense and the prosody of the German texts, as well as their musical rhythm.[44] The original versions of these translations are now lost, but on 10 September Mendelssohn wrote a detailed and quite favorable letter in

French to Benacci, requesting that he convey his gratitude to "the distinguished poet, . . . who has shown himself to be an able translator as well as an expert concerning our [German] language and our music." He then listed several "bagatelles" that he wished to have changed for the final version:

> To begin with, I cannot consent to calling the first song "*Chant de douleur*" [song of sorrow];[45] that is not the expression that it can or should have. It is a song of solitude, of silence in the forest, of silence, but not of sorrow. And this is why I do not like the rhymes of the second and fourth lines, "*le flot-noir*" [the dark gush] and "*sans espoir*" [without hope]. If there could be something somewhat sweeter, somewhat less bitter, I would prefer that. In the second song,[46] is there some way to go ahead and introduce the mountains and height in place of the two lines "*Aux danses des jeunes filles, les collines*"? It [height] is in the original German, and it is above all those tall mountains with their cries that I wished to compose. The same goes for the next line for "*au fond des bois*" [on the forest floor]. I would much prefer something like "*sur les rochers*" [above the rocks] or something comparable. I very much admire the translation of the third [song],[47] especially the fourth verse, but I feel strongly critical of the name *Emile*. Suleika's lover could not have been called *Emile* and his name is not *Emile*. I hope that that name can be retracted in any case; it is also not in question in the original, and what does a given name matter anyway? And then in the last song[48] I am a little repulsed by the word "*hourra*" [hurrah], which occurs just before the close. At least this is neither the shout that I wished to compose nor the feeling that inspired it. But if it is impossible to change this word without changing the end of the poem I would prefer to leave it alone, because the ending is so well- and literally translated that no one could improve it or replace it [with anything better].[49]

The surviving correspondence thus shows that the Benacci and Peschier edition of op. 57 not only obtained the approval of the composer, but also reflected his own evidently meticulous input into the textual revisions. Mendelssohn certainly also appreciated Benacci's assurance (issued in a letter of 16 October) that he had entered the requested alterations into the proofs and deposited the volume in the copyright office again, and that he would ensure that it was not released until the revisions had been fully met even if this necessitated a further delay in the publication date.[50] And at any rate, Mendelssohn offered his op. 71 songs to Benacci on 24 September 1846[51]— an offer that surely would have been withheld if he were not fully satisfied with the firm's and Delâtre's prior representation of him and his music.

Italian Translations

There are no authorized Italian translations of Mendelssohn's music, at least not in the sense that applies to the various French translations that appeared during his lifetime. As Pietro Zappalà has established, Benacci and Peschier recognized the untapped commercial potential of Mendelssohn's music in Italy and petitioned the composer for the exclusive rights to publications of his music there, but Mendelssohn was unable to grant such sweeping permission because it would have constituted a conflict of interest with his German publishers (especially Breitkopf & Härtel) who exported their editions to Italy.[52] This does not mean that at least some of Mendelssohn's vocal music did not circulate in translation in Italy, however; nor does it preclude at least a measure of authority for those texts. It simply means that issues of authority are often genuinely murky.

The issue of Italian translations of Mendelssohn's music involves many of the same problems posed by the French ones. In the Italian-speaking countries as in France, Mendelssohn became a viable musical commodity only relatively late, and initially only through indirect channels. Mendelssohn's vocal music also had to overcome a certain prejudice among Italian musicians: the publisher Ricordi explained why his firm's eagerness to publish any of Mendelssohn's works except those including the voice by stating that most of "our Italian dilettantes" wished to sing only excerpts from operas that had been performed in "our [Italian] theatres," and the knowledgeable musicians who could appreciate German and French vocal works were too few to offset the costs of production.[53] Despite these issues, after the mid-1840s a genuine rivalry for the Italian rights to Mendelssohn's music developed between Ricordi and the Milan firm of Lucca. This rivalry involved not only legitimate Italian original editions of Mendelssohn's music (vocal as well as instrumental), but also a more clandestine culture of manuscript copies with Italian texts and even a pirated printed edition of at least one major work, *St. Paul*. This underground culture—which resulted in the composer being sent a handsomely produced manuscript copy of *St. Paul*, while an utterly unauthorized version was published without any involvement of any sort on the part of the composer[54]—laid the groundwork for the substantial increase in Italian interest in his vocal works in the second half of the century.

Works Composed in Languages Other Than German

The last group of works to be discussed here are those compositions that Mendelssohn composed not in German, but in English, French, or Italian; to these we must also add works written in Latin (a category not applicable to the works written in German, since Mendelssohn translated none of those into Latin). In some instances Mendelssohn eventually provided a German translation or counterpart to the original text, but in others he never did. The

Table 11.2. Works Originally Composed in Latin

Date	Brief Title	Publication /MS / Leipziger Ausgabe der Werke von FMB (LMA)	Remarks
1819/20	In secula seculorum amen (vocal fugue) (4 vv).	In R.L.Todd, *Mendelssohn's Musical Education* (Cambridge: Cambridge University Press, 1983) [LMA VI/3]	Composed for Pauline Anna Milder-Hauptmann
1822 (?Mar.)	Gloria in E flat (2SATB, ch, orch)	In K.E. Hatteberg, *Gloria* (1822) and "*Große Festmusik zum Dürerfest* (1828) . . ." (D.M.A. diss., U. of Iowa, 1995); P. Zappalà (Stuttgart: Carus, 1998); R. Wehner, 2001 (LMA VI/4)	
1822 (Mar.–May)	Magnificat in D (SATB, ch, orch)	P. Zappalà (Stuttgart: Carus, 1997) / R. Wehner, 1997 (LMA VI/5)	
1822 (Oct.–Nov.) (1st vers.) [LMA VI/3]	Jube dom'ne (solo vv and 2 4-pt ch)	G. Graulich (Stuttgart: Carus, 1980) (2nd vers.); R. Wehner (Leipzig: Deutscher Verlag für Musik, 1993) (1st Verso.) [LMA VI/3]	2nd version ded. Cäcilien–Verein Frankfurt am Main
1824 (Apr.) 1826 (Dec.)	Salve Regina (S, str) Te Deum in D major (2S 2A 2T 2B, dbl ch, bc)	G. Graulich (Stuttgart: Carus, 1980); [LMA VI/6] W. Burkhardt, LMA vi/1 (1966; rev. ed. 1988); W. Burkhardt (Stuttgart: Carus, 1976); B. Mohn (Stuttgart: Carus, 1996) [LMA VI/1]	
1827 (July) or 1828	Salvum fac populum tuum (soloists, ch, orch)	D-B MN 46 [LMA VI/6]	Probably intended as autonomous; later inserted into autograph for *Te Deum* as alternative to its "Salvum fac populum"
1827 (Nov.)	Tu es Petrus, op. posth. 111	J. M. Cooper (Stuttgart: Carus, 1996); [LMA VI/6]	

(continued)

Table 11.2. (*continued*)

Date	Brief Title	Publication /MS / Leipziger Ausgabe der Werke von FMB (LMA)	Remarks
1828 (July)	Ave maris stella (S, orch)	H. Ryschawy (Stuttgart: Carus, 1993) [LMA VI/6]	
1828 (Nov.–Dec.)	Hora est (bar, 16 vv, org).	M. Hützel (Stuttgart: Carus, 1981) [LMA VI/2]	
1830 (Dec.)	O beata et benedicta (Zum Feste der Dreieinigkeit) (motet) (2S, A, org).	P. Horn (Stuttgart: Carus, 1978) [LMA VI/2]	
1830 (publ. 1832, 1838)	Ave Maria, op. 23 no. 2 (T, dbl ch, org/orch).	G. Graulich (Stuttgart: Carus, 1977); [LMA VI/2]	1832 edn. is parts and figured b.c. part; 1838 edn. is orch
1829–30 (publ. 1835)	Non nobis Domine [Nicht unserm Namen, Herr] (Psalm 115), op. 31 (S, ch, orch)	R. L. Todd (Stuttgart: Carus, 1994) [LMA VI/8]	
1830 (Dec.) (publ. 1838)	Surrexit pastor, op. 39 no. 3	G. Graulich (Stuttgart: Carus, 1977); [LMA VI/2]	
1830 (Dec.) (publ. 1838)	Veni Domine, op. 39 no. 1	G. Graulich (Stuttgart: Carus, 1977); [LMA VI/2]	
1833 (Feb.)	Ad Vesperae Dominicae XXI post Trinitatis, Responsorium e Hymnus "Adspice domine," op. posth. 121	G. Graulich (Stuttgart: Carus, 1979); [LMA VI/2]	
1837 (Feb.)	[2 Sacred choruses], op. posth. 115	G. Graulich (Stuttgart: Carus, 1980); [LMA VI/3]	No. 1: Beati mortui in Domino morientes; No. 2: Periti autem fougebund, ut fulgor aethenes
1837 (Aug.)	Laudate pueri, Dominum, op. 39 no. 2	G. Graulich (Stuttgart: Carus, 1977); [LMA VI/2]	
1846 (Feb.–Mar.)	Lauda Sion, op. posth. 73 (solo vv, ch, orch).	R. Larry Todd (Stuttgart: Carus, 1996); [LMA VI/6]	

Date	Brief/Title	Text Source	First English Publication / Leipziger Ausgabe der Werke von FMB (LMA)	Remarks
1829 (May) (publ. 1841)	By Celia's Arbour All the Night ("The Garland")	T. Moore (Eng.)	London: Ewer, [1841]; [LMA VII/6]	Autogr. also contains German text (An Celias Baum in stiller Nacht, "Der Blumenkranz") beneath Eng. Also published simultaneously by Braunschweig: Spehr, with German text.
1830	Far from the moveless dark bright eye (Charlotte to Werther).	W. F. Collard, after Goethe	In *Apollo's Gift, or the Musical Souvenir for 1831* (London: S. Chappell, [1830]): [LMA VII/6]	Autograph incl. inc. German text beneath Eng. Music reused for text "Seemanns Scheidelied" (H. v. Fallersleben, 1850); Mendelssohn had nothing to do with that contrafactum.
1832 (Aug.) (publ. 1846)	Te Deum ("We praise thee, O God," for the Morning Service) (SSATB solos, chor, org)		London: Ewer, [1846]; [LMA VI/2]	Composed at invitation of V. Novello for Anglican morning service. Also publ. 1847 with Jubilate Deo (see below)
1833 (Feb.) (publ. 1842)	Lord have mercy upon us (ch, org)		London: Ewer, [1842]; [LMA VI/2]	Also erroneously as "Evening Service" or *Abendsegen*.
1833 (Aug.)	There be none of beauty's daughters	Byron	*Album Musical auf das Jahr 1837* (Leipzig: Breitkopf & Härtel, 1836), and independently (Leipzig: Breitkopf & Härtel, [1837]); [LMA VII/6]	Not published in England during Mendelssohn's lifetime. German text probably by K. Klingemann.
1839 (Feb.)	Lord, hear the voice of my complaint (SATB)	N. Tate and N. Brady, metrical arr. of Ps. 5 (1696)	H.E. Ditbdin, comp., *The Standard Psalm Tune Book* (London: D'Almaine, [1851 or 1852]); [LMA VI/3]	

(continued)

Table 11.3. (continued)

Date	Brief Title	Text Source	First English Publication / Leipziger Ausgabe der Werke von FMB (LMA)	Remarks
1839 (Feb.)	Defend me, Lord, from shame (SATB)	N. Tate and N. Brady, metrical arr. of Ps. 5 (1696)	C.D. Hackett (comp.), *The National Psalmodist* (London: Coventry & Hollier, 1839); [LMA VI/3]	
1840–43	Anthem: Why, O Lord, delay (A, ch, org or orch)	Ps. 13, paraphrase by C.B. Broadley	Mvts 1–3 only (without fugual finale) as *Anthem for a mezzo soprano, with chorus* (London: Cramer, Addison, & Beale, [1841])	Orch. Version posth. publ. as *Hymne*, op. 96. See discussion in text (pp. 234–235)
1844–45	Hear my prayer (S, ch, org or orch).	W. Bartholomew, after Ps. 55	London: Ewer, [1845] (version with org acc); London: Novello, Ewer & Co., [1880] (version with orch); [LMA VI/2]	
1847 (Apr.)	Jubilate Deo ("O be joyful in the Lord," for the Morning Service), op. 69 no. 2 (SATB solo, ch, org)		London: Ewer, [1847]; [LMA VI/3]	Published with Te Deum (see above) as second part of Morning Service. German text fitted by Mendelssohn; Ger. vers. publ. 1848 as a cappella motet, with doxology from 17 Jan. 1844
1847 (Jun.)	Magnificat ("My soul doth magnify the Lord," for the Evening Service), op. 69 no. 3 (SATB solo, ch, org)		London: Ewer, [1847]; [LMA VI/3]	Composed with Nunc dimittis (see below) for Anglican Evening Service. German text fitted by Mendelssohn; Ger. vers. publ. 1848 as a cappella motet.
1847 (Jun.)	Nunc dimittis ("Lord, now lettest Thou Thy servant," for the Evening Service), op. 69 no. 1 (SATB solo, ch, org)		London: Ewer, [1847]; [LMA VI/3]	Composed with Magnificat (see above) for Anglican Evening Service. German text fitted by Mendelssohn; Ger. vers. publ. 1848 as a cappella motet.

Note: Lists only most important source-critical editions; identifies the appropriate series and volume of the Leipziger Ausgabe der Werke von Felix Mendelssohn Bartholdy (LMA); where LMA volume is not yet published as of this writing, projected series and volume numbers are given in [brackets].

latter group thus comprises works whose existence with German texts must be considered unauthorized translations, even though German was the composer's native tongue. Inventories of these works are provided in tables 11.2–11.3;[55] the following remarks single out a few instances for clarification.

Mendelssohn composed works in Latin throughout his career (see table 11.2). Accordingly, the issues of translation raised by these works vary from case to case. On the one hand, there are works such as the two large-scale motets for voices and orchestra, *Tu es Petrus* (op. posth. 111), and *Lauda Sion* (op. posth. 73). Neither the autograph, the contemporary copies, nor the posthumous editions of the 1827 *Tu es Petrus* employs anything other than the Latin text, whereas the *Lauda Sion,* composed and completed in the last year of Mendelssohn's life, almost immediately acquired German and English translations as well as its original Latin one. Because of the brevity and the general nature of the text of *Tu es Petrus* (the Vulgate's reading of part of Matthew 16:18),[56] Mendelssohn's setting could easily have been translated into virtually any other language; while the *Lauda Sion* employs the venerable Catholic sequence for Corpus Christi by Thomas Aquinas and the melody by Adam of St. Victor, and thus seems if anything more inherently imbued with Latin/Catholic elements. Yet the later work quickly became polylingual (and thus implicitly pan-denominational, with the composer's full authorization), while the early one never received a translated text, even when it was posthumously published as Mendelssohn's op. 111 in 1868.

The reason for this disparate treatment probably lies once again in the deep-seated affinity between verbal language, musical language, and religious connotation and function in these two Latin works. *Tu es Petrus,* which Mendelssohn in 1828 called his "most successful piece" (*mein gelungenstes Stück*)[57] represents a tightly woven amalgamation of historical and liturgical references—elaborate *stile antico* polyphony in the context of a modified ternary form in which the modified return of the "A" section offers a dazzling display of the *ars combinatoria,* all with full-sized Romantic orchestra and chorus.[58] These elements are bound together by the text, whose underlying idea symbolized the concept of Catholic Church as both an ecclesiastical institution and a historical fact.

By contrast, the *Lauda Sion,* composed in 1846 to commemorate the six-hundredth anniversary of the Feast of Corpus Christi, carries a lengthy text (80 lines) that is explicitly didactic and communal.[59] It exhorts all to praise the Blessed Sacrament, celebrates the founding of the institution, and concludes with a prayer of supplication and invocation of mercy in the glorious grace of God. Mendelssohn composed the work with Latin and French texts before him, and wrote only the Latin text in the score. Although he asserted that the work would "hardly do . . . without the Catholic church and its ritual,"[60] he proceeded apace with arrangements for an English first edition, to be issued simultaneously with the German one. William Bartholomew prepared an English paraphrase for the former, but Mendelssohn was unable to review it because it reached him only in his final days.

The first publication of the *Lauda Sion* was the English piano-vocal score, published early in 1848. This edition included Bartholomew's English text and the Latin original. It was followed in 1849 by the German first editions of the orchestral and piano-vocal versions. Both piano-vocal scores provided the Latin text, and the full score provided the English as well. More significantly, both now included a German translation of unknown provenance. Most problematic of all, through a fluke of the work's source-history and chronology, all three omitted an important movement that Mendelssohn wrote (with Latin text) in the autograph, temporarily removed, and ultimately reinstated for the premiere. The edition included in the series of Mendelssohn's collected works edited by Julius Rietz and published by Breitkopf & Härtel in the 1870s omitted both that movement and the English text, but did include the spurious German translation. Only in 1996 did the work finally appear in its complete form.

The *Lauda Sion* thus raises significant issues of translational authority. Certainly the Latin text is authoritative, but the English version by Bartholomew (omitted from almost all editions since the English one issued a few months after Mendelssohn's death) probably should also be considered valid, since Bartholomew was by then thoroughly familiar with Mendelssohn's ideas and standards for translated texts.[61] The French text might, theoretically, be next in line, but it appears in no manuscripts or published editions. But the German text that has been a fixture of all editions since 1849 carries no authority at all. Neither written, solicited, nor approved by the composer, it is an anonymously composed and posthumously applied contrivance. In other words, aside from the Latin version, the textual authority of the English and German editions of the *Lauda Sion* is precisely the opposite of what all editions currently in print would suggest.

Despite certain parallels with *Tu es Petrus,* then, the *Lauda Sion* represents a second class of Mendelssohn's Latin compositions: those in which the (still common) German translation ranks as the most suspect and unauthorized version. To these must be added a third class comprising works composed in Latin but ultimately published with German text as well, with Mendelssohn's authorization. The most notable works in this class are the three op. 39 motets for high voices with accompaniment of piano or organ. Composed with Latin text in December 1830 for the nuns of the Convent of Trinità de Monti in Rome, these works languished among Mendelssohn's manuscripts for seven years. After the firm of N. Simrock

(Bonn) accepted his offer of publication in April 1837 he decided that it would also be necessary to provide them with German texts. In this instance, he wrote the German texts himself—an undertaking that brought him much difficulty.[62] By the time he submitted the manuscript to the German publisher he had already arranged for their publication in England by Novello, and thus requested that the corrected proofs be sent immediately to the English firm. The motets were published individually with separate listings under the single opus number "39" early in 1838. The German edition carried both Latin and German texts; the English edition, Latin and English texts.

The smallest group of the remaining non-German compositions is those written in French. It is probably coincidental that the French compositions fall at the outer ends of Mendelssohn's career, but the chronological difference may also be seen as a function of Mendelssohn's development. The early song "Pauvre Jeanette" (1820)[63] probably was set in consequence of Abraham Mendelssohn's well-known Francophilia, while the late canticle "Venez et chantez" was written for the French Reformed Church in Frankfurt am Main and intended for inclusion in a new hymnal to be published by that church.[64] The earlier work was intended for strictly familial use;[65] the later one, for communal use among French Protestants in Germany.

Both the autograph and the first edition of the *Cantique* carry only French text. Because the form of the only text that Mendelssohn aligned with his melody is incompatible with what he would have considered a chorale,[66] "Venez et chantez" should neither be considered a chorale nor sung in German: its linguistic identity, functional identity, and music are mutually interdependent. Yet for all its stylistic simplicity, the canticle also offers its share of subtle but artful musical responses to the ideas and emotions of its text.[67]

Mendelssohn's few surviving patently Italian compositions comprise the bulk of his concert arias. The earliest of these works, *Che vuoi mio cor?* for soprano and piano (1823; text by Metastasio) was composed and circulated in manuscript copies with Italian text only, but with its posthumous publication in 1880 it also acquired a new German text attributed to a certain "A. Matthias." Three more concert arias, likewise based on *opere serie* by Metastasio, exist with Italian texts only and remain unpublished: the 1825 aria for baritone and piano, *Ch' io t'abbandono,*[68] the incomplete aria for soprano and orchestra *Tutto è silenzio* (1829), and the 1834 aria for soprano and orchestra with obbligato violin, *Infelice! / Ah, ritorna, età dell' oro* (written for Maria Malibran). The last of these provided a general compositional starting point for the later concert aria *Infelice! / Ah, ritorna, età felice,* written for mezzo-soprano Sophie Schloß in January 1843 and premiered with

Italian text in February 1843.[69] At some point Mendelssohn also entered a German translation of the text into the autograph for the 1843 aria, and Schloß performed the aria with that text in London on 26 May 1845. The German version may have been used for the final performance during Mendelssohn's lifetime, again given by Schloß with the Leipzig Gewandhaus Orchestra under Mendelssohn's direction. The posthumous publications of the 1843 aria as Mendelsson's op. 94 (issued by Breitkopf & Härtel and Ewer and Co. in 1851) again introduced a new translational element: the German editions offered both the Italian and German texts, as is proper, but the English editions dispensed with the German text and replaced it with an English one by Bartholomew. Bartholomew was certainly well-placed to provide such a translation. But since Mendelssohn neither published the work nor imagined it as having an English text, the English version in this instance must be considered spurious.

The final group of Mendelssohn's non-German compositions—those written in English—is in some ways the most complicated, for despite compelling artistic (and, in some instances, biographical) merits, most of these works remain little known (see table 11.3). Those that are more familiar often circulate in versions with German texts. Most unimposing among these English compositions, but hardly artless, are Mendelssohn's hymn-like settings of Psalms 5 and 31. Twenty-eight and twenty-six measures long respectively, these a cappella settings were composed on 26 and 27 February 1839, pursuant to a commission from Coventry and Hollier. The setting of Psalm 31 was published later that year in the London firm's *The National Psalmodist*. It was republished along with the setting of Psalm 5 in 1852, in a collection titled *The Standard Psalm Tune Book,* compiled by Mendelssohn's friend Henry Dibdin. Both works escaped the attention of the Breitkopf & Härtel collected-works series of the 1870s and have remained largely unknown. They were first published in a modern edition in 1997, including the original English texts and a newly written German translation by Heidi Kirmße.[70]

More obviously important but still obscure is the solo anthem "Why, O Lord, delay," for mixed chorus with organ or orchestra.[71] Mendelssohn composed this anthem for mezzo-soprano solo, chorus, and organ at the invitation of Charles Bayles Broadley on 12 December 1840, using Broadley's metrical English paraphrase of Psalm 13. As a complement to the planned English edition he arranged to have the work published by Simrock, in "a very good German translation" (presumably penned by himself).[72] He also added that he would have nothing against it if the publisher wished to add a Latin text for use in Catholic churches.[73]

According to plan, the privately published English edition of the anthem was published ca. 15 April 1841; Simrock, for his part, was first able to publish the "very good German translation" of the anthem in August (with English text also included) as *Drei geistliche Lieder für eine Altstimme mit Chor und Orgelbegleitung* (no opus number). Both of these versions were in three movements and called for organ accompaniment. In the meantime, however, Broadley had requested an orchestrated version—and when Mendelssohn undertook to compose this he decided to include a new final movement, a fugue on the text from the closing verses of Broadley's text. The composer's friend Ignaz Moscheles then retroactively arranged this fugue for organ accompaniment, and this arrangement was published ca. June 1843 as the "fourth movement of an anthem . . . composed . . . by Felix Mendelssohn Bartholdy."[74] It was not, however, published in Germany. Finally, in 1852 Breitkopf & Härtel published the complete orchestral and keyboard versions—now assigned the new title of *Hymne* and the opus number "96" and still carrying the English text beneath the German one. The keyboard version of the fourth movement was not attributed to Moscheles. Eventually the English version—the text that had occasioned the work and inspired its music—was left behind. Despite its inclusion in David Brodbeck's fine edition,[75] the work evidently continues to be performed and recorded only in its German version. The musical world seems unaware of the existence of an English version that is more authoritative than the familiar German one.

Outside the realm of sacred music, the most important English works belong to the genre of the concert aria and the solo song. The concert aria in question is *On Lena's Gloomy Heath* (1846) for baritone and orchestra, based on an English text from James Macpherson's legendary Ossianic forgeries—a text, ironically enough, that purported to be a translation from ancient Gaelic.[76] The existence of at least three contemporary manuscript copies—all with English text only—suggests that *Lena* enjoyed some measure of popularity in the mid and late nineteenth century.[77] It certainly stands as a musically rewarding contribution to the nineteenth century's legacy of evocative musical responses to the Ossianic texts, and a document of continental/insular cultural interactions of the day. Unfortunately, it remains unpublished even today.[78]

A final important example of the English works retroactively fitted with German texts occurs in the Two Romances on Texts by Byron, composed in 1833–34.[79] Because of Byron's erratic lifestyle, his social isolation, and his engagement as advocate for radical social change, many continental artists (including composers, of course) found in him the personification of the Romantic ideology that led to the wave of revolutions at mid-century. This was the persona evoked (and invoked) in works such as Berlioz's *Harold in Italy,* Liszt's *Tasso,* and Schumann's incidental music to *Manfred.* It is not, however, the persona that appealed to the urbane, cosmopolitan Mendelssohn. Instead, the first of his two romances, "There Be None of Beauty's Daughters," celebrates the delicate, sensually amorous aspect of Byron's poetry, while the second, "Sun of the Sleepless," is an intimate study in bleak melancholy.

Mendelssohn composed the first of these songs in English and the second to a German translation of Byron's English. After several revisions, both were published late in 1836.[80] The music, however, proved to be less of a challenge for Mendelssohn than the text—for in preparing to disseminate his musical responses to Byron's poetry to the German public, Mendelssohn struggled mightily to obtain a German text that would not stop at being a literal translation of the words of the poem. Instead, the German text had to endeavor to express verbally the ideas and feelings that Byron's poetry had aroused in him and inspired his music. When he began to consider publishing his settings he asked his close friend Klingemann (who had written original texts for several of Mendelssohn's songs and would frequently collaborate with him in interpretive and translational issues) to provide new words:

> I recently found my composition of Byron's "There be none of beauty's daughters" in Mde. Moscheles's song book, and I liked it very much, and I would like for the song to become known. But this is absolutely not possible with the English words—neither in England nor here. Also I could imagine different words, which would be much better suited for singing than the English ones, but I can only think of them, not produce them; you can do that, and I ask you, would you please do it for me? I will tell you what my thoughts were.[81]

Once his friend had undertaken the task, Mendelssohn described his thoughts on the general idea of the first song's text and sent him some "bumpy" verses of his own to serve as a starting point:

> The beginning should be "Denkst Du noch der sel'gen Stunde, wo Du sprachst, ich bleibe Dein," and later in the second part, where it modulates to C major. And at the return to the A-major theme I had instead of the verses "whose breast is gently heaving["] etc. etc. up to "adore thee" the following four:
>
> > "Und die Nachtigall mit süssen
> > Liedern wiegt uns flötend ein,
> > da sank ich zu Deinen Füssen
> > und Du sprachst, ich bleibe Dein.["]
>
> . . . I would like to have the mood of the song as it is in these horrible verses, it seems just right to me (that is, their sense) and for the return to A major I would like a word such as "da" [there] and a "Fussfall" [falling at feet], or an "ewig" [ever], or something else like that.[82]

The language of this letter, of course, anticipates that of Mendelssohn's correspondence with Bartholomew in the 1840s. The final irony, however, is that he never considered publishing the Byron settings in England. They were published only in Germany, by Breitkopf & Härtel, with both German and English texts. Only later (perhaps posthumously) did they begin to circulate in England as well.

The English compositions offer more such complicated case histories than can be discussed in these few pages.[83] Each case is unique. What they have in common is that they raise translational issues that stem from Mendelssohn's habit of creating music as a consummately subjective mode of expression whose task it was to express the sense he perceived in the words— and doing so clearly enough for different listeners to understand the ideas he found in the poem better than would be possible with the words alone. Because of his persistent avoidance of "red roofs" and his simultaneous efforts to clarify the idea he perceived in the text, the authorized translations of his works are generally no less successful than were the original ones. These are translations of substantial artistic worth.

Conclusions

The above observations permit some instructive observations concerning the merits and weaknesses of various translations of his music. As is always the case, translations for all the posthumously published works (all works with opus numbers higher than 72, as well as those published without opus number after early 1848) bear no direct authorial input—although those by Bartholomew obtain a measure of presumable credibility because of his extensive collaboration with the composer. Among the works published in English translations during Mendelssohn's lifetime, most of those by Bartholomew were subject to very real authorial scrutiny and bear the stamp of the composer's (well-certified) approval. William Ball's translation of *St. Paul* and the various uncredited translations of Mendelssohn's music that appeared before the collaboration with Bartholomew begun in the 1840s may be generally free of outright errors, but they bear a lesser stamp of substantive authority. The same is true of the posthumously issued French editions of Mendelssohn's music by Bélanger and Bourges. Certainly those translators' efforts profited from their having worked with the composer on projects that he oversaw and/or implicitly approved. Still, their remaining translations should also be reviewed more critically and are more susceptible to alteration at the performer's discretion.

Most importantly, modern performers and scholars should recognize the limited usefulness of usual modern assumptions regarding versions of Mendelssohn's music in languages other than his native German. We should neither automatically privilege the authority of the German-language versions of his works nor unthinkingly dismiss or downplay settings in other languages. With the surge of documentary scholarship concerning nineteenth-century music and the unprecedented accessibility of electronically transmitted bibliographic data in the information age, most of the necessary tools are within reach of every mature musician. Mendelssohn insisted on his identity as a *deutscher Komponist,* as witness his numerous posthumously published and still unpublished solo songs, part-songs, concert arias, and choral works with German text only. But his well-known cultural breadth and lifelong compositional engagement with English, French, Italian, and Latin texts suggests that he viewed that identity as inviting or even requiring linguistic and cultural diversity and pluralism. The editions most inherently spurious are those that deny or diminish those central aspects of his identity. And the real challenge to performers interested in a faithful rendering of his music is to strive for that same cultural, linguistic, and musical comprehensiveness.

Appendix 11A. Successive versions of Bartholomew's text for "Vaterland, in deinen Gauen"

First version[1]	Second version[2]	Third version[3]	Final version
Man. No. 3	Proposed alteration for No. 2	No. 2 Jubilate	No. 2
Let our theme to heaven ascending	Let our theme to heaven ascending	Mortals, all your voices blending	Let our theme of praise ascending,
Fly in music's holy strain	Fly in music's holy strain:	Sound His praise in joyous lays!	Blent in music's lofty strain,
Soaring through the starry main	Soaring through the starry main	Let the song to heav'n ascending	Soaring thro' the starry main,
Blessed with echos [sic] never ending!	Blessed with echos [sic] never ending!	Waking echos [sic] never ending,	Peal in echoes never ending.
"Heaven and earth appear!" he said—	Heaven inspired the wondrous man	Praise the Lord! let all the earth	Learning dawn'd, its light arose;
Stars heaved with astral throes,	Who devised the graphic plan;—	Sound His praise in strains of mirth!	Thus the Truth assail'd its foes.
Order from disorder rose!—	Heaven inspired the hand that wrought		
Thus the heavens and earth were made!	Signs that first embodied thought.		
Light, from darkness disentangled,	By the pen, our feelings worded—	Vale and mountain, stream and ocean,	Faith and Hope began to banish
Morning dawned serenely bright;	Heard in sounds that breaking die,—		Doubt and soul-appalling Fear:
And when evening brought the night,	Clad in forms, before the eye	Fragrant flow'r and fruitful bow'r,—	Spreading, shining still clear,
Heaven appeared with stars e'er spangled!	Stand indelibly recorded!	All, instinct with life and motion,	Error in their beams will vanish,
He ordained the glorious Sun,	Heaven inspired the wondrous man	Aid the lay of pure devotion,—	Learning dawn'd, its light arose;
Day by day his course to run;	Who defined the graphic plan,—	Praise the Lord! let all the earth	Thus the Truth assail'd its foes.
With the "lesser light" appear	Heaven inspired the hand that wrought	Sound His praise in strains of mirth!	

Appendix 11A. (*continued*)

First version[1]	Second version[2]	Third version[3]	Final version
"Signs and seasons, days and years"!	Forms imbued with living thought.		Mortals roam'd without a guide,
Fruitful verdure clad the land; All was instant life and motion.	Traced at Sinai's cloud cap'd brow, Great Jehovah's code was given:	Praise His greatness, praise His might,	Darkness clouded ev'ry nation; Not a ray could be descried, All was gloom and desolation: Learning dawn'd, its light arose; Thus the Truth assails its foes.
From the hollow of his hand, Poured he forth the teeming ocean!	We behold it graven now Brought by man, and taught by heaven.	In the firmament, adore Him, In His temples day and night,	
Last, and best of all he wrought, Man was made, endued with thought!	Thus inspired the favoured Sage Multiplied the sacred page,—	Homage Him and bow before Him,— Him, whose mercy far exceeds All His wonder-working deeds,	
Wondrous Man's immortal soul,	Gutenberg, with art divine,[4]	Praise the Lord! let heav'n and earth	Till the earth with one accord,
Formed the climax of the whole!	Stamp'd the first metallic line,	Sound His praise in strains of mirth!	Shall adore and praise the Lord.
Angels shouted—"Godlike man,	Gutenberg, the wondrous man,		
Crowns Jehovah's glorious plan!"	Thus improved the graphic plan!		

Notes

1. Bodleian Library, Oxford, GB 18: 302.
2. Bodleian Library, Oxford, GB 17: 251.
3. Bodleian Library, Oxford, GB 17: 285.
4. Originally: The wondrous man.

Appendix 11B. Mendelssohn, "Vaterland, in deinen Gauen" from Gutenberg *Festgesang*: English translation and original German.

(continued)

Appendix 11B. (*continued*)

Appendix 11B. (*continued*)

NOTES

1. For the German text of the surviving lines, see Felix Mendelssohn Bartholdy, *Paphlëis: Ein Spott-Heldengedicht,* ed. Max F. Schneider and Ursula Galley (Basel: Internationale Felix-Mendelssohn-Gesellschaft, 1961). Excerpts are translated and aptly discussed in Clive Brown, *A Portrait of Mendelssohn* (New Haven: Yale University Press, 2003), 64–73. See also R. Larry Todd, *Mendelssohn: A Life in Music* (Oxford: Oxford University Press, 2003), 70–73.

2. For three of his translations of Dante's sonnets, see August Reissmann, *Felix Mendelssohn-Bartholdy: Sein Leben und seine Werke* (Berlin: J. Gutentag, 1867), 319–21.

3. For a more detailed discussion of these issues with regard to Mendelssohn's songs, with additional documents, see my "Of Red Roofs and Hunting Horns: Mendelssohn's Song Aesthetic, with an Unpublished Cycle (1830)," *Journal of Musicological Research* 21 (2002): 277–317; further, Douglass Seaton, "With Words: Mendelssohn's Vocal Songs," in *The Mendelssohn Companion,* ed. Douglass Seaton (Westport, Conn.: Greenwood, 2001), 661–700.

4. The earliest known example of a piano miniature designated "Lied" is the little-known Lied [ohne Worte] in E-flat major written on 14 November 1828, entered in Fanny Hensel's *Noten-Album.* See Hans-Günter Klein, ". . . dieses allerliebste Buch: Fanny Hensels Noten-Album," *Mendelssohn-Studien* 8 (1993), after p. 152.

5. The English term "songs without words" evidently caught on only unofficially and after Mendelssohn's death. The first volume (op. 19[b]) was published as "Original Melodies for the Pianoforte" by Alfred Novello (London) late in 1832, and as *Lieder ohne Worte* by N. Simrock (Bonn) in 1833. The English edition of the second volume (op. 30) was published as "Romances for the Piano Forte" in 1835. With Volume 3 (op. 38, published in London by J. A. Novello in 1837) the official English designation had become "The celebrated 'Lieder ohne Worte': Book 3 of Original Melodies for the Piano Forte." See Peter Ward Jones, *Catalogue of the Mendelssohn Papers in the Bodleian Library, Oxford,* vol. 3: *Printed Music and Books* (Tutzing: Hans Schneider, 1989), 121–26.

6. Letter from Berlin to Josephine von Miller, Munich, 30 January 1833 (Bayerische Staatsbibliothek Munich, shelfmark Stieleriana I,2). For a facsimile of this letter, see *Felix Mendelssohn Bartholdy: Brief an Josephine von Miller, Berlin 30.01.33* (Biberach/Riss: Dr. Karl Thomae, GmbH, 1980).

7. Translated from letter of 12 October 1842 from Souchay to Mendelssohn, held in the "Green Book" collection of the Bodleian Library, Oxford. Items from this collection are cited by the appropriate volume in the series and item within the volume. This letter is GB 16: 69.

8. Translated from letter from Mendelssohn to Marc-André Souchay, 15 November 1842. The autograph for this letter is currently in private possession; the text as given here is based on a contemporary copy in the Bodleian Library, Oxford (MS M. Deneke Mendelssohn c.32, fol. 56–57).

9. Letter from Mendelssohn to Henriette von Pereira-Arnstein, July 1831; quoted from *Felix Mendelssohn Bartholdy: Reisebriefe aus den Jahren 1830 bis 1832,* ed. Paul Mendelssohn Bartholdy, 5th ed. (Leipzig: Hermann Mendelssohn, 1863), 205–206.

10. Letter of 2 January 1831 from Mendelssohn to Carl Klingemann, printed in Carl Klingemann [Jr.], ed., *Felix Mendelssohn Bartholdys Briefwechsel mit Legationsrat Karl Kingemann in London* (Essen: G. D. Baedecker, 1909), 86. The translation is adapted from Susan Youens, "Mendelssohn's Songs," in *The Cambridge Companion to Mendelssohn,* ed. Peter Mercer-Taylor (Cambridge: Cambridge University Press, 2004), 192.

11. See Jeffrey Kallberg, "Chopin in the Marketplace," in his *Chopin at the Boundaries: Sex, History, and Musical Genre* (Cambridge, Mass.: Harvard University Press, 1986), 161–214.

12. For an earlier but otherwise entirely applicable case study in this problem, see Patricia Stroh, "Evolution of an Edition: The Case of Beethoven's Opus 2," *Notes* 57 (2000): 289–329; *Notes* 60 (2003): 46–129.

13. Peter Ward Jones, "Mendelssohn and His English Publishers," in *Mendelssohn Studies,* ed. R. Larry Todd (Cambridge: Cambridge University Press, 1992), 245.

14. On this and Mendelssohn's other orchestral psalm-settings, see Wolfgang Dinglinger, *Studien zu den Psalmen mit Orchester von Felix Mendelssohn Bartholdy* (Cologne: Studio, 1993).

15. Mendelssohn's correspondence with the German publisher of op. 36 (N. Simrock, Bonn) shows that he carefully checked the English text (see Rudolf Elvers, ed., *Felix Mendelssohn Bartholdy: Briefe an deutsche Verleger* [Berlin: Walter de Gruyter, 1968], 207–208). There is, however, no evidence that he was directly involved in its production or application to the proofs.

16. Mendelssohn himself initiated this series in a letter to Edward Buxton of Ewer and Co. on 14 March 1843 (Bodleian Library, Oxford, MS M. Deneke Mendelssohn c. 42, fol. 68v.

17. See Douglass Seaton, "Mendelssohn's Cycles of Songs," in *The Mendelssohns: Their Music in History,* ed. John Michael Cooper and Julie D. Prandi (Oxford: Oxford University Press, 2002), esp. 203–206.

18. See Ward Jones, "Mendelssohn and His English Publishers," 240–52.

19. Perhaps the most valuable surviving documentation of Mendelssohn's collaboration with his English translators would require explanation and discussion beyond the scope of this short article: the proof sheets for most of the first English edition of the choruses from the *Antigone* incidental music, op. 55, which contain extensive corrections, comments, and cross-references in Mendelssohn's hand as well as well as alterations in the hand of the translator, survive in the Bodleian Library, Oxford (shelfmark Deneke 96). See Peter Ward Jones, *Catalogue,* 87.

20. *Festgesang für Männerchor zur Säcularfeier der Erfindung der Buchdruckerkunst* (Leipzig: Breitkopf & Härtel, [1840]). The German version of this Festgesang is for male chorus only, with double brass choir; for the 1844 English publication Mendelssohn reworked it for mixed chorus. See Peter Mercer-Taylor, "Mendelssohn's 'Scottish' Symphony and the Music of German Memory," *Nineteenth-Century Music* 19 (1995): 68–82.

21. Manuscript copy of letter in English from Mendelssohn to William Bartholomew, 18 April 1843 (Bodleian Library, MS M. Deneke Mendelssohn c.42, fol. 103–104).

22. Letter of 2 May 1843 from Bartholomew to Mendelssohn (Bodleian Library, Oxford, GB 17: 233, p. 2): "I am sorry the words I wrote to your Festgesang Choruses have failed to please you. Music, in my humble opinion, is but a colour for words, which are as definite forms in a picture. The suitability of words and music varies as the minds of the hearer. . . . I have no objection to praise Guttemburg [*sic*], or any man who merits it, but if the originator of printing is to be extolled, we must seek his name in the Chinese empire—where, I believe centuries before Guttemburg [*sic*] was born, letters were cut and multiplied on wooden blocks."

23. Bodleian Library, Oxford, GB 17: 251.

24. Letter in English from Mendelssohn to Bartholomew, 12 June 1843 (Bodleian Library, Oxford, MS M. Deneke Mendelssohn c. 42, fol. 105r–v).

25. Bodleian Library, Oxford, GB 17: 285.

26. Letter in English from Mendelssohn to Bartholomew, 16 July 1843 (Bodleian Library, Oxford, MS M. Deneke Mendelssohn c.42, fol. 107r).

27. Bodleian Library, Oxford, GB 18:26.

28. A reference to mm. 17–21 in the second verse of the "Jagdlied," op. 59 no. 6 (text by Goethe). In his letter of 18 July 1843 Bartholomew had asked whether "O Lieb, O Liebe" was "addressed to Love, a Mistress who is endeavouring to detain . . . the speaker" (Bodleian Library, Oxford, GB 18: 26, p. 3).

29. Bartholomew's original text for the poem's last stanza (Bodleian Library, Oxford, GB 18: 26, p. 1) read: "Feeling impels me / now to impart;—/ Coridon tells me, / I have his heart!" Corydon is the archetypal lovesick youth, as represented by the shepherd in Virgil's *Bucoloics* (or *Eclogues*) II.

30. "Mächtiger rühret bald sich ein Hauch," mm. 63.

31. Letter in English from Mendelssohn to Bartholomew, 31 July 1843 (Bodleian Library, Oxford, MS M. Deneke Mendelssohn c. 42, fol. 108–109). "The altered notes" refers to slight alterations Bartholomew had suggested to accommodate the English diction in mm. 32–33 of the "Jagdlied" (op. 59 no. 6).

32. See ch. 14 ("Portrait of a Prussian Musician") in Todd, *Mendelssohn*, 447–84; and especially the prefatory essays to Christian Martin Schmidt's editions of the orchestral and piano arrangements of the *Midsummer Night's Dream Music*, series 5 vols. 8 and 8a of the Leipziger Ausgabe der Werke von Felix Mendelssohn Bartholdy (Leipzig: Breitkopf & Härtel, 2000 and 2001, respectively).

33. Bodleian Library, Oxford, GB 19: 164, 1–2.

34. Letter from Mendelssohn to Edward Buxton, 28 March 1844 (GB-Ob MS M. Deneke Mendelssohn c. 42, no. 39 (copy by Marie Beneke).

35. Mendelssohn conducted selections in concert with the Philharmonic Society in London on 27 May and 10 June 1844 and 26 April 1846, and at the Birmingham Festival on 27 August 1846. See Todd, *Mendelssohn*, 472–73, 545–46, 528.

36. Research into the publication history of Mendelssohn's music outside Germany and the British Isles during his lifetime is only nascent. The following discussion is deeply indebted to information kindly provided by Cécile Reynaud (Bibliothèque nationale de France) and Pietro Zappalà (Università di Pavia, Cremona).

37. See Peter Ward Jones, "Mendelssohn's Opus 1: Bibliographical Problems of the C Minor Piano Quartet," in *Sundry Sorts of Music Books: Essays on the British Library Collections, Presented to O. W. Neighbour on His 70th Birthday*, ed. Chris Banks, Arthur Searle, and Malcolm Turner (London: British Library, 1993), 264–73.

38. See Elvers, 69, 211, 229.

39. GB 24: 61.

40. Léon Kreutzer, "Société des Concerts et Société Saint-Cécile (2e article)," *Revue et gazette musicale de Paris* 20, no. 14, 3 April 1853, 121–23. Kreutzer's review, along with other issues concerning the translations of *Die erste Walpurgisnacht*, are discussed at length in my *Heathen Muse: The Walpurgis Night, Goethe, and Mendelssohn* (forthcoming).

41. Letter from Goethe to Mendelssohn, 9 September 1831, translated from Christoph Hellmundt, "Mendelssohns Arbeit an seiner Kantate *Die erste Walpurgisnacht:* Zu einer bisher wenig beachteten Quelle," in *Felix Mendelssohn Bartholdy: Kongreß-Bericht Berlin 1994*, ed. Christian Martin Schmidt (Wiesbaden: Breitkopf & Härtel, 1997), 105: "This poem is intended to be symbolically elevated in the literal sense. For in the history of the world it must eternally be repeated that something old, established, proven, [and] reassuring will be compacted, pushed aside, dislocated, and, if not abolished, then corralled into the tightest space. The middle period, in which the hatred is still capable of reacting, and still may do so, is presented here succinctly enough, and a joyous, indestructible enthusiasm flares up once again with brilliance and clarity."

42. See Goethe's letter of 3 December 1812 to Zelter, printed in Karl Robert Mandelkow, *Goethes Briefe, Hamburger Ausgabe in 4 Bänden, Band II: Briefe der Jahre 1786–1805*, 3rd ed. (Munich: C. H. Beck, 1986), 215–16.

43. The program distributed at the premiere of the revised version of the *Walpurgisnacht* (2 February 1843) offered this explanatory note: "During the last years of paganism in Germany, the Christians declared that the druids' sacrifices were punishable by death. Nevertheless, at the beginning of springtime the druids and the populace sought to regain the peaks of the mountains, make their sacrifices there, and intimidate and scare off the Christian warriors (usually through the latter's fear of the devil). The leg-

end of the first Walpurgis Night is supposed to be based on these attempts." For the original German and further discussion of this program, see my *Mendelssohn, Goethe, and the Walpurgisnight: The Heathen Muse in Western Europe, 1700–1850* (New York: University of Rochester Press, 2007), 80–96.

44. GB 18: 52.

45. "Altdeutsches Lied" (Es ist in den Wald gesungen), on a text by "Heinrich Schreiber" (Henricus scriptor). See Seaton, "With Words," 671.

46. "Hirtenlied" (O Winter, schlimmer Winter), on a text by Ludwig Uhland.

47. "Suleika" (Was bedeutet die Bewegung), on a text by Goethe / Marianne von Willemer.

48. "Wanderlied" (Laue Luft kommt blau geflossen), on a text by Eichendorff.

49. Translated from "Una lettera inedita da Felice Mendelssohn," *Boccherini* 7, no. 1 (15 April 1868): 6–7: "D'abord, je ne puis pas consenter à appeler la 1er mélodie, *chant de douleur;* ce n'est pas là l'expression qu'elle peut ou doit avoir. C'est un chant de solitude, de silence dans le forêt, de silence mais non pas de douleur. Et voilà pour quoi je n'aime pas les rimes de la 2e et 4me ligne *'le flot-noir'* et *'sans espoir.'* S'il pouvait y avoir quelque chose de plus doux, de moins amer, je l'aimerais mieux. Dans la 2e mélodie, est-ce qu'il y a moyen d'introduire déjà les montagnes et la hauteur au lieux des deux lignes *'Aux danses des jeunes filles, les collines'*[?] Elle est dans l'original Allemand et ce sont surtout ces hautes montagnes avec leurs cris que j'ai voulu composer. C'est la même chose à la ligne suivante *'au fond des bois.'* J'aimerais bien mieux *'sur les rochers'* ou quelque chose semblable. J'admire beaucoup la traduction de la 3me, surtout de la 4re strophe; mais je trouve fort à redire au nom d'*Emile*. L'amant de la Zuleika ne saurait s'appeler *Emile*, et, il ne s'appelle pas *Emile*[.] J'espère bien que le nom pourra se retrancher tout à fait, aussi n'en est-il pas question dans l'original, et qu'import le nom de baptême en général? Et puis dans la dernière mélodie, j'ai une petite repugnance pour le mot *hourra* qui vient peu avant la fin. Du moins ce n'est pas ce cri, ou le sentiment qui l'inspire que j'ai voulu composer; mais s'il est impossible de changer ce mot sans changer la fin du poème, j'aimerais mieux laisser le tout parceque la fin est si bien et si littéralement traduite que rien ne saurait l'améliorer ou la remplacer."

50. GB 18: 145.

51. Letter from Benacci to Mendelssohn, 1 October 1846 (GB 24: 61). See also the discussion of Bélanger, above.

52. Pietro Zappalà, "Mendelssohn Reception in Nineteenth-Century Italy," paper given at the conference *Mendelssohn in the Long Nineteenth Century,* hosted by Trinity College, Dublin, 15–18 July 2005. I wish to thank Prof. Zappalà for sharing the text of his paper with me in advance of its printing.

53. Letter from Ricordi to Mendelssohn, 22 November 1844 (Bodleian Library, Oxford, GB 20: 182).

54. An Italian translation of *St. Paul* by the Marquis Dominico Capranica was published in 1844 (see Ward Jones, *Catalogue,* 149–50). Mendelssohn was informed of this translation (and publication) only after the fact (letter of 8 January 1845 from Capranica to Mendelssohn, Bodleian Library, GB 21: 169). A lavishly produced manuscript copy of the vocal parts in a translation by L. Mazzini, used for a performance in the Palazzo Vecchio, Florence, on 28 June 1846, was sent to Mendelssohn by the Marquis Marbellini, on 13 May of that year (GB 23: 269).

55. These remarks do not include Mendelssohn's "Kyrie" settings or canons.

56. The Latin text is "Tu es Petrus / Et super hanc petram / aedificabo ecclesiam meam," rendered in the King James version of Matthew 16:18 as "Thou art Peter / and upon this rock / I will build my church."

57. Letter from Mendelssohn to Klingemann, 5 February 1828 (Klingemann, *Briefwechsel,* 48). On *Tu es Petrus,* see especially Ralf Wehner, *Studien zum geistlichen Chorschaffen des jungen Felix Mendelssohn Bartholdy* (Sinzig: Studio, 1996), 188–99.

58. See my edition in the Stuttgarter Mendelssohn-Ausgaben (Stuttgart: Carus, [1996]).

59. The bulk of the following discussion concerning the genesis and publication history of the *Lauda Sion* derives from the "Vorwort" to R. Larry Todd's magisterial edition published in the *Stuttgarter Mendelssohn-Ausgaben* (Stuttgart: Carus, [1996]).

60. Letter from Mendelssohn to Klingemann, 19 January 1847, translated from Klingemann, *Briefwechsel,* 319: "Es (kann) sich kaum ohne katholische Kirche und Zeremonie gut ausnehmen."

61. Unfortunately, the English text is omitted from the otherwise exemplary Carus edition of the *Lauda Sion.*

62. Letter of 23 August 1837 from Mendelssohn to Simrock, printed in Elvers, 213–14.

63. Edited by R. Larry Todd in his *Mendelssohn's Musical Education: A Study and Edition of His Exercises in Composition* (Cambridge: Cambridge University Press, 1983), 148.

64. The *Cantique* was first published in the *Recueil de cantiques chrétiens* (Frankfurt am Main, 1849) under the title "Cantique 103"; neither Mendelssohn nor the author of the text is named. A new edition by Pietro Zappalà (with newly created German translation of the French text) was published as part of the Stuttgarter Mendelssohn-Ausgabe (Carus-Verlag, 1997).

65. See Hans-Günter Klein, trans. Julie D. Prandi, "Similarities and Differences in the Artistic Development of Fanny and Felix Mendelssohn Bartholdy in a Family Context: Observations Based on the Early Berlin Autograph Volumes," in Cooper and Prandi, 238–41.

66. Each strophe comprises six lines and carries the syllabic distribution 9-9-8-9-9-8.

67. See the Vorwort to Pietro Zappalà's edition (n. 63), 6.

68. See Charles Turley, " 'Ch'io t'abbandono' by Felix Mendelssohn Bartholdy: A Dramatic Image of the Education and Aptitudes of the Composer" (D.M.A. diss., University of North Texas, 2002).

69. See my "One Aria or Two? Mendelssohn, Metastasio, and *Infelice,*" *Philomusica Online* 4–5 (2005) at http://philomusica.unipv.it/ (accessed 31 August 2005); further, "Mendelssohn's Two *Infelice* Arias: Problems of Sources and Musical Identity," in Cooper and Prandi, 43–97.

70. See *Felix Mendelssohn Bartholdy: Neun Psalmen und Cantique,* ed. Pietro Zappalà (Stuttgart: Carus, 1997), 12–13.

71. The bulk of the information below is derived from David Brodbeck, "Some Notes on an Anthem by Mendelssohn," in *Mendelssohn and His World,* ed. R. Larry Todd (Princeton, N.J.: Princeton University Press, 1991), 43–64.

72. Letter from Mendelssohn to Simrock, 4 March 1841, in Elvers, 227–28.

73. Mendelssohn to Simrock, 31 March 1841, in Elvers, *Verleger,* 229.

74. Exemplar in the British Library (London), quoted from Brodbeck, 63n23.

75. Stuttgarter Mendelssohn-Ausgaben, CV 40.166 (Stuttgart: Carus, [1998]).

76. See R. Larry Todd, "Mendelssohn's Ossianic Manner, with a New Source: *On Lena's Gloomy Heath,*" in *Mendelssohn and Schumann: Essays on their Music and Its Context,* ed. Jon R. Finson and R. Larry Todd (Durham, N.C.: Duke University Press, 1984), 137–60.

77. In addition to the exemplars in the Bodleian Library and British Library (discussed by Todd), there is at least one exemplar currently housed in an Italian library. I wish to thank Prof. Pietro Zappalà for bringing this exemplar to my attention.

78. *On Lena's Gloomy Heath* has been recorded by Francine van der Heiden and the Robert-Schumann-Philharmonie (Chemnitz) under the direction of Ingo Caetani, using the unpublished edition prepared by R. Larry Todd (Claves 50-9912).

79. For an excellent exploration of both Byron romances and their geneses, see

Monika Hennemann, "Mendelssohn and Byron: Two Songs Almost without Words," *Mendelssohn-Studien* 10 (1997): 131–56.

80. *Album musical: Sammlung der neuesten Original Compositionen für Piano und Gesang von F. Chopin, F. Hünten, F. Liszt, C. Löwe, F. Mendelssohn, G. Meyerbeer, Panseron, L. Spohr. Poetisch eröffnet von Fr. Rückert* (Leipzig: Breitkopf & Härtel, [1836]).

81. Letter of 31 January 1836 to Carl Klingemann, printed in Klingemann, *Briefwechsel,* 199–200. Translation quoted from Hennemann, 131.

82. Translation lightly modified from Hennemann, 139–40.

83. The most important further instance is that of the three choruses op. 69, which were conceived and composed in English and adapted for publication in Germany (with German text) at the last minute. See my edition published by Bärenreiter-Urtext; further, David Brodbeck, "*Eine kleine Kirchenmusik:* A New Canon, a Revised Cadence, and an Obscure 'Coda' by Mendelssohn," *Journal of Musicology* 12 (1994): 179–205.

CONTRIBUTORS

Clive Brown is Professor of Applied Musicology and Head of the School of Music at the University of Leeds. He has published books, including the first critical biography of Louis Spohr, articles, critical editions, and contributions to reference works. His most recent books are *Classical and Romantic Performing Practice 1750–1900* and *A Portrait of Mendelssohn*. He is also an active performer and conductor.

John Michael Cooper is Margarett Root Brown Chair in Fine Arts at Southwestern University in Georgetown, Texas. He is editor of Mendelssohn's *Paulus* and Op. 69 and Op. 78 motets for Bärenreiter Urtext Editions, and author of *Mendelssohn, Goethe, and the Walpurgis Night: The Heathen Muse in Western Europe, 1700–1840* and *Mendelssohn's "Italian" Symphony.*

Kenneth Hamilton, a member of the music faculty of the University of Birmingham, UK, is well known internationally as a concert pianist and writer on music. He is author of *Liszt: Sonata in B Minor* (Cambridge University Press) and editor of *The Cambridge Companion to Liszt.* His latest book, *After the Golden Age: Romantic Pianism and Modern Performance*, has recently been published by Oxford University Press.

Monika Hennemann is Visiting Lecturer in Music at the University of Birmingham. Primarily a specialist on Mendelssohn, she has also published on Liszt, Berlioz, and other aspects of nineteenth-century music. She is presently preparing *The Piano in Prose,* a co-authored annotated anthology of textual and musical sources related to the development of the piano for publication.

Peter Ward Jones has been Head of the Music Section of the Bodleian Library since 1969, where his responsibilities include curatorship of the library's great Mendelssohn collection. His many publications have included an edition of the illustrated diary that Mendelssohn and his wife kept jointly during their honeymoon and first months of marriage in 1837. He is also active as an organist and harpsichordist.

David Milsom is an AHRC-funded Research Fellow at the School of Music, Leeds University, UK. His primary research area is late-nineteenth-century violin performance practice, with particular reference to Joseph Joachim. Aside from his research work, David is an experienced instrumental teacher and violinist.

Siegwart Reichwald is Associate Professor of Music History at Converse College. His principal research interests are the music of Felix Mendelssohn, narrativity in music, and orchestral performance practice. He is author of *The Musical Genesis of Felix Mendelssohn's Paulus* and conducts the Converse Symphony Orchestra.

Douglass Seaton is Warren D. Allen Professor of Music at The Florida State University. In addition to Felix Mendelssohn Bartholdy, his research interests center on the interactions between music and literature. He is editor of *The Mendelssohn Companion* and of the critical edition of Mendelssohn's *Lobgesang.*

Ralf Wehner is director of the Leipzig Edition of the Works of Felix Mendelssohn Bartholdy at the Sächsische Akademie der Wissenschaften zu Leipzig. He has written extensively on Mendelssohn and published six volumes for the *Gesamtausgabe.* He is author (with Friedhelm Krummacher) of the Mendelssohn article in *Die Musik in Geschichte und Gegenwart.*

INDEX